SEA-CHANGES

SEA-CHANGES:

American Foreign Policy in a
World Transformed

EDITED BY
NICHOLAS X. RIZOPOULOS

COUNCIL ON FOREIGN RELATIONS PRESS
NEW YORK • LONDON

COUNCIL ON FOREIGN RELATIONS BOOKS

The Council on Foreign Relations, Inc., is a nonprofit and nonpartisan organization devoted to promoting improved understanding of international affairs through the free exchange of ideas. The Council does not take any position on questions of foreign policy and has no affiliation with, and receives no funding from, the United States government.

From time to time, books and monographs written by members of the Council's research staff or visiting fellows, or commissioned by the Council, or written by an independent author with critical review contributed by a Council study or working group are published with the designation "Council on Foreign Relations Book." Any book or monograph bearing that designation is, in the judgment of the Committee on Studies of the Council's Board of Directors, a responsible treatment of a significant international topic worthy of presentation to the public. All statements of fact and expressions of opinion contained in Council books are, however, the sole responsibility of the author.

For more information about Council publications, please write the Council on Foreign Relations, 58 East 68th Street, New York, NY 10021, or call the Publications Office at (212) 734-0400.

Library of Congress Cataloguing-in-Publication Data

Sea-Changes : American foreign policy in a world transformed / edited by Nicholas X. Rizopoulos.
  p.   cm.
  ISBN 0-87609-087-0 : $14.95
  1. United States—Foreign relations—1989– I. Rizopoulos, Nicholas X.
  E881.S43 1990
  327.73–dc20
                                         90–3891
                                         CIP

96   95   94   93   92   91   90   PB   10   9   8   7   6   5   4   3   2   1

CONTENTS

FOREWORD

Peter G. Peterson

Foreign policy often undergoes transitions, but rarely does it experience genuine transformation. We are living in a time of transformation and are groping to find new answers, or at least to invent new questions, that will help us make sense of the sea-changes around us. Not since the immediate postwar years has the Council on Foreign Relations experienced so great a need and opportunity to further its critical educational role. In this spirit, the Council's Board of Directors asked Nicholas X. Rizopoulos, Vice President of Studies, to commission a series of essays from leading experts that would try to give coherence and meaning to the stunning events around the world that we view nightly on our TV screens. While the resulting essays in *Sea-Changes: American Foreign Policy in a World Transformed* are indeed perceptive, they demonstrate that even the experts do not begin to have full answers. Yet these studies succeed in raising a number of daunting, tantalizing, and often original questions.

For example, it is clear that American foreign policy now consists of several overlapping realms, each calling for a distinctive style of leadership and each of whose relative importance has been shifting dramatically. Traditionally, "high politics," involving military/national-security/strategic considerations, predominated. When the threat was tangible and freedom itself was at stake, consensus "beyond the water's edge" was relatively easy to sustain—on U.S. exceptionalism, anticommunism, and working toward a democratic, capitalist world order. Guided by these precepts, the American leadership acted largely in a bipolar context. In important ways, however, "containment" itself was reactive, rather than affirmative, because U.S. foreign policy was based on fears for our security and values.

Now, as the essays in this volume vividly illustrate, a greatly demilitarized world has dramatically elevated the importance of other international considerations. Primal survival fears have given ground to simple hopes—often stimulated by global media—for a better life. As a result, new and formidable challenges confront us in, for example, the areas of economic security and global economics, where we have experienced discomfiting relative decline. And it is hard to know where a foreign policy consensus begins and ends when national borders have less bearing on a global economy characterized by integrated financial markets, multinational corporations, and internationalized production, as well as proliferating foreign direct investments and cross-border transactions. What should our *national* role be in this inherently *global* context?

Concerns that we have regarded mainly as domestic now may be the central stuff of a successful foreign policy. While global economic interdependence has become one of our newer clichés, we have rarely considered that this phenomenon might make real differences in how we live our lives at home. We have known for some time how difficult it is for a democracy to sustain, over any period, a strong foreign policy without a strong domestic economy and a stable society. Now, however, given the urgent need to invest in our economic future, we have already seen direct Gramm-Rudman effects on foreign affairs: major cuts in vital international programs; embassies and consulates being shuttered; desperate efforts to fund modest commitments to the very international institutions that we ourselves founded; and a deep reluctance to fund new initiatives.

Furthermore, many of the new global issues—the environment, immigration, terrorism, drugs, to name a few—have unfamiliar qualities. They are frequently influenced by technological developments outside the purview of traditional foreign policy concerns. Their benefits and costs are often unevenly, even unfairly, spread from one area of the world to another. For instance, even though the future world environment may suffer from a Brazilian's decision to cut down a stand of rain forest, that activity may be quite profitable locally. Addressing such problems will require creative linkages among seemingly disparate issues, including environment, debt, technology transfer, and development finance. Such interconnectedness poses complex questions—how these issues are to be negotiated, in what settings, and through which old or new institutions. Perhaps ironically, the global institutions that might appropriately address these emerging new core issues of foreign policy are precisely those, such as the United Nations, that have for some years been relegated to distinctly secondary status. Moreover, this intimate connectedness prompts us to revisit basic constitutional questions of executive (versus legislative) predominance in foreign affairs that, in the eighteenth century, were largely understood as making wars and concluding treaties. (Happily, these no longer seem to be growth industries.)

The evolving foreign policy agenda may be increasingly global, but our allies remain quite regional in their outlook. America, therefore, still has a vital role to play, but a very different kind of leadership will be required in a transformed world. Making tough choices in an era of constraints, thinking globally, thinking pluralistically, thinking in terms of consensus, thinking of partners rather than of dependents, thinking multilaterally— these do not come naturally to Americans. We sometimes fantasize that others will provide the money and that we will enjoy the power and privileges. Alas, with burden sharing will come unsettling new issues of power sharing and glory sharing.

I suppose that many of us instinctively react against the notion of national limits, trade-offs, and the constraints of cooperative action. We much prefer the more unilateralist approach, which is often tinged with populist tendencies. After all, the Western cowboy riding horseback on the limitless plain remains a kind of nostalgic role model for many of us. Multilateralism, consensus building, and power sharing might well strike some as downright un-American.

In sum, we are confronting a world of transformed foreign policy. Indeed, the Council, with its tradition of quiet and private policy deliberation, faces conceptual and institutional questions of its own, given the developing agenda and process of making foreign policy that is highly public, partisan, and ideological.

The questions resulting from these sea-changes, and the answers that we require have barely begun to surface. This book is a part of the Council's contribution to that vital process.

July 1990

ACKNOWLEDGEMENTS

This study was originally suggested to me by Peter G. Peterson, chairman of the board of directors of the Council on Foreign Relations, and was made possible through a generous grant from Mr. Peterson to the Council specifically for this purpose. We are grateful to him not least for his unflagging interest in all aspects of this project during the past year.

I would also like to take this opportunity to thank a number of my colleagues at the Council, all of whom were wonderfully supportive at every stage of this enterprise: the senior staff of the Studies Program; Peter Tarnoff, president; Harold Brown, Strobe Talbott, and John C. Campbell, members of the Committee on Studies; David Kellogg and Suzanne H. Hooper of the Publications Program; and Carol Rath, as always the ideal administrative assistant. In addition, the copy editor, Dore Hollander, should also be recognized.

Needless to say, this volume would have never seen the light of day were it not for the authors' patience, cheerful cooperation, and careful attention to detail. They rightly deserve the lion's share of the credit for whatever merit this collection of essays will be judged to possess.

Nicholas X. Rizopoulos
July 1990

INTRODUCTION

Nicholas X. Rizopoulos

Pan metron ariston ("nothing to excess"), said the ancient Greek philosopher. Wise words, to be sure, in almost any context. Yet if truth be told, at least a few among us—conscientious students of international politics that we may be, though perhaps more accurately described as belonging to that endangered species, the "educated layman" with no pretensions either to specialized knowledge or to privileged access to the proverbial Corridors of Power—have, for over a year now, gorged ourselves on a steady diet of schadenfreude as we have watched many of the "experts" (particularly those so anointed by the media) look rather silly both in attempting to explain their failure to predict most of the stunning events that have transpired, in Europe and elsewhere, and in resorting to obfuscating platitudes while trying to make some sense out of what can truly be described as sea-changes in the workings of the international system. Then, too, for those of us with a more parochial interest in monitoring the vicissitudes of U.S. policymaking, perhaps nothing captured more poignantly (or as wittily) the peculiar predicament of the current American administration during this Year of Revolutions than the cartoon (by James Borgman, published in the *The Cincinnati Enquirer*) that showed a bemused President Bush, sitting at his desk in the Oval Office, looking at his watch and thinking: "Communism is dead, the Wall is down, Apartheid is falling, Mandela is free, the Sandinistas are ousted, Germany is reuniting, the Cold War is over, I've returned all my calls, and, heck, it's not even lunchtime."

Still, it obviously behooves us—and not least those of us directly involved with the educational activities of an institution such as the Council on Foreign Relations—to keep asking the difficult questions of those genuinely qualified to provide coherent answers. In this instance, that means a small group of uncon-

1

ventional thinkers and writers—many drawn from the university world; some (though by no means the majority) former professional colleagues of the present editor; all (without exception) chosen by him as much for their habitual candor as for their impeccable "academic" credentials.

As the title of the volume suggests, this collection of original essays is an attempt to look beyond the (new) "German problem," the (diverse) upheavals in Eastern Europe, or the (putative) end of the North Atlantic Treaty Organization; to describe, and evaluate, the wider-ranging transformations—in the strategic, economic, political, demographic, and environmental spheres— that had already been set in motion before the "Gorbachev phenomenon" burst upon us; and to assess, if only for the short-to-medium term, some of the new challenges that will inevitably confront U.S. policymakers.

It should also be pointed out that the specific contents (and overall structure) of this volume reflect in good measure the editor's personal preference for the historians' "long view" when dealing with "current events." When this project was formally initiated almost a year ago, all of the contributing authors were asked, inter alia, to address themselves—to the extent that they deemed appropriate in terms of the specific topics assigned to them—to a cluster of four sea-changes that (it was readily agreed) were already in the process of radically transforming the international system that we had grown accustomed to during the preceding 45 years:

- The erosion of strategic bipolarity through the waning of the Cold War, combined with a diminution in the perceived utility of military force

- The upsurge of populist/democratic opposition forces to authoritarian rule (seen most dramatically—but not exclusively—in Eastern Europe), combined with a discrediting of Marxist models of socioeconomic reform

- The emergence of a global economy—increasingly market-oriented, less dominated by the United States (and conversely more attuned to pressures emanating from a united

Europe and Japan), yet also threatened by the real possibility of renewed trade wars

- The growing interconnection between debt and development problems in the Third World, on the one hand, and questions of economic stability and quality of life in advanced industrial societies, on the other.[1]

What this volume includes, then, is—to begin with, in Part One ("A Look at . . . ")—twelve relatively short articles that are meant to provide the reader with "regional," rather narrowly focused, overviews—of both the traditional ("Europe," "Africa," "The International Political Economy") and the not-so-traditional sort ("Science and Technology," "Democracy Resurgent")—that would also assess cause-and-effect relationships (or, in certain instances, the lack thereof) between the larger sea-changes mentioned above and such more limited, "topical" developments as nevertheless deserve our attention. What the reader will *not* find here—for that was never the editor's intention—is a series of lengthy "briefing papers," similar to those generated with regularity within the State Department or the National Security Council: studies overloaded with factual data, contradictory intelligence estimates, and cleverly hedged policy prescriptions. The authors of this collection were urged to express their personal opinions freely, unfettered by any obligations to produce "balanced" judgments; they were also encouraged to write pieces that could properly be described as old-fashioned *essays*—informative, to be sure, but a pleasure to read in their own right.

In Part Two ("Reconsiderations"), several well-known scholars and longtime commentators on contemporary affairs, all of them historians of the first rank (irrespective of their official academic accreditations), were commissioned to write "overarching" (and considerably lengthier) essays, unashamedly informed by the authors' own most recent research and writing. These essays would, ideally, identify—and expand upon—such recent historical currents, and the transformations these have effected on the international system, as each of the authors believes to be of truly lasting significance. Finally, in sketching out what from the beginning was conceived as the concluding chapter of this volume, Stanley Hoffmann was asked to respond, if only in passing, to some of the views expressed by the other authors, as well as to look ahead at the more immediate foreign policy challenges facing the American people.

NOTE

1. Purposely excluded from this initial list were such "supranational" threats to international "law and order" as terrorism, the drug trade, and nuclear proliferation, since these (admittedly worrisome) developments did not qualify as sea-changes per se—at least not according to the editor's restrictive definition of that term.

PART ONE:

A Look At . . .

A Look at ...
EUROPE AFTER THE SUPERPOWERS
Ronald Steel

The Europe of the Cold War has dissipated into the background of history. None of the ineluctable "realities" we took for granted during the past four decades carries much meaning any longer. The division of Europe, the partition of Germany, the hegemony of the superpowers, the deadly competition of rival alliances—all this is now outdated. The old American role as Europe's protector and power broker is finished. Much of this change has happened so fast that few on either side of the Atlantic can grasp its scope, let alone its meaning and consequences. As the galloping pace of German unification proceeds, it has made clear that no nation can control the pace of change, and that few can even see it coming. Much of American policy toward Europe has, like the assumptions that guide it, become irrelevant.

While the Cold War divided Europe into two hostile blocs, one dominated by the United States and the other by the Soviet Union, it also imposed order and stability on a Continent that for much of this century has known neither. Throughout most of the Cold War, Europe was remarkably quiescent, one of the few areas of stability in a world rocked by regional, tribal, and post-colonial warfare. The rival pacts into which Europe was divided, the evident determination of the giants to shield the heartland from their joustings for influence, indeed their contentment with a status quo that ensured their preeminence over a divided Europe—all these factors reinforced a structure of stability.

But the ending of the Cold War removes the very structure of European stability. Imposed from the outside, that stability was maintained by a European psychology of acquiescence to the superpowers and reinforced by the arms race. The collapse of the Soviet Empire in Eastern Europe and the emergence of a unified German state have eroded the political balance on the Continent. Europe, for so many decades an instrument of the policies of others—willingly so in the West, unwillingly in the East—has forced Washington and Moscow to the sidelines. Rather than setting the agenda for Europe and deciding the parameters bounding the new Europe, they have become little more than spectators in the great unfolding drama of Europe's future.

For the first time since 1945, the question for these two great powers is not the place that Europe plays in their rivalry. Rather, it is how they can protect their interests in, and ultimately even against, a Europe that is defining itself independently of them. For American policymakers, lulled by more than four decades of Atlanticism into assuming an identity of purpose between the United States and Western Europe, an adjustment to the new realities of power will be wrenching. But such an adjustment is urgent if the power to influence events, and thus to protect the future, is not to be dissipated.

If we step back even a bit from the avalanche of recent events, we can see at least the outlines of the Europe that is emerging. The Germans will be united into a single state, the North Atlantic Treaty Organization (NATO) and the Warsaw Pact will have lost much of their relevance, a cohesive Europe will become a challenging economic and political competitor to the United States, ethnic and regional rivalries will threaten the stability of the Soviet Union and its former empire, the Soviets will be drawn into the European economic orbit as an "under-developed" country, and American political influence on the Continent will wane sharply.

The end of the Cold War means not only the abatement of tensions, but the demise of the entire political order that stemmed from it. The political order, insofar as Europeans were concerned, was dominated by the United States and the USSR. It is finished. For some time it has been both politically and economically obsolete. Its continuation over the past decade has been a result of cultural lag and of unimaginative, uninformed leadership by both superpowers. But it took the action of the Soviets and the Eastern Europeans finally to bring it down.

The Cold War world has collapsed, first of all, because of Mikhail Gorbachev. His determination to respond to the economic needs of Soviet society, to reform rigid ideological and political structures, and to reinterpret the requirements of Soviet security has transformed the relationship of the Soviet Union to Eastern Europe and to the nations of the Atlantic Alliance. He set in motion forces far more powerful than he or anyone else could have imagined even a few months ago. He surely did not intend that communists would be discredited and forced from power in Eastern Europe; that East Germany, the star of the Soviet diadem, would be swallowed up whole by the Federal Republic; that republics of the Soviet Union itself would demand independence from the Kremlin; or that the scepter of power in Europe would pass from Moscow to Berlin. Yet this is now happening, and the Soviets, like ourselves, are powerless to prevent it.

The second force that undermined the Cold War is the declining importance of military power. Nuclear weapons have proved to be not only a great equalizer—making the Soviet Union, a nation with a third-rate economy, the "equal" of the United States—but a great neutralizer as well. The superpowers find their nuclear might unusable not only against each other, but even against recalcitrant lesser states they seek to control, such as Afghanistan and Vietnam. Unlike previous technological innovations, such as tanks or dreadnoughts, nuclear weapons are not even useful to intimidate the weak. The kind of military force marshaled by the so-called superpowers (even the term has begun to sound ironic) is no longer an effective measure of global influence. Power today is measured increasingly by productivity, trade surpluses, and technological innovation rather than by nuclear throw weight. Effective, usable power has been shifted from the nuclear musclemen to the more agile trading states.

A third factor is the economic fatigue of the superpowers. The weapons race has left them, like exhausted gladiators in an arena abandoned by a bored crowd, less—rather than more—

able to influence events and defend their broader interests. This is dramatically so for the Soviet Union, but also true for the United States. The profligate rearmament programs of the 1980s, combined with unfavorable trade balances and an unwillingness to tax for public expenses, weakened American competitiveness and with it the economic base of American power. Even without a Soviet initiative, the United States must inaugurate its own version of perestroika. The challenge to American economic interests, both from the actions of the United States itself and from its allies and clients, dictates an about-face from an obsession with the Cold War.

The dissipation of the psychology of the Cold War has, like an earth tremor rumbling beneath a seemingly impregnable building, shaken the mighty structures we have taken for granted. Foremost among these structures is a Europe divided between the United States and the Soviet Union. It has become as anachronistic to speak of the "communist bloc" today as it would be to refer to the "Axis" or the "Central Powers." It is even getting difficult to speak with clarity of Eastern as distinct from Western Europe. Day by day we witness the transformation of the "other Europe" into what must be called simply Europe. Not long ago it was considered arrogant or insensitive to speak of "America's Europe" or "Russia's Europe." Today such terms are simply meaningless. History has, in the space of a few months, passed them by.

As the Cold War power blocs have crumbled, the structures that delineate them—NATO and the Warsaw Pact—have become functionally irrelevant. A Soviet leadership that allows communist parties to be swept from power in Eastern Europe cannot expect Warsaw Pact membership to be a high priority for the hard-currency nationalists who have replaced them. The Kremlin has already undercut the logic of the Pact in its quest for markets and bankers in the West, and for legitimacy at home. The Pact, which ironically bears the name of the city where the anticommunist revolution of Eastern Europe began a decade ago, is an embarrassing reminder of Moscow's weakness, rather than a symbol of its strength.

While the Pact is virtually defunct, NATO could remain formally intact for some time longer. It asks little of its members, except for military expenses many today consider redundant, and the Europeans are now finding a new use for it as an insurance policy against one of its members: Germany. For some time, it has been inertia rather than fear that has held the Alliance together. Once the door to political change in the East was opened, the issue of Europe's defenses took a back seat to the question of Europe's political future. NATO is by nature a reactive alliance. By reacting to the decline of the Soviet threat, it unavoidably undercuts the reason for its own existence.

The result of this has been to magnify a development that has been gathering force for more than a decade, but has been masked by Cold War rhetoric and the inflation of Cold War rhetoric during the last years of Carter and the first term of Reagan: the reduction of America's dominant place in Europe's affairs. Our control over Europe was directly related to the degree that Europeans believed they needed our protection. What was once so eagerly solicited by them now seems a bit of a nuisance—even though the desire for some form of American connection remains. With the Soviet threat retreating into the history books, with Germany rising to become one of the world's great powers, and with Europe itself—like some restless adolescent—proclaiming its independence and demanding gratification of its needs, the notion of Europe as a junior partner and dependency of America seems as quaint as it is self-deluding.

Atlanticism—the organizing principle of U.S. postwar policy toward Europe—was built on such dependency. It was the form in which the United States saw itself in relation to Western Europe, and it inspired a host of institutions and bureaucracies that encouraged and managed that relationship. NATO, the linchpin of Atlanticism, was always conceived as the instrument by which the United States, with Europe's consent and assistance, would provide for the protection of its allies. In so doing, it also retained ultimate direction of Europe's defense and diplomacy. This is the system that such European nationalists as General de Gaulle inveighed against and labeled "hegemony." But it also served Europe's interests. Atlanticism worked so long as Europe's division seemed insurmountable and Europe's dependency inescapable. As these conditions have eroded, so has Atlanticism. With the Soviet Union transformed from a present menace to an impoverished and confused supplicant, the United States has become less important to Europe and exerts less influence over it. The end of the Cold War has meant the extraction of the United States from the European equation. As we assume the role of bystander at the political and economic reorganization of Europe, we find ourselves having moved, however regretfully, into a post-Atlantic world.

The passing of the old order signals the resolution of certain problems—such as a Soviet Union that threatened to impose its will on Western Europe. But it also unleashes others: some new, some until now repressed or concealed. These are likely to replace the Cold War as a focal point of our anxieties toward the external world.

First among these is the emergence of a European entity, constructed on the base of the European Community (EC), that will be a serious economic and political competitor. Already the EC is a larger market than the United States, its industries often more productive, and its standard of living at least comparable. In an earlier time the United States could, and often did, use Western Europe's military dependency as a lever to gain economic or political concessions. But beginning in the early 1980s, with the Soviet gas pipeline imbroglio, the Europeans made it clear that they would pursue their interests even where this risked straining relations with Washington. This focus on self-interest at the expense of Atlanticist pieties will inevitably increase after the creation of a single European market in 1992. Europe may speak in one voice, or perhaps in several, but its cues will not come from Washington.

Second, it is abundantly clear that European nationalism, at least in the East, is growing. Together, we and the Soviets imposed an unnatural calm upon Europe. Peoples who had been at one another's throats for centuries lived together in peace, if not in harmony. Europe has been a tranquil place for the past 45 years, whether under democratic governments in the West or imposed communist dictatorships in the East. But the relaxation of central control in Eastern Europe and the removal of the fear of Soviet intervention have allowed long-suppressed resentments and ambitions to burst open. Deep-seated ethnic fevers have not abated in the East, and even national frontiers are once again being called into question. These fevers will be hard to confine to Eastern Europe. Indeed, as German unity proceeds, they could shake even the hitherto stable and pacific Federal Republic as it tries to absorb 16 million people who have lived for three generations under totalitarian systems. The "peaceful revolution" that shook Eastern Europe in the fall of 1989 could yet come to bear some resemblance to its forebear of two centuries earlier. We may come to look back with some nostalgia on these past decades as a time when Europe was stable.

Third among the problems posed by the waning of the Cold War is the reemergence of the German Question. Long confined to the realm of the hypothetical by the U.S.–Soviet competition and Europe's partition, it has once again become an active issue. The German Question was never resolved, but merely repressed. It was always at the center of Europe's stage, like the rhinoceros in Ionesco's play that everyone walked around and pretended did not exist.

NATO was brought into being not only to deter a marauding Soviet bear, but to reassure the other Europeans that the Germans would be kept in place. The division of Germany was, in the eyes of most Europeans, the one happy result of World War II. Germany's postwar partners refrained from saying this openly, and gave lip service to the dream of unification so long as it seemed infinitely distant and unlikely. They learned to live quite comfortably with a democratic West Germany of roughly the same size and economic strength as Britain and France.

Just as Germany was crucial to NATO, so did the trans-Atlantic Alliance play an important part in dealing with the German issue. For the Americans, it offered a way of harnessing German industry and manpower in the struggle against the Soviet Union. For the Europeans, the presence of a large American army on German soil gave reassurance against all potential aggressors. Thus, just as partition reduced German power and ultimately served to "contain" it, so did an American-dominated

NATO keep Germany within an Atlantic framework tied to U.S. leadership.

The Germans, too, benefited from such an arrangement. They gained protection from the Soviets, U.S. economic assistance, reconciliation with their Western neighbors, sanction for rearmament, and leverage—on that distant day, from which their gaze never fully strayed, when the Soviet hold on East Germany loosened—for the ultimate unification of Germans under a common flag. Thus, in an apparent paradox, it was only by unflinching allegiance to the West and the incorporation of the Federal Republic into Western military and economic institutions that the ending of Germany's partition and her reconciliation with the East might one day be brought about.

That seemingly unattainable time has now come, and the long-dormant German Question is upon us. NATO cannot define Germany's interests, as it has in the past. It has not prevented even the most Western-oriented Germans from looking east and dealing with the new opportunities. The German Democratic Republic, having lost its legitimacy in the eyes of most of its own citizens, has virtually ceased to exist. It was a state with no identity other than that imposed by Stalinist-style communism. When that lost its authority and legitimacy, the state itself collapsed. All that was left were people who defined themselves as Germans, and for whom the most urgent goal was to share the prosperity of their fellow Germans in the West. Although a number of factors seemed to stand in the way of early unification—concern on the part of Germany's neighbors, Soviet security interests, anxieties in the Federal Republic itself about diluting or imperiling the respect and prosperity it has won—none of this has been enough to hold back a tide that has escaped the control of even the erstwhile superpowers.

As unification proceeds, we are witnessing the emergence of what was once called Mitteleuropa: an Eastern Europe dominated economically, culturally, and politically by the powerhouse of Germany. Germany's interests, like its sense of identity, require it to look east as well as west, and in the East it has no serious economic or even political competition. In a German-dominated Eastern Europe there would even be a special place for the Soviet

Union, most likely as a workshop and source of raw materials. In its role as economic junior partner, or even apprentice, the USSR would, like any semi-developed country, benefit from German know-how and investment. The Cold War relationship between these two countries would, in other words, be turned upside down; or, looking at it another way, they would return to their pre-1941 relationship.

This raises the question of whether it is possible to construct a Europe large enough to channel and dilute German power. The EC, impressive though it is, lacks the weight. A unified Germany will dominate the Community, encouraging separatists in Britain and elsewhere who are already wary of European integration. In one sense the problem is not that Germany is too large, but that Europe is too small. The reason for this is that it is divided and that the Soviets were, during the entire Cold War, written out of the equation as though the USSR were a non-European power. But historically, culturally, and geographically it is a part of Europe. More important, it is central to the creation of a viable European balance.

Cold War politics dictated that the only way the USSR could be brought back would involve opening the entire Continent to Soviet military dominance. Such a fear has always been exaggerated, given the Soviet Union's economic backwardness and military caution. But today the very notion seems fanciful. The Soviet Union is a troubled, ethnically divided, semi-industrial country. It needs association with Europe in order to emerge from its backwardness and pursue the democratic evolution of its political system.

A quarter-century ago de Gaulle envisaged a Europe extending "from the Atlantic to the Urals." At that time, in the heyday of Atlanticism and of American expansionism, such a concept was deemed unrealistic and even anti-American. But today, as the United States grows increasingly preoccupied with its own social and economic problems, the notion of a Europe responsible for its own security and stability is more than appealing. It is necessary. It provides the best hope for avoiding the breakdown of the European idea into a congeries of contentious and jealous power groupings of the kind that have been so disastrous in Europe's past. It also offers a framework for enveloping Germany in a structure it cannot dominate and that is not threatening to it.

For the United States, the challenges posed by an evolving and potentially volatile situation in the heart of Europe are clear. The first is to keep Europe stable at a time when the Cold War blocs have become unraveled. Second, the United States needs to maintain its influence on the Continent in a situation where the Western Europeans, less dependent on U.S. protection, are also less responsive to U.S. economic and political interests. Third, the United States must assist the liberalization of the Soviet Union in order to prevent its regression to Cold War militancy. The fourth challenge is to ensure that the evolving European balance will not become hostile to U.S. interests. Although the United States is not a European power, it is very much of Europe, and it has a crucial stake in the manner by which Europe emerges from the Cold War.

How these goals can be accomplished will involve considerable argument, shoving, and reordering of priorities, for an adjustment to new realities cuts to the heart of long-cherished assumptions and entrenched bureaucracies. In every area the most ruthless "new thinking" will be essential.

NATO. Here it will be impossible to carry on as before, even with sharply reduced U.S. forces on the Continent and the "devolution" of more responsibilities to the Europeans. The Alliance is simply worth far less than it used to be: both to Americans and to Europeans. An American troop presence is desirable in the short run to reassure both Europeans and Soviets that the old balance will not suddenly be overturned. It also serves as an instrument of American influence in Europe. But the purpose of the Alliance has to be redefined from primarily one of deterrence to that of mutual security.

In the long run, however (where long means two or three years), NATO is as doomed as the already virtually defunct Warsaw Pact. It is simply not possible to sustain an alliance such as NATO without an enemy such as the Soviet Union has been. We will have to stop thinking about how to reform NATO and start thinking about how to move beyond it. This means moving from a relationship of power and authority to one of equality and mutual dependency. This will not be an easy adjustment, especially for U.S. national security bureaucracies grown rich and fat on nearly a half-century of imperial management.

Eastern Europe. For all the justifiable euphoria that has greeted the downfall of Stalinist dictatorships in most of the region, the fact remains that the states of this region are, for the most part, without a democratic tradition or modern economy. Some are quite likely to revert to previous forms of militarism and authoritarianism. All will probably be plagued by unemployment, inequality, and the consequent social unrest. The states of this traditionally unstable region have been frozen in an authoritarian mold for at least four decades, and some for many more. They have been cut off from the forces of democratization and modernization that have transformed Western Europe. They have a long history of anarchy, ethnic violence, endemic hatreds, regional warfare, and authoritarianism. The fact that they have been liberated from communist dictators does not mean that they will be pacific or democratic. For the time being Eastern Europe is a no-man's-land, detached from Soviet control but not yet capable of being absorbed into the democratic West without dangers for all concerned. It needs to be put into a political quarantine while its fevers subside. The Soviets kept the peace in Eastern Europe, albeit at terrible human cost, for more than four decades. The region will not be stabilized easily now that Soviet, and even communist, control has been removed. Stabilization requires not only Western patience and firmness, but also the cooperation of Moscow. This means a return to some of the principles of great power peacekeeping that were enunciated in the World War II conferences at Yalta and Potsdam but ignored and then repudiated by the passions of the Cold War. Eastern Europe may well need some external force to keep the peace and prevent nationalism from destroying the emerging European union. Historically, this role has been played by Germany, but this has also posed problems of hegemony. For that reason it would be desirable to bring both the United States and the Soviet Union into the equation.

Western Europe. Although U.S. influence has been sharply reduced by the decline of the Soviet threat, it is not negligible. The Europeans continue to need the United States for balance: not only against the Soviets, but against each other, and particularly to counterbalance the ascending weight of the Germans. It is not in the interest of the Europeans to lock the United States out of the emerging new power balance, and they should be made aware of this. The U.S. role in Europe is not only to nurture and protect, but also to participate in the Continent's evolution. American policy should be directed toward keeping the EC open, not only to U.S. trade and investment, but also to Eastern Europe and the Soviet Union. Within the framework of a wider European community open to the East lies the possibility for bringing an evolved Soviet Union into a continental balance.

Germany. The Cold War began with Germany, and it is ending with Germany. Because the World War II allies could not agree on the political orientation of Germany, along with that of Eastern Europe, they partitioned the former reich and built fortresslike spheres of influence on either side of it. The unification of Germany marks not only the end of the Cold War, but the expulsion of both America and the Soviet Union from the positions of power they have occupied for more than four decades. Confronted with a resurgent Germany that seems likely to dominate the Continent, they seek to maintain their privileges and, more important, some measure of control of a renascent great power capable of challenging them both. The postwar "occupation" countries—the United States, Britain, France, and the Soviet Union—now once again meet in self-conscious session to deal with the German Question. The Western allies, led by the United States, insist that a unified Germany be a member of NATO. The logic behind this is not that NATO needs Germany as a barricade against the Soviet Union, but that the Alliance will tie Germany down, preventing it from becoming a "loose cannon" between East and West. The Soviets are told that this is good for them as well. Maybe they will come to believe it. But whether a unified Germany is inside or outside of NATO is irrelevant. It will not consent to be occupied by foreign armies, and in short order both the Americans and the Soviets will be sent home. To try to contain a unified Germany through NATO is like trying to contain Bismarck through the Congress of Vienna. The framework is outdated and functionally meaningless. If Germany is to be "contained," that must be accomplished through a political, economic, and even military structure of which it is a determinant part. This means a wider European security order that would supersede the outdated Cold War alliances and would include the two declining superpowers, America and the USSR.

Soviet Union. If the Cold War was the confrontation between the United States and the USSR, the post–Cold War period will be marked by their guarded cooperation in pursuit of common interests. It will mean, in effect, a return to the logic of the World War II alliance, into which Washington and Moscow were forced because they faced a greater threat to their interests. During the 40 years of the Cold War they defined the world as being divided between them. That definition was never accurate, and now it has no meaning at all. Other challengers are rising—Japan, Germany, a unifying (or perhaps splintering) Europe—and more will follow. The Soviets need the United States to keep Europe calm, to restrain a revived Germany, and to prevent the creation of an anti-Soviet alliance that would threaten their existence. But the United States also needs a cohesive Soviet Union that does not itself become a "power vacuum" sucking in foreign intervention. It is not in our interest that the Soviet state collapse into a congeries of bitterly feuding ministates organized around ancient ethnic hatreds. American security requires not anarchy and violence, but stability and calm in Eastern Europe. This means the maintenance of a power in the East to flank and to balance the turbulent forces of nationalism now roiling what was once the Soviet Empire.

The balance of power is not an outdated concept. If we need a strong Germany to balance the Soviet Union and help keep order in Eastern Europe, so we need a stable Soviet Union to contain the forces in its former empire unleashed by the end of the Cold War. In other words, just as the Soviets have begun to realize that we are not so much the "enemy" as we are a potential partner in a quest for security that has assumed very different forms than it took during the Cold War, so we must readjust our thinking. Instead of devoting our energies to devising ways of weakening and disrupting the Soviet Union, we will, because of the radical changes in the world power structure that have become unavoidable, grow increasingly preoccupied with efforts to strengthen and stabilize our former nemesis. We will, that is, have to start thinking about the Soviet Union the way we did about Germany and Japan once World War II was over and a new challenge to our interests began to emerge.

The focal point of the U.S.–Soviet competition has been Europe, and it is concern over the future of Europe that must force the United States and the USSR into at least a tacit cooperation. The United States does not need, and cannot expect, a compliant Europe. But it does require a stable one, as do the Soviets. We should use our waning authority over our European allies to attain this objective. We cannot lackadaisically assume that the Europeans will work things out among themselves. They have not done so well at this in the past. Nor can we assume that whatever the Europeans—or the strongest powers in Europe—decide will be in our interests as well as theirs. We shall have to play as active a role in the coming European settlement as we played in building a Western European Cold War bloc. We have interests in Europe, for Europe, and in some cases against Europe. To say merely that we want a strong, unified Europe is simplistic and even possibly self-defeating. We need a Europe that is peaceful, prosperous, open to trade and investment, and a menace neither to itself nor to others. We need, as do the Soviets, a Europe that will not return to its patterns of ethnic violence, revanchism, and civil war.

We are witnessing today in Europe a return to history: a return to ethnicity, to nationalism, to self-determination, to the struggle for influence and power. Such goals in the past have not always led to tranquility. They may not do so now unless the

Europeans show restraint, unless a workable power balance is established, and unless the United States recognizes and acts upon its interests in the coming European settlement. This is an astonishing moment in European history, one comparable to that of the eruption of the great forces in 1848. Whether it leads, as earlier revolutions have, to disillusion and reaction or to a freer and more peaceful Continent depends to a significant degree on our own ability to readjust our ways of thinking, discard obsolete relationships and ideological blinkers, embrace new opportunities, and act upon a wider and more imaginative concept of our interests. To say that the Cold War is over is simply to express a cliché; to act upon it unsentimentally and in response to the new forces of change will require that rarest of qualities: statesmanship.

A Look at . . .

EASTERN EUROPE AND THE
SOVIET UNION

Robert G. Kaiser

Energies suppressed for decades by the arbitrary power of communist parties have suddenly erupted in every nation of the old
Soviet Empire, causing a political earthquake. Earthquakes in
nature occur when pent-up energy in two plates of the earth's
surface becomes so powerful that the plates must move. In the
old Soviet bloc, the energies are political, economic, sociological,
even psychological. If there were a Richter scale for disruptions
in modern societies, the temblor we are witnessing might well set
a record for the entire history of nations.

The forces being released are so great that their consequences are genuinely unpredictable. Uncertainty about what
comes next is the subtext of nearly every public pronouncement
by the new leaders of Eastern Europe, including Mikhail Gorbachev. Uncertainty should also be the theme of any outsider's
attempt to analyze these changes. What began in 1989 will be a
feast for students of politics and economics, probably a font of
great literature, too, and certainly a splendid intellectual entertainment. But it will take years to see these changes whole; now
we have only clues about where they may lead.

The world, East and West, got so used to the old arrangements that most of us lost sight of just how unnatural they were.
Arbitrary, authoritarian regimes, dependent for their power on
secret police forces, and large communist parties, insisting on
counterproductive economic policies and demanding adherence
to an irrational orthodoxy, created bizarre societies. All of these

societies have missed out on most of the dramatic technological changes that have transformed the capitalist world in the last generation. We called the Soviet Union a superpower without regard for its total failure to adapt to the computer age, for example. We agonized about the military threat from the East without seriously calculating the disarray in Soviet-bloc armed forces whose troops were appallingly trained, demoralized, badly equipped. As the shrouds and blinders have fallen away, all in the West can finally see these countries more or less as they were: poor, corrupt, stupidly run, spiritually bankrupt, mired in a bureaucratic morass, committed to economic programs that destroyed the environment of each of the seven nations of the Soviet bloc while failing to make any of them remotely competitive by international standards.

The collapse of ancien régimes throughout Eastern Europe and the crumbling of the old order in Moscow are rightly a source of jubilation, but none of the changes now occurring can wash out the stains of 45 years, or 75, of Marxism-Leninism. Throughout the old Soviet Empire, workers have learned how to prove the accuracy and relevance of the old Russian joke: We pretend to work, and they pretend to pay us. Economies that have so long devalued both work and money cannot be quickly turned around. All crave the silver bullet of Western investment, and all are likely to get it. Then all will also learn that investment cannot undo the consequences of so many years of mismanagement and bad work habits.

Can Soviet peasants who have never managed a piece of land from season to season—or taken responsibility for decisions about what to plant, how to fertilize, and the like—learn to be efficient farmers? Can workers protected from economic discipline by ideology adapt to conditions where hard work is required and laziness is severely punished? Can workers unfamiliar with insecurity cope with unemployment? Can managers at every level of society, from the factory canteen to national ministries, learn to manage on their own initiative, without reference to higher authority or an ironclad rule book? Can a new class of politicians learn the value of tolerance and the ability to endure criticism or attack from rivals without resorting to repression? Can journalists learn to report information that the authorities would prefer to suppress, and will the authorities tolerate its publication? These are huge questions; the fate of the nations of Eastern Europe will depend on how they are answered.

The Soviet Union, Poland, Hungary, Czechoslovakia, Romania, and Bulgaria will now become a giant laboratory of politics, economics, sociology, and psychology. (East Germany seems destined simply to be absorbed into the Federal Republic.) A series of fascinating experiments will be conducted in this new lab. Consider some of the subjects to be explored.

How significant a role do national character and distinctive national experience play in the modern age? The nations of the Soviet bloc may have appeared as a unitary blur in Western imaginations for the last generation or so, but the differences among them are actually immense. Will those differences significantly alter their individual prospects in their shared struggle to create modern, democratic societies—and if so, how?

Russian national character and the burden of Russian history are powerful factors impinging on Gorbachev's efforts to modernize and democratize the Soviet Union. We may discover that the damage done by Stalinism to the fabric of that society is simply too great to overcome. In countless respects, the Soviet Union has been despoiled. The consequences are now vividly on display in the liberated Soviet news media, which record excruciating examples of the collapse of health care, the destruction of the environment, the indifference of workers and managers to the quality of the goods they produce, the petty tyranny of bureaucrats at all levels, the mindless "leveling" that deprives high achievers of higher rewards.

Sixty years of Stalinism have produced profound pessimism in the Soviet Union. There was a striking example of this amid the journalistic hoopla that greeted the opening of Moscow's first McDonald's in early 1990, a commentary by one of *Izvestia*'s best-known columnists, Stanislav Kondrashev.

"I don't know if the heads of the McDonald's corporation realize the trials that await them in Moscow," he wrote. The new store—the world's largest McDonald's—might be "swept away by crowds of curious people" or collapse in a mire of corruption. "As a realist, I do not exclude the possibility that, in six months, McDonald's will run away from the most ambitious project in its history. The manager will be lifted out by helicopter, straight from the roof of the cafeteria, just as American diplomats were lifted out of the U.S. embassy in Saigon."[1]

Kondrashev wrote ironically, but he meant to be taken seriously, too. His implicit pessimism—suggesting that his countrymen could not actually sustain an efficient, clean, modern, service-oriented institution even on the simple level of a hamburger store—is typical of many well-informed Soviets. It reflects a peculiar cultural fatalism of which we will see a good deal more in the near future.

McDonald's decision to do business in the Soviet Union is instructive. The experiment actually cost $50 million before the first hamburger was sold. McDonald's had to bring potato seed to the Soviet Union (where potatoes and bread have been the basic diet for centuries), teach farmers to grow and harvest the spuds properly, then import equipment and train workers to produce every single ingredient and piece of equipment the chain uses. All of this is now done in a campus of factories surrounded by wire fencing, an isolated island of efficiency. Some problems could never be solved; McDonald's finally decided to import its special mustard from Canada, tomato paste from Portugal, and apples from Bulgaria.

Sixty years of Stalinism have largely crushed individual initiative—not that it was ever a prominent feature of the Russian character. Perestroika is unlikely to throw up a new cohort of thousands or millions of entrepreneurial individuals willing to take responsibility for independent enterprises, schools, farms, and so on. But without new leaders to assume those responsibilities, there is no real hope of fundamentally reforming the Soviet Union. As Gorbachev has discovered, a successful reform movement cannot simply be willed from Moscow.

The forced absorption of dozens of non-Russian peoples into the Soviet Union has left ethnic divisions that will also frustrate political and economic reform. Gorbachev has accepted the rule of thumb that reform and decentralization are inseparable, but in the Soviet context, decentralization encourages the expression of repressed local nationalisms. Lithuania's attempt to secede from the USSR will be followed by others; in time, it seems inevitable, parts of the country will break away from Moscow's control. Whether a recognizable Soviet Union can survive this century is an open question.

National characteristics in Eastern Europe will also prove critically important. Czechoslovakia may have the best prospects for success as a free-market social democracy, thanks to its tradition of high-quality manufacturing and a well-educated, relatively disciplined work force. The Hungarians have similar advantages, and a strong agricultural sector, but they are burdened with scores of large and hopelessly inefficient state-owned enterprises that will have to be closed or radically restructured. The Poles' early success with draconian austerity measures is hopeful, but Poland starts far behind East Germany, Czechoslovakia, and Hungary. Rural backwardness, a weak communications infrastructure, and huge and probably unsalvageable state enterprises will all slow Poland's progress. So will the exhaustion of the 1980s, a tumultuous decade that drove many of the country's most talented citizens to emigrate.

The poorer countries of the Warsaw Pact, Romania and Bulgaria, appear now to have the worst prospects. Romania particularly was devastated by the cruelest dictatorship in the region; its population is less educated than the richer Eastern European countries, its industry less sophisticated. Bulgaria has a stronger agricultural tradition, but Bulgarians, like Romanians, have been isolated for decades, and they are far less advanced than Czechs or Hungarians.

Yugoslavia offers—as it has for 40 years—a special case. The chaos there seems virtually endemic, though beneath it are signs of economic recovery. Serbia is now one of the last redoubts of communism in the region; Croatia seems to have set off on its own, democratic path. The other republics continually jockey for position, and for prosperity. The possibility that the country will break apart seems real, but perhaps economic success will provide new adhesive. Yugoslavia has already had many years to try to demonstrate the benefits of independence from Moscow; so far, the demonstration has been unpersuasive.

Can the technologies of the information age—and the values of honesty and openness that they foster—compensate for the absence of democratic and legal traditions? New information technologies accelerated the collapse of Stalinism throughout the Soviet Empire by undermining the monopolies on information that are necessary for any leadership seeking to impose absolute political controls. Shortwave radio, VCRs, computers, faxes, and photocopiers all broke down the isolation of the socialist countries. Over time the governments of every Warsaw Pact nation concluded that they had to open up to the outside world to relieve internal pressures. But the myths that sustained Stalinist systems could not survive exposure to the outside world. Intelligent people within the Soviet bloc began to realize not only that their system was *not* the wave of the future, but that it was impoverishing their countries.

Gorbachev and his allies in Moscow understood the power of information from the moment he came to power in 1985. Soon new editors of a handful of journals were providing a new brand of honest journalism, and winning millions of new readers for the *Moscow News, Ogonyok,* and others. Then, under the banner of glasnost, Gorbachev permitted the first full airing of Stalin's fearsome crimes. Revelations published and broadcast beginning in late 1987 utterly discredited the surviving Stalinists in the party apparatus; soon Gorbachev had routed them, apparently eliminating the threat of a hard-liners' coup d'état.

In a different but equally effective way, Poland's Stalinists were undermined by years of truth-telling, first in underground "free universities" and samizdat publications, later in open pronouncements from leaders of Solidarity and its allies and leaders of the Catholic church. The East German regime was eroded by West German television, a constant reminder to the citizens of the East that their government's propaganda was hollow.

Now the peoples of Eastern Europe will have opportunities to use the information newly available to them to pressure their governments to behave fairly and democratically. Already they have demonstrated this capacity.

During the first months following the collapse of the Eastern European dictatorships, the East German public forced the pseudoreformist Egon Krenz from office, forced the old-line party apparatchiks to step aside, and ultimately forced the issue of reunification. Crowds in Romania kept pressing the National Salvation Front to abandon its authoritarian methods. In Poland, amazingly, the first public reaction to painful austerity measures was favorable. In Hungary, skeptical voters headed off the efforts of reformist communists to dominate democratic politics.

The tolerance and respect for an independent judiciary that has to mark any real democracy will be harder to come by in these newly liberated countries. In our complicated times democracy does seem to offer practical advantages, however. No government relying on force can solve the problems of a complex modern society—a critical reason why the Stalinist model has collapsed. Democratic governments also seem incapable of sweeping success in managing industrial societies, but democratic governments can at least share, and thus diffuse, the blame for failing to manage them more effectively. Rising expectations are more easily contained in a democracy; so are dissidents.

Can the psychological damage caused by 45, or 75, years of tyranny be overcome? The peoples of Eastern Europe have lived for decades in authoritarian societies featuring secret police forces, informers, bugged telephones, arbitrary justice, and cruel punishment for nonconformists. Popular sovereignty, individual civil rights and human dignity, privacy and religious tolerance had virtually no place in a Stalinist system. But these are the very values that must be embraced now if these societies are to be successfully democratized, and then to prosper economically.

We in the West have been moved by the spectacle of countless Eastern Europeans rushing into the streets to express their frustrations and aspirations, even to bring down governments that once seemed invincible. Somehow, during a few months in 1989, people who had been too scared even to disclose their own thoughts to a friend or colleague suddenly found the courage to shout their opinions in public, often at great personal risk. Fear melted away, and not just in Leipzig, Prague, and Bucharest.

Soviet mothers in remote cities of the USSR forcefully resisted a call-up of their sons who were to be sent to Azerbaijan to quell ethnic disorders there. Young Armenians took up arms to defend their villages against pillaging Azerbaijanis. Leaders of Lithuania's communist party looked Gorbachev in the eye and refused to do his bidding when he insisted they not withdraw from the Soviet communist party.

Can this kind of courage endure? Can people raised to believe that individuals were of no great consequence now act like resourceful, responsible, sovereign persons? This is a great deal to ask of human beings.

Can centralized, Stalinist economies that have fallen far behind their capitalist rivals be converted into modern and efficient engines of prosperity? This question looms largest for the Soviets, partly because they have the largest economy. The scale of their difficulties now is daunting: that Gorbachev could squander five years in power without confronting them proves the point.

But all of these countries are ill prepared to compete in a global marketplace. Their standards of manufacturing quality are far below international norms. They have weak economic infrastructures, miserable telephone systems, primitive banking sectors, nonexistent capital markets. They will have to make giant strides quickly to avoid prolonged economic crises. We will see talented people struggling against endemic backwardness and inefficiency, and for many years they may be unequal to the struggle.

Can the nations of central Europe rearrange themselves in a new and stable order? This final question will not be answered by the Eastern Europeans alone. Outsiders from the West will play an important role. The traditional blocs seem destined to collapse into each other. A united Germany in Europe's center will inevitably dominate the economic, and perhaps also the political, life of the Continent. But will the smaller powers in the West fit easily into a new European order?

George Kennan recently noted an important paradox: Though the Eastern Europeans have been able to throw off the

Soviet yoke with the help of powerful nationalistic sentiment, now that they are gaining their independence, they will have to learn to suppress nationalism to cooperate with one another and with the rest of Europe.[2] But can Romanians and Hungarians really learn to cooperate? Will Polish animosities toward Germany diminish or intensify? Can Poles and Hungarians fruitfully work together? Eastern Europe is an ancient incubator of conflicting nationalisms, many of them artificially suppressed for half a century. The removal now of political constraints could invite a revival of destructive national rivalries.

Those rivalries have never been entirely rational, which means their future intensity is not predictable. In the spring of 1990 a fight broke out in Czechoslovakia about how to rename the Czechoslovak Socialist Republic. Czechs proposed the Czechoslovak Republic; Slovaks preferred the Czecho-Slovak Republic. Tens of thousands of Slovaks took to the streets of Bratislava to press their case for a hyphen. The history and emotions that make such arguments possible will confront the old Soviet Empire regularly in the years to come.

The nations of Eastern Europe must now transform themselves. Countries do transform themselves, but only with the greatest difficulty—or under the greatest pressure. Japan and Germany transformed themselves after being devastated in war; conceivably, the devastation caused by Stalinism will give Eastern Europeans a similar combination of incentives and opportunities. But this is far from certain. What has occurred so far—a stunning historical turn, totally unexpected a year before it began—has been due largely to Soviet influence. Gorbachev and his colleagues took the critical step when they decided to forswear the use of force to preserve the regimes of Eastern Europe. Gorbachev began in 1987 to say publicly that force would not be used, but only in 1989 was his word tested. When the Eastern Europeans realized that he actually meant what he said, spontaneous combustion ensued.

Like the other proprietors of twentieth century empires, the Soviets decided that the costs of maintaining a far-flung empire outweighed the benefits. The mythical security zone that Stalin sought to create in Eastern Europe had long since become an insecurity zone, where destabilizing events beyond Moscow's direct control continually threatened international stability, as well as communist control.

It has been no great trick for the Soviets to relinquish control. What has happened so far is likely to be remembered as the easy part of the counterrevolution in Eastern Europe. Soviet influence will play a much smaller role henceforth, unless there is a sharp turn backward in Moscow, a possibility that cannot be ruled out. It was revealing that Václav Havel, the playwright-president of Czechoslovakia, used his speech before a joint session of Congress to tell America that the best way to help democracy in Eastern Europe is to help Gorbachev succeed in the Soviet Union.

In his remarkable "inaugural" address, Havel observed that in achieving their splendid velvet revolution of 1989,

> both our nations [Czechs and Slovaks], after hundreds of years, have raised their heads high on their own initiative, without relying on the help of stronger nations or powers. It seems . . . that this constitutes the great moral asset of the present moment. This moment holds within itself the hope that in the future, we will no longer suffer from the complex of those who must constantly express their gratitude to others. Whether this hope is realized, and whether our civic, national and political self-confidence will be awakened in an historically new way, now depends only on us.[3]

Help from the West, particularly in the form of capital investment and technical expertise, will be useful in Eastern Europe, but Havel is right that the biggest challenges, political and economic, can be met only by the peoples of these countries. Yet for half a century or more, they have had no real opportunity to practice or prepare for the tasks they face.

NOTES

1. As quoted in Michael Dobbs, "Moscow Plays Ketch-Up," *The Washington Post,* February 1, 1990, p. A1, 18.
2. George F. Kennan, "On the Soviet Union and Eastern Europe," *New York Review of Books,* vol. xxxvii, no. 3 (March 1, 1990), p. 7.
3. Václav Havel, "Our Freedom," *The Washington Post,* January 1, 1990, p. A15.

A Look at . . .

THE MIDDLE EAST

Itamar Rabinovich

The profound political and economic changes that have recently been taking place in much of the world have, ironically, resulted in a reversal of roles between Europe and the Middle East.[1] During most of the post–World War II era change in Central and Eastern Europe was governed by rigid Soviet control (and the tenets of the Yalta agreement), while the Middle East arena, not regulated by similar treaty arrangements between the superpowers and far more affected by internal upheavals, became the scene of far more rapid and compelling change and intense Soviet-American competition.

Today, it is in Europe and in the Soviet Union itself that momentous changes are taking place; by way of contrast, the patterns of Middle Eastern politics seem to have rigidified. This need not necessarily remain the case even in the near term, and the main purpose of this essay is to examine both the actual and the potential impact that the recent global sea-changes have had in the Middle East—with a particular emphasis on U.S. policy implications.

Official American interest and interests in the Middle East, as a region of direct governmental concern and as an important component of the international geopolitical system, crystallized in earnest toward the end of World War II as the United States began to assume its role as a superpower. During the past half-century the region's growing importance in the eyes of U.S. policymakers has been the result of a number of factors:

General geopolitical considerations. The Middle East lies astride three continents; is the single most important source of oil and oil reserves; occupies a critical position for international communications by land, sea, and air; and represents a significant proportion of the membership of the United Nations. It houses the whole Arab world and is effectively the center of the larger Muslim community.

An arena of Soviet-American rivalry. The United States asserted itself as the new protector of Western interests in the Middle East in the immediate aftermath of World War II (and during the gradual devolution of the British Empire) and spent the next decade trying to prevent what was then seen as a Soviet "penetration" of the region. In the early 1950s the United States and Britain cooperated in organizing the defense of the Middle East, but as time went by, differences in their respective outlooks surfaced. The United States preferred to rely on a "northern tier" of the Soviet Union's immediate Middle Eastern neighbors, while Britain wanted an alliance comprising its Arab clients so as to perpetuate its traditional influence. The net result was the Baghdad Pact of 1955—a compromise of the two approaches that was unsuccessful and out of tune with Middle Eastern realities. But before the year's end, the Soviet Union leapfrogged over the Baghdad Pact, established its presence and influence in Egypt and Syria, and subsequently did the same in such Arab countries as Iraq, Algeria, Libya, and the People's Democratic Republic of Yemen (PDRY). The Soviet breakthrough of 1955 was followed by eighteen years of fierce competition between the superpowers. At stake were immediate and concrete issues— military bases, arms sales, political influence—but also the success of the respective Western-liberal and Soviet-Marxist models. For a good while, the West appeared to be largely on the defensive, while the Soviet blueprints for rapid modernization, a socialist economy, and a "people's democracy," combined with the exportation of Russian arms and military doctrine and the construction of such spectacular projects as the Aswan and Euphrates dams, were the foundations of the Soviet Union's success in the region. In addition, Egypt's President Gamal Abdel Nasser emerged as one of the three principal leaders of what was essentially an anti-Western, nonaligned movement primarily among Third World countries.

Oil. Middle Eastern oil has been vital for the United States as well as for its European and Far Eastern allies and has been a source of enormous revenues for American oil companies. The oil crises of the early and late 1970s dramatically demonstrated the disruptive potential available to Middle Eastern oil producers, and for a whole decade (1973–1982) the huge profits of the members of the Organization of Petroleum Exporting Countries turned them into all-important actors on the world financial arena.

Threats to international security. A series of Arab-Israeli wars and (to a surprisingly lesser degree) the recent war between Iran and Iraq presented actual or potential threats to the precariously balanced international security system and repeatedly threatened to draw the United States into direct military involvement in the area and into a confrontation with the Soviet Union.

A setting for spectacular diplomatic successes and failures. The relative fluidity of the Middle Eastern political arena, the high stakes involved therein, and the symbolic as well as emotional and ideological dimensions of the ongoing confrontations have endowed superpower successes and failures in the region with a particular significance and resonance. Thus, Egypt's defection from the Soviet orbit in 1972–1973 and the orchestration of the Arab-Israeli peace process in the mid-1970s (leading to the Camp David accords in 1978) were viewed as spectacular achievements for the United States and its policymakers. Conversely, the debacles in Iran and Afghanistan in the late 1970s and the "Irangate" scandals of 1986–1987 were seen as humiliating failures for two successive administrations.

The "special relationship" with Israel. The United States developed in the course of the past four decades several "special relationships" with Middle Eastern states—Saudi Arabia, Iran, and

Egypt have been three such states—but the special relationship with Israel, recent tensions notwithstanding, seems to be in a category by itself. The American-Israeli relationship has gone through several significant changes, but during much of the period it has consistently rested on three principal elements: broad public and political support in the United States, shared values, and "strategic cooperation" against the Soviet Union and radical elements in the Middle East. The relative importance of these three elements is a matter of debate between supporters and critics of the "special relationship" with Israel in the United States. The unusual closeness, intensity, and intimacy of the American-Israeli relationship for more than two decades have now turned it into a very salient dimension of the U.S. position in the Middle East.

II

It is against this background that the significance of the larger sea-changes in world affairs as they pertain to the Middle East, and of that region's relationship to the rest of the world, will be evaluated.

To begin with, it is the changes occurring in the Soviet Union that have the greatest potential for affecting developments in the Middle East; for it is the Muslim dimensions of the changes now taking place *within* the Soviet Union that could matter most to certain Middle Eastern actors. More specifically, the large Muslim population residing along the Turkish, Iranian, and Afghan borders has ethnic as well as religious ties with those living across the Soviet border. For almost 70 years the Soviet border was a very effective barrier separating the two groups, and the Soviet system as a whole seemed to have placed an effective lid on both nationalist and religious agitation among the Soviet Union's Muslim population.

But should present trends—nationalist and ethnic agitation throughout the Soviet Empire, combined with a comparatively meek response from Moscow—continue, and should these trends be reinforced by other, and closely related, developments, such as the transformation of the present tight borders with

Turkey and Iran into "porous" borders, the repercussions for the Middle East could indeed be far-reaching. For more than a century now, Turkey and Iran have felt menaced by powerful and expansionist czarist Russian and Soviet empires. They also have been separated from kindred groups living on the other side of the border. In the Turkish case this facilitated the decision to abandon in the early 1920s the "Pan-Turkish" option and to focus instead on the effort to develop a well-defined Turkish territorial nationalism and to ally the Turkish Republic to the West. In Iran the same fear cemented the Shah's Western orientation and kept the specter of a Soviet intervention alive in the event of a severe domestic crisis.

The removal for the time being of the Soviet threat and the establishment of new links between, say, Turkey and the Uzbeks, and Iran and the Tajiks, could have important ramifications for the international orientation of these two states. In Turkey, for instance, coupled with unhappiness with Washington's and the European Community's policies, a loosening of ties with the North Atlantic Treaty Organization could be seriously considered.

Of greater direct impact on the Middle East has been the blunting of the Soviet-American competition in the region. Given the fact that for nearly 40 years the larger Soviet-Western or Soviet-American rivalry had been a cardinal feature of Middle Eastern politics, the dissipation of that rivalry and its replacement by a different type of relationship could have far-reaching consequences for the region. So far, the change and its impact have been limited.

To some extent this limited effect has derived from the fact that the original symmetry of the Soviet-American confrontation in the Middle East had already been spoiled by earlier developments. By the mid-1980s, it was no longer a case of the United States allied with Israel and the conservative Arab and Muslim states against the Soviet Union and its radical Arab clients. Egypt crossed the lines to the pro-American camp in 1972–1973; the Islamic revolution in Iran in 1979 replaced the Shah's pro-American regime with a regime hostile to both Washington and Moscow (but more so to Washington); and as a by-product of the ensuing war between Iran and Iraq, the latter changed its orientation from an essentially pro-Soviet line to a quest for American support. The Palestine Liberation Organization, considered a pro-Soviet force, was actually keen to enter into a dialogue with the United States and did so at the end of 1988 when the United States changed its policy and decided to engage in such a dialogue. In the mid-1980s the superpowers remained rivals and competitors in the Middle East, but the pattern of their rivalry changed. Both superpowers had difficulties in formulating an effective policy toward Iran and the Gulf War. In the Arab-Israeli part of the Middle East, the United States had an advantage—it was allied with Israel and a diversified group of Arab states, and considered the only superpower capable of effecting an Arab-Israeli settlement; while the Soviet Union was allied with a problematic client, Syria, and was considered barely relevant to the Arab-Israeli peace process. In reality, though, that peace process had been stalled since 1980, and all U.S. efforts during the decade to effect another Arab-Israeli breakthrough failed.

The new Soviet policy in the Middle East has been predicated on, and conducted as part of, a larger Soviet effort to shift from a policy of "confrontation" with the United States to a "balance of interests" posture. In the current Middle Eastern context this means that the Soviet Union would like to become a status quo power, with its own position and interests fully recognized, and to no longer be perceived as the radical outsider seeking to upset the status quo in order to create strategic advantages for itself. Beyond a change in rhetoric and style, the change has manifested itself primarily in a change of attitude toward Syria and Israel, and toward the issue of an Arab-Israeli settlement.

Since Egypt's defection from the Soviet camp in 1972–1973, Syria has been Moscow's principal ally in the region, but their relationship has never been warm, particularly intimate, or free of tensions. More recently relations have been exacerbated by the Soviet Union's new initiatives—slowing down, though not ceasing, the delivery of weapon systems to Damascus, the improvement of relations with Israel and with Syria's conservative Arab rivals (Saudi Arabia, Kuwait), and the patent quest for a partnership with the United States in orchestrating the Arab-Israeli peace process. The single most dramatic measure taken by the Soviet Union vis-à-vis Syria was the statements made by the Soviet ambassador to Syria, Alexander Zotov, in late November 1989. Zotov publicly advised Syrian President Hafiz al-Assad's regime to relinquish its quest for strategic parity with Israel and to seek instead adequate defensive capability. Zotov further explained that the "new realities" in the Soviet Union meant that Moscow would have to take into account "the limits of our capabilities" to provide advanced weapon systems, as well as Syria's "ability to pay for them." The Soviets had always maintained a deliberate ambiguity regarding the nature of their security commitment to Syria in the event of war with Israel. Zotov's statement was meant to serve as a public warning to Syria not to rely on such a commitment in formulating its policies and has, indeed, been received as precisely such by the Syrians.

A second dimension of the Soviet Union's new policy in the Middle East has been a change of official attitudes toward, and in the tenor of overall relations with, Israel. So far the Soviets have stopped short of renewing full diplomatic relations with Israel, but they have gone a long way toward normalizing informal and semiformal contacts and have acquiesced in a renewal of diplomatic relations between Israel and Warsaw Pact members. Hungary, Poland, and Czechoslovakia have restored full diplomatic relations with Israel, and others are on the verge of following suit. Moscow has also practically abandoned the insistence on an international conference as a condition for supporting an Arab-Israeli settlement and supports the current American effort to effect a Palestinian-Israeli settlement. The Soviets maintain that the policy of opening the gates to a massive wave of Jewish emigration, which for reasons beyond their control is presently directed almost exclusively toward Israel, is a matter of domestic and not foreign policy, but the practical effect of this large and highly qualified immigration is to strengthen Israel. Its continuation at the same pace, let alone on a grander scale, could transform Israel's society and political system.

Thus far Moscow's actions have served to blunt the edge of its competition with Washington in the Middle East, to reduce the danger of a Syrian-Israeli war, and to improve Israel's international position. The Soviets may not have sought to improve Israel's standing, but the influx of large numbers of highly qualified immigrants, the opening of Eastern Europe to Israeli diplomacy and economic activity, and the new role played in international politics by the Eastern European states did have this effect.

These changes in Moscow's Middle Eastern policies have been important but limited. Some of the impediments to the adoption of bolder policies have had to do with the Soviet Union's own considerations—an understandable reluctance to appear as a retrenching power and to make unilateral concessions, and a feeling that given the fact that the Soviet political system can absorb a limited amount of change, priority should be assigned to radical changes in more vital areas.

The actual course of events in the Middle East since 1987 has had a similar effect. There were no dangerous crises or sweeping breakthroughs that called for a new level of Soviet-American cooperation or tested the depth of the Soviet Union's commitment to its new Middle Eastern policy. Such developments as the end of the Gulf War, the Iranian succession, the Palestinian intifada, and the ensuing effort to set in motion a Palestinian-Israeli peace process, as well as the most recent events in Lebanon, could all take place within the context of a much milder Soviet-American competitive environment and did not call for a radical definition of the ground rules.

Two situations that could force difficult choices upon the Soviet leadership would be a war involving Syria and Israel, and a breakthrough in the current effort to promote a Palestinian-Israeli settlement. The Soviets abhor the prospect of a Syrian-Israeli war and have, as we have seen, invested efforts in preventing it. They do not support the notion of a Palestinian-Israeli settlement, though they must be aware of the consequences that any substantial progress in Palestinian-Israeli negotiations must have. Syria would then be likely to either sabotage the negotiations or seek to join them; in either event it would confront the Soviet Union with a serious challenge.

Limited as the changes in the Soviet Union's Middle Eastern policies have been, their impact on the Arab world's mood has been considerable. The single most telling articulation of Arab reaction to and thinking on these changes can be found in a speech delivered by Iraq's president, Saddam Hussein, on February 24, 1990. "We . . . Arabs, on the basis of the long-standing friendship with the Soviet Union," he stated, "did not expect the Soviet Union to capitulate to American pressure in such a fashion which leads to consequences dangerous to the Arab[s] and their national security." He envisions a period of "five lean years" of an unbalanced international system dominated by the United States.[2] That period will end when Japan and other new forces find their proper place in a new international order. Until then the Arabs will have to find ways—primarily by closing ranks—for contending with the challenges that the next five years are going to present.

Washington's relationship with its own principal allies in the Middle East has likewise been affected by the developments since 1987. Relations with Israel have changed on two different levels. In more immediate terms, the intimacy and warmth that characterized much of the Reagan-Shultz period have been replaced by acrimony and chill. The change derived from Bush and Baker's different attitude toward Israel, the cumulative effect of the intifada, and the Yitzhak Shamir government's failure to formulate and implement a policy responding effectively to the new circumstances. It was indicative of the change in relations that criticism and pressure by the Bush administration expedited the fall of Shamir's government in March 1990.

On a more fundamental level, the profound changes of the past few years are likely to affect Washington's view of the region and Israel's place in the scheme of things over time. As the Cold War in the region is waning, Israel's importance as a strategic ally is likely to diminish. But as the region's overall importance declines, the pressures generated by Washington's close association with Israel—the other side of strategic cooperation—are likely to decrease as well.

It is interesting to note that the Egyptians are as worried as are the Israelis that the current developments in Europe and in

East-West relations could have an adverse effect on their relationship with the United States. Egypt, together with Israel, is a major recipient of U.S. foreign aid. Its claim to that aid is predicated on its geopolitical importance. A blunting of the Soviet-American competition in the Middle East, and the need to divert aid money to Eastern Europe, could result in the reduction of U.S. aid to Egypt.

On a different level, the apparent discrediting of the Marxist model of socioeconomic reform has had a minor effect in the Middle East for the very simple reason that in that part of the world, the Marxist mode lost much of its appeal more than a decade ago. A full-fledged communist regime had never been established in the region. (The radical regime of the PDRY came closest to fitting the model; but the PDRY is a rather small state situated in the region's periphery and has been marginal to its politics.) True enough, Marxism had an important influence on Arab thought and politics in the late 1950s and during the 1960s, but the revolutionary governments that emerged in Egypt, Syria, Iraq, and Algeria had—by the early 1970s—failed or been transformed into Thermidorian regimes. Since then, Marxism has been replaced either by well-articulated Islamic ideologies or by an inarticulate acceptance of the ways of the West.

But the growth of populist/democratic opposition to authoritarian/totalitarian rule in Eastern Europe (and the Soviet Union itself) is likely to have a more significant effect in the Middle East. The retreat or collapse of formerly formidable regimes in the face of popular resistance in communist countries occurred, as far as Middle Easterners are concerned, in the immediate wake of a series of successful challenges presented in the Middle East by popular movements to powerful governments—the Islamic revolution in Iran, the Palestinian intifada, the riots in Algiers and in Jordan. After two decades during which Middle Eastern states appeared far more powerful than the societies inhabiting them, both governing elites and the people at large must have been impressed by the ability of popular or even spontaneous movements to defy entrenched regimes and by the ruling establishments' loss of nerve. Yet analogies and inferences drawn— regarding the Middle East—could be misleading: popular groups may become emboldened, but beleaguered regimes could also conclude that an immediate and brutal reaction to any popular uprising would be necessary for their survival.

In addition, Middle Easterners have been less impressed than Western Europeans or North Americans by the revival of nationalist, ethnic, and communal sentiments in Eastern Europe and the Soviet Union itself: such sentiments have been potent in the Middle East throughout the twentieth century. As for the liberal-democratic aspects of recent developments in Eastern Europe, they will probably *not* have an immediate or striking effect on the course of events in the Middle East. The tenets of liberalism and constitutional democracy were brought to the Middle East from the West. Unhappily, they were grafted in the wrong fashion, and the British and French record of promoting these ideas and forms of government in the Middle East was far from impressive. The current democratic experiments in Eastern Europe will have to become well-established success stories before they can become new sources of inspiration for Middle Easterners. The powerful Islamic wave of the late 1970s and early 1980s and its anti-Western edge have been weakened in absolute terms; but when it comes to alternative models, should any of the present authoritarian or semiauthoritarian regimes in the Middle East collapse, Islamic movements, enjoying the advantages of authenticity and at least a measure of organization, do stand a good chance.

When it comes to issues of economic development, it appears that for the Middle East the crucial issue will continue to concern the oil industry rather than shifts in the global balance of economic power from the United States to a "United" Europe and Japan or to a renewal of trade wars. Since the end of World War II the economic hegemony of the United States had been perceived in the Middle East as a dimension of the country's overall leadership as a superpower projecting political and military power, and serving as both the source of inspiration and the focus of resentment. The transfer of economic leadership is likely to affect but not totally erode this position.

In economic terms most Middle Eastern countries have lived since 1982 in the shadow of the oil industry's decline.

During the 1973–1974 "oil crisis," the launching of the "oil weapon" and the dramatic rise in oil prices provided Middle Eastern producers with huge revenues and financial reserves and with hitherto unfamiliar political and economic influence. In the region itself, new lines of division were created between "rich" and "poor" states, though the latter also benefited, at least indirectly, from the oil revenues. The subsequent decline of the oil industry, particularly since 1982, has had a different impact on these two categories of states. The "rich" states have been forced to trim their expenditures, cut budgets, and use at least part of their reserves while "poor" states—like Egypt, Syria, and Jordan—have all suffered economic and attendant political difficulties.

Several reports have predicted that a new "energy crisis" is looming and that Middle Eastern oil producers are likely to regain the crucial position they enjoyed a decade ago. Should these predictions be realized, a fresh infusion of revenues into the region's economies should be expected. Should they not, further economic and political difficulties in both "rich" and "poor" states are likely to emerge, and in the context of the densely populated countries of the Middle East, this could mean greater immigration flow to Europe and, to a lesser extent, to North America.

III

Seen from a U.S. policy perspective, the changes that have occurred during the past few years in the Middle East—and in the region's role and place in international politics—have been rather limited. The competition with the Soviet Union has been blunted but not eliminated; the importance of Middle Eastern oil is rising and may rise further, perhaps dramatically so, in the 1990s; Islamic fundamentalism as a political force has peaked but has not disappeared, and the sense of antagonism toward and resentment of American power is still affecting the attitude of many Muslims; the feeling that the "liberal West" or "America" won the contest with the Soviet Union (and its Marxist model) seems to reinforce that sense of antagonism. The Middle

East continues to be the source of threats to international security; the danger of a conventional war does not seem imminent, but the Arab-Israeli and Iranian-Iraqi military buildups continue, unconventional weapon systems proliferate, and the phenomenon of terrorism lingers.

Against this backdrop the advancement of an Arab-Israeli—more specifically, a Palestinian-Israeli—settlement remains an important U.S. policy goal. In theory it should have been facilitated by the cumulative effect of the Palestinian intifada and the other changes in Arab-Israeli relations that occurred in the late 1980s. But in reality, progress has been blocked by a number of factors: Palestinian pressure and initiative, through the intifada and the attendant political strategies, have been routinized and weakened; Israeli politics have been paralyzed by a systemic crisis and by a genuine dissension over the Palestinian issue; and the Bush administration has failed to pursue a persistent and clear-cut policy in this area. Furthermore, some of the progress that had been made in the 1980s toward an Arab acceptance of the Israeli state has been undone by hostile Arab reactions to the new wave of Jewish immigration from the Soviet Union.

The next few years may well see greater changes occurring at a quicker pace in the Middle East either as a result of such internal changes as a domestic upheaval in a key state or as a by-product of the broader changes that are reshaping international politics. But even if this is the case, it is difficult to envisage a decline in the saliency of the Arab-Israeli problem as the principal U.S. policy concern in the Middle East.

NOTES

1. For the purpose of this essay the term "Middle East" denotes the area comprising the Arab world, Turkey, Iran, and Israel.
2. Speech at the Fourth Summit of the Arab Cooperation Council, Amman, Jordan, February 24, 1990.

A Look at . . .

EAST ASIA

William H. Gleysteen, Jr.

Until talk of a "Pacific century" was pushed out of American minds by the fascination with dramatic developments in Europe, most commentators pointed to East Asia as the most striking case of sea-changes in recent history. An area known for chronic war and economic backwardness has been transformed within less than half a century into the world's foremost model of rapid development. The transformation, much of it centering on Japan, is, of course, far from complete or uniform. China and the other communist regimes are bogged down with massive internal difficulties, trying to resist inevitable change or suffering through painful transitions. Economic performance has overshadowed far less impressive progress—and, indeed, frequent regression—in political development. Nevertheless, East Asia's accomplishments have been stunning.

These changes have fundamentally altered the contours of American policy. The United States has lost the overwhelmingly powerful position it used to enjoy as the region's protector and benefactor, along with some of the respect accompanying that position. Moreover, East Asians are now far less anxious about security protection from what they see as diminished military threats and are far more preoccupied with economic prowess. Although U.S. policy has evolved enough to reflect some of this change, it continues to be excessively focused on the Soviet Union and the People's Republic of China (PRC) without showing enough concern about the cost—and danger—of a deteriorating relationship with Japan. Nor do many Americans recognize that their own country's economic revival is a prerequisite for implementing an effective strategy in the East Asia of the future.

II

The international alignments and balance of power—even the elements that undergird national power—in East Asia today differ strikingly from the situation of the 1950s, when the United States felt a compelling need to stabilize and protect a poor and war-torn region from the powerful threat of communism centered in the Soviet Union and the PRC. Unless militarily deterred, as in Korea, communism seemed poised to expand through the use of massive military force, organizational skill, subversion, and pure ideological appeal—particularly through the promise of rapid and egalitarian economic development. We assumed that the Soviet Union and Communist China had mutually reinforcing objectives and were in full control of their communist cohorts in Korea and Southeast Asia. In contrast, noncommunist Asia was on the defensive, apparently bogged down in a battle of survival against enemies who seemed effective in taking advantage of widespread systemic weaknesses. Most of the region was suffering from underdevelopment, as well as from the political fighting that had accompanied the collapse of the old colonial order.

Washington's response to this situation was reasonably coherent and certainly vigorous. Building on the earlier decisions to strengthen Japan and to hold the line against Communist China in Korea and the Taiwan Straits, the United States sought to contain the communist threat through new alliances and the deployment of a powerful military presence around China. Together with a program of military and economic assistance, we hoped that this forward posture would shield East Asia and buy time to develop the region—as it did. Although at times progress seemed unnecessarily slow and costly, by and large the American public accepted the burden. In the process the United States made major military sacrifices and extended massive amounts of help in ways that played a fundamental role in East Asia's subsequent burst toward rapid economic development.

Despite the generally constructive nature of this American policy, it was often encumbered by emotionalism, ignorance, and a faulty perception of Sino-Soviet solidarity and of relations among communist forces in Asia. These factors caused a remarkably long delay in our efforts to see whether the communist regime in China might be interested in reducing tensions with the United States—and this despite suggestive evidence of Sino-Soviet friction going back as early as the mid-1950s and more obvious public indications of the same a few years later. These same factors, combined with an exaggeration of communist military and organizational capabilities, also led ultimately to our costly engagement in Vietnam. Ironically, misperceptions and exaggerations of communist power tended to obscure for most Americans—although less so for Asians—the extent to which the United States dominated the Pacific during the two decades after World War II—the only time we enjoyed something approaching hegemony.

In the late 1960s and the 1970s American policy in East Asia underwent significant change. The definition of primary potential "enemy" was narrowed down and fixed on the USSR. We also recognized our own tangible limitations—stemming more from the clash of domestic priorities than from ultimate capacity—in maintaining a preponderant position in the region. North Korea remained a continuing source of regional concern. Focusing our main strategic concern on the Soviet Union's rapidly growing military strength, the United States sought to offset our own relatively diminishing power by courting at least tacit cooperation from China, which was by this time vehemently anti-Soviet, as well as by relying more explicitly on Japan's growing strength. The war in Vietnam, combined with a considerable oversimplification about the motives of China's behavior, confused this neat picture of mutual alignment against the USSR. Some Americans, for example, thought that China might help us pull our chestnuts out of the fire in the Vietnam peace process by applying heavy pressure on North Vietnam—even at the risk of undermining its still substantial relationship with Hanoi. An even larger number of Americans naively assumed that a weak China—having lowered the danger to its own security by a transformation of its relations with the United States—could be enticed or manipulated back into adopting a high-risk posture against the USSR.

Generally, however, the new American strategy was far more realistic than its immediate predecessor. The concept of an informal coalition of states—including a communist China—aimed against the USSR clearly reflected an awareness of substantial shifts in the way national power was being distributed, or redistributed, in Asia: Americans now demonstrated a better, if still imperfect, appreciation of divergent relations among communist countries; and they understood, at least to some degree, the relative decline of U.S. power and of Japan's growing importance beyond its role as a supplier of consumer products.

Moreover, by the 1970s many conditions in East Asia were becoming favorable to the United States. Despite the doomsayers, the collapse of South Vietnam in 1975 not only failed to trigger the falling of the rest of the dominoes but, indeed, invigorated the Association of Southeast Asian States (ASEAN), thus effectively reducing the communist threat in Southeast Asia, except in Indochina. Throughout East Asia, including the communist nations, communist ideology was losing its luster. Following closely in Japan's footsteps, a number of market-oriented economies in the region were now in the process of spectacular takeoffs toward rapid economic development. Although by now curtailed, the massive U.S. aid programs of earlier years finally seemed to be bearing fruit. True enough, Americans were no longer willing to support large assistance programs; but these were no longer needed, because the developing countries of East Asia had reached a point where access to the huge American market was more important than aid for their export-driven economies.

The 1980s brought further realism to U.S. strategic thinking, as well as more favorable shifts in regional conditions. The buildup of American military forces in response to hard-line Soviet policies, particularly the invasion of Afghanistan, effectively checked concern over comparative U.S. and Soviet power in the Pacific. In any event, the Soviet Union has not been able to use either its military power or its emerging diplomatic flexibility to make damaging gains at American expense. While the PRC has revealed a logical preference for a more equidistant position between the United States and the USSR, thus disappointing those who were mesmerized into thinking that the Chinese would become American surrogates against the Soviets, the shift has not negated the fundamental strategic attraction between Beijing and Washington. Other developments in the area seem equally encouraging. Much of East Asia has registered dramatic economic growth, with many countries headed for promotion to "developed" status within a decade; and progress toward political liberalization has also begun far sooner than most had thought possible, with major movements toward political pluralism occurring in South Korea, Taiwan, and the Philippines. A mood of optimism, reflected in talk of a Pacific century, has emerged in noncommunist East Asia—despite an awareness that economic growth may yet run into new barriers, while political progress will almost certainly prove fragile in certain cases, as already demonstrated in China in 1989.

III

This rather benign picture of largely constructive development in East Asia—and generally sensible American responses—reflects, but also obscures, a number of profound changes that must be addressed by planners of U.S. policy.

First, East Asia has been transformed from a region known for its poverty, political instability, and recurring wars to one of the world's economically most dynamic and stable areas. Although, as already noted, political progress has been less than spectacular, a generally favorable trend has emerged—limited so far largely to noncommunist Asia, where economic development has engendered a mushrooming of middle-class values. Japan is the centerpiece in this developmental transformation. The economic and political accomplishments that underlie that country's surge of national strength are a more solid foundation for international strength in today's world than the brute military power possessed by the Soviet Union or China. Given a growing appreciation of this reality, it is hardly surprising that the prime concern of most East Asians is for continued rapid economic development. Fortunately for them, many of these countries have sufficient general education and technical skills to be able to take exceptional advantage of progress made in science and technology, in effect leapfrogging over traditional stages of modernization. This pattern of growth—through foreign trade and interdependence with other countries for resources, capital, technology, and markets—has, of course, also made East Asia singularly dependent on a functioning system of relatively free trade.

Second, in striking contrast to the situation of the 1950s, no East Asian country, with the possible exception of Korea, foresees the likelihood of a military attack by a hostile power in the next five to ten years. Although some East Asians may continue to underestimate the helpful role U.S. global strategy has played in the past, most do feel that the general communist challenge has been blunted. More so than most Americans, they also see a confirmation of their long-standing conviction that historical rivalries and national enmities have tended to keep communists divided. They believe that the leading communist powers in Asia have been weakened, if not crippled, by internal turmoil. Above all, the Soviet military threat, which always seemed more remote to them than it did to Americans, now strikes East Asians as rapidly diminishing in this era of global détente and of radically changing policy priorities in Moscow.

Japan may be an exception to this rule in the sense that its government still justifies the gradual strengthening of its self-defense forces on the grounds that East-West détente has not significantly reduced Soviet military deployments in East Asia. Japan has, moreover, suffered from the Soviet Union's relatively clumsy handling of the dispute over the Northern Territories (the four islands north of Hokkaido occupied by the USSR but claimed by Japan). Despite these important qualifications, as well as long-term concerns about China, the Japanese do not feel they are under imminent military threat from any quarter. This reality would manifest itself even more clearly were the Soviet

Union to promise to hand back the four disputed islands in the Northern Territories.[1] Similarly, although many East Asian countries have long been wary of China because of its proximity and its past domination of the region, today few among them feel much of a military threat from a country that has downgraded military priorities and is so troubled by internal unrest.[2] Even Vietnam no longer appears a worrisome security threat to most of its neighbors (except to some elements in Cambodia). North Korea remains the exception to such an optimistic overview of the region. Yet most Asians, including most South Koreans, expect North Korea to remain deterred from any serious military adventurism by South Korea's newly developed strength—and by continuing evidence of the American commitment to that country's defense.

Third, communism in East Asia no longer carries any popular appeal in the face of the success of so many market economies in contrast to communist failures. Any attraction that the communist model held for others was completely negated by knowledge of the disastrous results of China's Cultural Revolution, the regimentation and dangerous goings-on in North Korea, and the remarkable hollowness of North Vietnam's "victory" over the South. Recent events within the Soviet Union and the cascading changes taking place in Eastern Europe have only helped underscore this point. The binding power of ideology has been severely weakened even in East Asia's communist countries, although this should not be interpreted to mean that communist rulers in Asia will soon lose control in the manner of their Eastern European counterparts. Terrified by the combination of popular protest in China and the crumbling of communist authority in Europe, the aged leaders of East Asia's communist regimes have resorted to old techniques of repression and control that may allow them to hold the line for the time being. If they should fail in this, and even if they are replaced by more liberal-minded leaders, Western-style democracy is not likely to bloom quickly in societies where authoritarian rule has been the norm, and may remain so in the absence of the sort of economic transformation that has benefited political reforms in other parts of the region.

Finally, there is a profound change taking place in the very character of international relationships within East Asia, as well as in the region's orientation to the rest of the world. For the better part of the postwar era, military concerns weighed more heavily than economic ones in the calculus of national power. With America's capacity to project both military and economic strength, noncommunist countries in the region tended to look to the United States as a provider of military security, as well as for capital, technology, and markets. Americans were known for their generosity, and the United States was viewed as a country in control of its own destiny, as a model for economic development. The United States was, in effect, the hub of the Pacific.

Not enough Americans appreciate how much the situation has changed. The United States remains East Asia's principal guarantor against external threats, and American markets continue to provide the main avenue for the export-driven growth of many of the region's countries. But as economic considerations have come increasingly to overshadow military ones, there has been a relative decline in U.S. power—and leverage. Japan has largely replaced the United States as the region's creditor, as the source of the most useful (but not always available) technology, and as a more appropriate model for economic development. With a huge economy no longer so dependent on exports, Japan. is also becoming a major market for other East Asian states, not only for those resources Japan lacks, but increasingly for manufactured items produced in other parts of the region by Japanese or foreign firms. For countries such as South Korea and Taiwan, the Japanese market promises within a few years to parallel the American in importance. Japan has effectively replaced the United States as the major source of assistance in the region, and the yen is considered a safer, if less convenient, currency than the dollar. There is little prospect of a formally organized East Asia "bloc" headed by Japan. But Japan has become a second hub of relationships in East Asia, in some cases complementing, in others rivaling the American role. American prestige and respect have declined, while Japan's have risen to a considerable extent.

Nevertheless, Japan is not about to replace the United States as the principal power in the Pacific, if only because other Asian states would not tolerate such a fundamental role change with the memory of Japan's expansionist policies of the 1930s and 1940s still fresh in their minds. Indeed, not many Japanese are imbued today with a sense of "manifest destiny," and most find it difficult even to broaden their vision enough to appreciate the global role most other countries believe Japan should be playing. Moreover, the Japanese may be more aware than any outsiders of the many shortcomings in their political institutions that, together with other domestic conditions (such as inadequate housing, high retail prices, and excessive regulation), may make Japan's emergence as a world power far more difficult than might be assumed. Thus, the United States will almost surely remain the single most important power in East Asia, retaining enormous economic clout and alone able to offset Soviet military power. No other major power has the credibility and capacity to undergird stability in the region by buffering latent tensions between China and Japan, Korea and Japan, Southeast Asia and Japan—or China.

IV

This brief look at how U.S. policy has accommodated itself to a gradual but profound transformation in East Asia since the Korean War leads one to suggest some generalizations about the next stage of American involvement in the region.

The first condition for a successful adjustment of U.S. policy to the new East Asian realities is for some movement to take place toward the self-discipline and painful repair of American fiscal management, tax structure, industrial policy, and educational performance that alone can improve U.S. competitiveness and eventually overcome the inferiority complex that underlies so much of our present fear of Japan and of Germany.

A second and related requirement is to stop the current drift toward a virulent antagonism in American attitudes toward Japan. Our alliance with Japan has been a fundamental feature of the postwar balance of power arrangements in Asia, permitting both our own forward defense strategy and Japan's extraordinary economic growth. If this cooperation were transformed into a "neutral" or, conceivably, adversarial relationship, Japan would inevitably become less accommodating to U.S. geopolitical needs and strike a more independent course in international affairs. The Japanese, who generally sense the reality of interdependence more than Americans do, could probably be counted on to rein in their anger in an effort to sustain their country's prosperity. But some Japanese would undoubtedly begin to act just as nationalistically and xenophobically as current American critics predict they will—to the detriment of both nations' security. In a worst-case scenario, Japan might restrict or end our access to military bases on its territory, build up and equip its own military forces in ways that would alarm others, and resort to a kind of opportunism that would be greatly to our disadvantage.

Thus, U.S. leaders need to explain to the American people that our relationship with Japan is our most important one in East Asia: it is in strategic terms as fundamental as that with China; economically more productive than that with any other country; and in effect beginning to surpass in global significance even our ties with the Soviet Union. In short, we have become critically dependent on East Asia's stability and prosperity, and Japan has emerged as the decisive actor in sustaining these conditions. We must, therefore, find ways to live with the inevitable strains and frustrations that accompany such interdependency.

Our relations with Japan will continue to be difficult, since the element of economic rivalry not only will grow but is apt to become more and more preoccupying for both sides—assuming, of course, that traditional security concerns fade further away as a result of developments within the Soviet Union and other communist countries. Moreover, Japanese leaders will certainly not encourage their people to adopt American patterns of high consumption, and we can assume they will continue to rely on some variety of industrial policy as a way of protecting their interests. Thus, periodic pressure, carefully focused on achievable targets, will be required if we are to accelerate Japan's movement toward economic liberalization and deregulation. But Washington policymakers will have to exercise enough care to preserve (basically) good relations with Tokyo, allow enough time for its still closed society to open up, and provide enough inducements (e.g., Japanese leadership of international economic organizations and Japanese involvement in major decisions affecting both the United States and Europe) to enhance Japan's leadership role.

Assuming the United States can do a better job of managing its relationship with Japan, it is then not hard to envisage an appropriate U.S. strategy for the entire East Asian region. This would be premised on the rather satisfactory strategic equilibrium that now exists, while allowing greater flexibility and less of a focus on "enemies" than did the "containment" policy of the past decades. Although such a strategy would require greater attention to economic concerns, prudence would call for a still significant—though reduced—American military component to cope with the threat of an adverse turn in Soviet or Chinese foreign policy, while also discouraging any other power, including Japan, from trying to replace the United States as the principal guarantor of regional stability. The United States has played this role effectively for a long time, has the capacity to continue doing so, and has far better credentials than any other imaginable candidate. The need for this buffering role by the United States will continue even with substantial evidence of Soviet-American détente in East Asia.

Such a revised U.S. strategy would, nevertheless, rely heavily on Japan, though not to the exclusion of important roles reserved for China, the Republic of Korea, and the ASEAN countries. It would, moreover, treat the USSR as a bona fide Asian power whose military, economic, and diplomatic involvement throughout the region is now a fact of life. Japan would continue to provide bases for U.S. forces, henceforth reduced to mostly naval and air elements (substantially smaller than those deployed today); and it would be responsible for all aspects of its own defense except for nuclear deterrence. In the economic sphere Japan would be treated as a coequal with the United States; and politically Japan would be accorded a "special relationship" with the United States, having the kind of access in Washington nowadays enjoyed by key North Atlantic Treaty

Organization partners—and often enough by the Soviets and the Chinese.

Although a far less significant economic power than Japan, the PRC would be an important factor in the success of such a strategic plan—given China's heavy weight in the region, its nuclear capacity, and its strategic location. These considerations were sufficient to prompt American leaders to begin normalizing U.S. relations with the PRC at a time when China's domestic policies were at their most repressive, and presumably they will continue to influence Washington as it tries to make the best of a difficult relationship with Beijing in the wake of the political crackdown in 1989. Since an uncooperative China would severely handicap any sensible U.S. strategic approach, Americans may well have to accept conditions within China that cause them—as well as many Chinese—considerable stress. In the long run, moreover, an American posture of relatively cooperative engagement with China is more likely to have a positive influence in China than is one of sharp confrontation.

Looking beyond Japan, China, and the Soviets, it is clear that a number of other relationships—or contingencies—will affect U.S. strategy in East Asia. Korea, for example, remains a danger point, perhaps even more so today because of the expected leadership transition in Pyongyang and the tension generated there by events in the Soviet Union and Eastern Europe. At the same time, however, these developments may trigger changes in North Korea that will eventually permit reduced confrontation. Complications may also arise from a new Soviet-Japanese relationship that could emerge if the USSR were to relax its hard line on the Northern Territories—especially if such a change coincided with a deterioration in U.S.–Japanese ties. Events in the Philippines could also deprive us of the option of maintaining our bases there; but with reduced global or regional requirements for the bases and the existence of alternative basing arrangements in the Pacific, the negative effect of withdrawing from Clark and Subic would be limited. Continuing civil war and unsettled political conditions in Indochina should inspire American policy planners to devise ways to entice as well as pressure an exhausted Vietnam into a better relationship with the United

States, as well as with other member-states of ASEAN. However, the impasse in our relations with Vietnam today is more a question of lost opportunities than a threat to major U.S. interests.

Finally, this new strategy would require the United States to undertake a serious effort toward the eventual reduction of the principal military forces currently deployed in East Asia. This will prove extremely difficult to achieve, because of many disparate factors, including the deployment in the area by the United States and the Soviet Union of forces considered by them to be necessary for purposes of the overall global strategic balance, but seen as excessive or threatening in regional terms; the lack of symmetry between Soviet and U.S. defense needs in East Asia; the crazy quilt of countries involved (in contrast to the clearly defined blocs that existed in Europe at the start of the arms control process there); the feeling among some influential Japanese leaders that their defense establishment has not yet reached the point of self-sufficiency (let alone of a proper projection of national power); the intensity of the hostile confrontation between the two Koreas; and the lingering civil war in Cambodia.

Nevertheless, the issue of force reductions should be pursued in earnest, because the danger of war in East Asia involving the Chinese or the Soviets has definitely diminished. South Korea has now reached a level of defensive strength where we can seriously contemplate the phased withdrawal of all U.S. ground forces, so long as we make it clear that our treaty commitment to Seoul remains, allow enough time to condition people in both South and North Korea—as well as neighboring countries—to such a withdrawal, and leave U.S. air and naval units in place. Ideally, any major ground force withdrawals should be phased with talks between South and North Korea to create an additional incentive for force reductions, but such talks need not be a precondition for U.S. withdrawals.

Americans are gradually learning of their nation's relative hegemonic decline in the Pacific. But it is apparent that they are not very confident about the next phase of the adjustment process that awaits them in Asia. And indeed there are good reasons for concern. One is a faltering domestic American economic performance, coupled with the absence of any signs of the kind of national self-reflection, commitment to hard work, and occasional sacrifice that are required to restore momentum. Another problem is that East Asia is evolving in ways that may deprive Americans of the kinds of targets, such as the Soviets and the Chinese, that helped mobilize past U.S. efforts to deal effectively with the region. In any event, Americans will be facing a complex East Asian arena, requiring a willingness to commit sufficient national energies to their dealings with a part of the world that already rivals Europe in importance.

NOTES

1. Nevertheless, to a certain degree Japan would always remain wary of the Soviet Union; and many Japanese would still wish to build up Japan's self-defense forces, because of Soviet-inspired—and other—considerations.
2. Even Taiwan seems reasonably confident of its security so long as it maintains strong forces and avoids provoking the PRC over the "independence" issue.

A Look at . . .

SOUTH ASIA

Thomas P. Thornton

South Asia[1] is an area that of late, and in terms of general interest, most of the world has relegated to the bottom of its priority lists. It plays a relatively small role in international affairs, and its internal conditions are of interest mainly to political scientists and development economists. Yet a quarter of the world's population lives there, and it is an area of immense potential in economic terms as well as military capability. There is little doubt that South Asia will over time become a much more important focus of American attention, but exactly when that will happen—and in what form—remains much less clear.

Although South Asia has played an important role in global history, and today is being drawn into this shared history at an increasingly rapid rate, the region's sheer size and strength enable it to navigate with considerable immunity from the set and drift of global sea-changes. India's future, especially, will be determined more by indigenous than by external factors. Pakistan and the lesser nations of South Asia are much more open to external influences—partially because they are smaller, but also because they see the outside world as a protection from the overwhelming presence of India. India, however, continues to dominate the region: not only "statistically," but also in ways that limit the influence of outside powers upon its smaller neighbors.

It is difficult to distinguish between South Asia and India. We talk and write of India and feel guilty about ignoring the other states of the subcontinent—but if we focus on them, we risk ignoring the central fact of South Asia. India, vast in population and area and complex in its culture and politics, is itself difficult to comprehend. Beyond that, it is a nation ambivalent about its very nature: Is India, in the international context, the least of the great powers or the greatest of the least? In domestic terms, is it the nation of more than 700 million of the world's poorest or of some 150 million middle-class persons within a rapidly developing consumer economy?

India, huge and diverse, is inert in both senses of that word: it demonstrates immense stability and resistance to manipulation, but also it is immensely difficult to get moving. The economic and social changes that have taken place over a generation of nationhood have been striking, but they have come about gradually and slowly, almost imperceptibly. Despite growing pressures, radical change is hardly more likely to occur in the last decade of this century than it was in the previous decades.

All of South Asia must, however, undergo some radical changes in its political, social, and (especially) economic orders— sometime. There are critical masses of discontent forming, and in each of the South Asian states the people's toleration of poor governance is wearing thin. In some cases we know where the future *must* lead; in others, much more numerous, we see a range of alternatives. Could the 1990s be the decade in which South Asia finally asserts itself on the international scene in ways commensurate with its size—for better or for worse? Or will this perhaps be the decade in which it slips inexorably down into destructive revolution or irretrievable depths of mass despair? There are prophets for either account.

II

None of the South Asian nations are now major actors on the international financial scene except as consumers of development assistance. Relatively speaking, they have been models of responsible international financial behavior. Had they, like some of the African and Latin American nations, borrowed recklessly a decade ago, they might now be the overwhelming focus of our concern about less-developed-country debt. That is mercifully not the case, but most of them do face difficult repayment problems. Pakistan, with a foreign debt of over $16 billion, was forced to turn to the International Monetary Fund for an SDR 273 million structural adjustment in December 1988. Although it has avoided default, it will continue to be plagued by repayment problems as long as it spends so much foreign exchange on military items and as remittances from Pakistanis working overseas lag. India's huge debt (over $46 billion) is supported by a large economy and has been managed soberly, but it is also worrisome. Throughout the region, needs for very large amounts of capital (whether as loans or as equity participation) will grow over the coming decades if these countries are to enter the international economic system successfully and make serious inroads on their development problems. Finding this capital is likely to be increasingly difficult, however, as South Asia—low on most national lenders' priority lists and frequently difficult to do business with—finds it has to compete with the politically more interesting demands emerging in Eastern Europe and, perhaps, China.

With the limited exception of Indo-Soviet relations, South Asia is insignificant in international trade. That, however, is one of the things that will inevitably change—and probably soon. Throughout the 1980s, India pursued policies of economic liberalization that encourage both imports and exports. There are populist forces in India that resist free-market developments (and these are well represented in the powerful bureaucracy and the coalition government led by Prime Minister Vishwanath Pratap Singh), but, if they can be fended off, India has the productive and entrepreneurial potential to become a claimant for a significant share of the international market for manufactured goods. This is a claim that the world will be hard put to accommodate, especially if it coincides with a major Chinese export thrust. The smaller economies of South Asia will present challenges of a lesser magnitude, but they, too, will have to be accommodated as they seek to export light consumer goods in a market that is already fiercely competitive. Even Bangladesh encountered problems of access to the U.S. market when it achieved some modest success in assembling clothing products as a subcontractor for East Asian exporters. To the extent that substantial growth makes these large and partially advanced nations into serious competitors on the international market, it will be logical to graduate them away from preferential treatment. In fact, however, they will under the best of circumstances remain extremely poor and in bad need of whatever advantages they can get.

The problems of coping with an increasingly prosperous South Asia could pale in comparison with the possibility of a South Asia mired in economic decay. The South Asian nations are making considerable progress in population control (Pakistan and Afghanistan are unfortunate exceptions), but no matter how effective these policies may be, huge growth is statistically inevitable through the rest of the century. India alone will have over a billion inhabitants by the year 2000. Rapidly growing populations inexorably eat up gains in production, and realization of frightening projections of famine and starvation sometime in the next century is possible. But Malthusian disaster is not inevitable. India's population has indeed doubled since independence, but overall growth of agricultural output in South Asia has been impressive. India has tripled grain production since 1950, and even Bangladesh has progressed toward self-sufficiency. The region can feed itself with ease if the political will exists to stimulate agricultural production. The immediate gains made under the Green Revolution technology are now leveling off, and a new thrust is needed. Above all, an integrated development program for the Ganges and Brahmaputra valleys is one of the crying needs not only for South Asia but for a world where food shortages and surpluses in one region can affect the price of bread globally.

Overall economic growth was encouraging in the 1980s through much of region. Pakistan and Sri Lanka, if they can put their political systems in order, might soon become middle-income countries. India's gross national product, recently growing at a 5 percent annual rate, could conceivably double by the year 2000. Yet combinations of bad luck (especially from the weather), bad management of the economy (especially government interference in the free-market process), and external economic forces over which India has no control (such as protectionism or a severe global recession) threaten these promising trends. Moreover, even if the more optimistic growth projections prevail, most South Asians will remain desperately poor well into the next century. The dimensions of the economic development challenge are so vast that replication of the East Asian newly industrializing countries' experience is just not feasible, except perhaps in Sri Lanka.

There may be more dire projections—billions of hungry South Asians explosively forcing their way into our attention— but that sort of contingency is probably far off. More likely is the continued persistence of inertia that yields only slowly to progress—important but irregular and inadequate growth, affected, but not dominated, by broader global trends.

III

South Asia is an economic anomaly compared with its increasingly prosperous neighbors to the west and east. Politically, too, it is odd man out, for within Afro-Asia it is in the subcontinent that democracy has secured its strongest foothold. India and Sri Lanka have long, virtually uninterrupted histories of free elections and relatively open societies, and while Pakistan and Bangladesh have had much more spotty careers, they too have the political infrastructure to support democratic rule. The restoration of democracy in Pakistan under Benazir Bhutto, following the long tenure of General Zia-ul-Haq, was, of course, one of the brighter instances of the global democratic resurgence that characterized the later 1980s. Although Bangladesh and Nepal still fall short of democratic practice, trends there are hopeful. The outlook for democratic evolution in the marginal states, Iran and Afghanistan, however, is bleak, and the military dictatorship in Myanmar (Burma) has, for the time being at least, ruthlessly crushed the nascent democratic movement.

In the core states of the region, however, the issue for the coming decade is less the emergence of open political systems than their preservation. Human rights and constitutional procedures are under stress from crushing economic and social problems that would threaten any political system. Basic law and order are breaking down, and in several of the countries regional separatism poses a severe problem. Sri Lanka hovers on the brink of Lebanonization as extremists from the Tamil and Sinhalese ethnic groups press their cases suicidally. Pakistan's fragile democratic renewal is held hostage by conflicting demands of the five ethnic groups that the country comprises, and the social order is threatened by the results of the Afghanistan war—the explosive spread of drugs and the ready availability of automatic weapons. India's problems include not only the regional separatism most sharply evident in the Punjab and Kashmir, but a deterioration in law and order resulting from caste strife and Hindu-Muslim animosities. Political party structure is in a state of flux as the Congress continues its decline, and the opposition has yet to demonstrate that it can pull together for positive policy goals.

The generation of leaders who brought South Asia's peoples to independence—Gandhi, Nehru, and Jinnah—were able to draw the masses into the political leadership in an evolutionary and constructive manner. The major states of South Asia now, however, are decapitated political societies. The successor generations have not been able to convey a sense of national purpose that would convince their countrymen that orderly progress is possible. Populist appeals have become more strident and are increasingly calling the tune. And it is often not a pretty tune, stressing issues of caste, religion, and ethnicity in ways that are disruptive both to national unity and to the achievement of a decent society. Atavistic pressures, rooted mainly in religion, could become the stuff of South Asian populism in a postdemocratic era.

The larger socioeconomic picture also gives cause for concern. While the relative incidence of poverty is diminishing in most of South Asia, the absolute number of poor continues to grow, as does the gap between the wretchedly malnourished and the emerging middle class, whose consumption concerns are VCRs and expensive parties. As traditional elites are replaced by a nouveau riche class that thrives on shady practices, explosive disparities in the social fabric are becoming ripe for exploitation.

Gruesome violence based on economic and social rivalries is common in countryside and city, and corruption is pervasive. The bureaucracy, the politicians, and, especially, the police are viewed as contemptibly venal, if not criminal. As these various pressures build up and threaten political and national integrity, law and order could become the overwhelming preoccupation of the state during the coming decade.

It would be bitterly ironic if South Asia were to enter a postdemocratic phase—one in which the constitutional forms might be maintained but their substance became a mockery—just as democracy was asserting itself elsewhere in the world. The potential for such an evolution is there. In all of the countries of the region, right-wing forces, often religiously inspired, have long been the main threat to centrist, open politics. Resurgent Islam poses serious problems for the region, but Hindu chauvinism has an even greater potential for undermining the open and secular political order that a diverse country such as India urgently needs. If unrest and disparity grow and religious prejudices continue to be fanned, it will take extremely effective political leadership to fend off pressures for increasingly authoritarian rule.

Inertia will probably keep India, at least, from descending into political chaos. India is not going to disintegrate in this century, and neither are its neighbors about to do so. Communal parties are likely to remain localized. Uncontrollable jacqueries are unlikely. By Third World standards, South Asia is uniquely blessed with political and administrative talent, and in several of the countries the electorate has come to appreciate the democratic system and shown considerable skill in manipulating it. As long as it believes that politics can be made to work, its tolerance will not snap. A global environment that fosters economic development and is increasingly populated by democratically ruled countries may also have some impact on South Asia. This will be only a secondary factor, however, for South Asia will continue to march to its own drummer. Unfortunately, the beat of that drum is increasingly ineffective in rallying the talented political leadership that South Asia needs to maintain and expand democratic rule.

IV

India is also ahead of the game in regard to some of the more important emerging international trends. It has long found the Soviet Union a cooperative partner and has been an advocate of reduced superpower tensions and of lessened U.S. and Soviet involvement in Third World affairs. That these Indian initiatives have been self-serving is beside the point; the world is now moving, tentatively at least, in ways that India has long believed that it would.

Indian foreign policy operates in three realms—the South Asia region, the global scene, and an intermediate, transregional zone in the Indian Ocean and neighboring areas of Asia. One of the more likely developments before the end of this century will be India's coming of age as a power. The questions are what kind of power, and in which of the three realms. One significant factor will be the growing irrelevance of nonalignment as a major foreign policy principle in a depolarized world. Another will probably be the decreasing interest of the United States and of the Soviet Union in South Asian affairs, so that the region will have to respond increasingly to its own dynamics. While this should be generally beneficial, there is also a significant draw-back: the two superpowers have often played constructive roles in moderating conflict in South Asia, and their restraining hands will become less effective.

Central to most of these considerations is the fact that through much of the 1980s, India's rate of growth of military expenditure was among the highest in the world. While Indian nuclear and missile capabilities have been well publicized, it is the increase in conventional weaponery that is most relevant to Indian security policy. India's military capability now far over-shadows that of all of its neighbors except China. Even China poses only a limited threat, however, and another transregional military power—Iran—has been much diminished by its recent war with Iraq.

While there has been a synergistic relationship between Indian and Pakistani (as well as Chinese) arms procurement,

India's ambitious program is now driven less by perceived security threats than by general assumptions about the overall level of military strength appropriate for a nation such as India. As nations acquire capabilities well beyond any established threat, they tend to look for challenges with which their newfound strength might be commensurate—not least of all to justify the unconscionable expenditure that they have made. India is now at that stage.

Fortuitously, India's military growth has come at a time when the United States and the USSR are relinquishing some of their global roles. If both of the superpowers continue to reduce their security involvement in distant areas of the world, India's *relative* position will be enhanced. This will not be of relevance at the global level, where India cannot match the superpowers' military strength; in the South Asian region India's growing capability is merely a case of piling on overkill against its weaker neighbors. The more interesting possibilities arise in the transregional sphere. In particular, a reduction of U.S. and Soviet naval power in the Indian Ocean will leave the Indian navy, with its several aircraft carriers and nuclear submarines, even more of a force than it is now: the nations of Southeast Asia, as well as Australia, are understandably following the Indian naval buildup with more than academic interest.

Concern over India's military capabilities is heightened by the possibility that a resurgent Hinduism could turn ugly not only at home but also abroad. Some Hindu nationalists see India as beleaguered by enemies, especially Muslims, in an arc stretching from the Gulf to Indonesia. This is scarcely a scenario credible to outsiders, but it is the kind of vision that would present challenge "appropriate" for a growing Indian military capability. That challenge would spell trouble for India's immediate neighbors (as it has in the past), but also in more distant parts of the Indian Ocean region where there are substantial numbers of overseas Indian residents (Mauritius, East Africa) or where India had an interest in earlier centuries (Indochina and Indonesia). Imaginative strategists have yearned for the capability to help the Indian minority in distant Fiji.

That much, however, is speculation. The most salient issues will continue to arise in South Asia. The recent painful experience in Sri Lanka may have stimulated some second thoughts about the use of force in the neighborhood, but India has a record of resorting to pressures and even military force in dealing with its neighbors when conciliatory diplomacy fails to yield results. There will be no dearth of problems that could result in conflict. Most dangerous is the unrest in the Punjab and Kashmir; if things go seriously wrong for India in either case, there will be a strong temptation to blame Pakistan and take actions that could trigger a new war. India's imposition of economic pressures on Nepal during 1989 and its continuing highhandedness in dealing with disputes in its relations with Bangladesh have been a discouraging sign that India will seek imposed hegemony rather than regional leadership based on consensus.

Again, there are brighter prospects as well. The South Asian Association for Regional Cooperation provides a vehicle for regional coordination if there are statesmen willing to use it, and the Singh government in India is committed to a more conciliatory line toward its neighbors than that of the Nehru-Gandhi family. The government will have its task cut out for it, however, for the Indian foreign affairs bureaucracy and strategic intelligentsia are ruthless guardians of old orthodoxies, determined that no new political thinking emerge.

The reduction in great power competition between the United States and the USSR offers both a model and an opportunity for India and Pakistan to rearrange their affairs constructively and free themselves from outside meddling. The winding down of the Afghanistan conflict will reduce some of the competitiveness in South Asia, and the special U.S. tie to Pakistan will also fade. Similarly, even though Moscow and Delhi value their mutual ties very highly, each will for economic reasons have to look more to the West than to the other. A South Asia relatively at peace internally could be an element of international stability—not least by being less troublesome itself, but also by playing a constructive role toward neighboring regions, notably the Gulf.

How this drama ultimately plays itself out depends, again, less on the impact of external forces (where the configurations are generally favorable) than on the internal dynamics of the South Asian region itself, where the going will be much more difficult. Above all, it will require all of the nations of the region to readjust their policies toward each other. India must learn to use its strength to lead rather than to compel; the smaller nations must learn to live with the reality of Indian power—all the more since foreign patrons will be less likely to come to their aid.

V

In sum, the outlook for South Asia is very much open to question, and in some cases it is quite disturbing. The 1990s *could* see a nuclear-armed subcontinent facing economic ruin, riven by ethnic and social unrest, swept by nationalism, abandoning the substance if not the forms of democracy, beset by intraregional conflict, and posing a threat to stability in the broader Indian Ocean region. Alternatively, South Asia *could* become a bulwark of stability—a well-integrated region with solidified and expanding democratic structures, moving toward a modest prosperity that is more fairly distributed than is now the case.

Two variables affecting the outcome are worth underlining. The first is the recent political evolution in India and Pakistan. In both countries there is potential for the consolidation of effective, multiparty democratic governments. Unfortunately, however, both the Bhutto and the Singh regimes are fragile, and it would be foolhardy to predict a bright, long-term future for either. Even if they do last, they may make little difference to the economic and social direction that their countries have been pursuing, for neither shows promise of differing greatly from previous governments.

Another variable is our own relationship to South Asia. The region should not be very high on our priority lists, nor is it likely that we (or others) can make any decisive, positive impact on developments in South Asia. We can, however, do two important things. First, we can provide the conditions that will make for a smooth entry of India and its neighbors into fuller participation in the international economy. That means keeping our own economy healthy and open, and ensuring that reasonable amounts of capital and technology are available. Second, we can pursue policies that strengthen trends toward regional cooperation in South Asia. That means avoiding involvement in regional disputes (especially between India and Pakistan) and, to the extent possible, working cooperatively with the Soviet Union in dealing with the region's problems, rather than competing for favor, as we have in the past.

Neither extreme projection for South Asia is likely to be realized during the rest of this century. On the basis of past performance, it appears far more likely that South Asia will look much as is does today in most regards. Important change will certainly continue to take place, but probably at an incremental level. The radical changes that seem needed and, at some time, inevitable can probably be once again postponed. We might find this an initially comforting thought; mostly what we want from South Asia is that it not be unduly troublesome and force its way up our list of priorities. The South Asian governments themselves find incrementalism preferable to radical change. Postponing problems will not, however, solve them; and as the people of South Asia store up resentment and the region itself edges ever more closely into the international community, these problems will impinge increasingly on our own concerns as we move toward and into the next century.

NOTE

1. For the purposes of this essay, the term "South Asia" denotes the area comprising India and Pakistan, together with Bangladesh, Nepal, Afghanistan, Sri Lanka, and Bhutan.

A Look at . . .

LATIN AMERICA
Mark Falcoff

Now that the Cold War is over, will the United States still need Latin America? If so, what will it need it *for*? And if we do need it, how much must we be prepared to pay—in attention and resources that would otherwise be directed elsewhere on the globe, including, by the way, to our own country. These are questions that American policymakers have not yet really begun to ask. But certainly they will not be answered by the litany of the old-time religion of Pan-Americanism—namely, that no matter what, "History, as well as geography, is destiny"; "the same problems that have preoccupied us over the past hundred years in Latin America will persist. Poverty, instability, lawlessness, violence and tyranny will continue to threaten our interests at some level and draw us into the region, whether we like it or not."[1]

Of course, at one point in our history the centrality of the area to U.S. interest was beyond debate. During the nineteenth century Latin America—or, rather, the northernmost portion of it—was our only important area of foreign policy concern. We fought our first two foreign wars there; and before World War I, Mexico, Cuba, and the five republics of Central America accounted for 90 percent of America's overseas investment. With the exception of the Philippines, Latin America was our only serious area of security concern, particularly after the opening of the Panama Canal in 1914.

From the Spanish-American War (1898) to the Great Depression (1929) and even beyond, Americans knew where Latin America fit in our scheme of things. Almost every aspect of our hemispheric policy could be subsumed under two simple headings—protecting our investments and denying geopolitical access to any external power. Both concerns were addressed by the Roosevelt Corollary to the Monroe Doctrine (1904), which claimed for the United States the right to preemptively assume authority in some of the smaller countries where irresponsible conduct by local governments would both endanger American nationals and property, and provide a pretext for European intervention.

This was the rationale under which U.S. navy and marine contingents intervened in Cuba (1906–1909) and established constabulary regimes in Nicaragua (1912–1926, and 1927–1933), Haiti (1915–1934), and the Dominican Republic (1916–1924). It also inspired U.S. diplomatic and military sanctions against Mexico during that country's civil war–cum–revolution (1910–1923). Although U.S. policy in these countries was never driven as sharply by private economic interest as many Latin Americans (and certain American revisionist historians) would have us believe, there was really no need for Washington to choose between economic and security agendas: they were seen as a seamless whole, reinforcing and protecting one another, and in fact largely did so.

Even when the focus and content of U.S. policy changed under Franklin D. Roosevelt's Good Neighbor policy (1933–1945), its components remained mutually reinforcing. U.S. interests remained the same—investments and security—but the terms of the hemispheric bargain were slightly altered. Security was now defined more broadly and also more creatively—an explicit trade-off that for want of a better term might be called a new hemispheric pact. In exchange for their implicit acceptance of U.S. leadership in global political affairs (a posture that proved of considerable value during World War II), the Latins received three major concessions: neutrality in investment disputes between local governments and American investors; automatic recognition of all regimes, whether elected or de facto (and whatever their conduct toward their own people); and privileged access to U.S. domestic markets through reciprocal trade agreements.

Since at least 1948, on the other hand, the organizing principle of U.S. hemispheric policy has been the Cold War and the
East-West struggle. This has been true whether the policy instruments chosen were predominantly "hard" (military assistance,
covert action) or "soft" (the Alliance for Progress, development
assistance, the Peace Corps, Fulbright scholarships). Different
administrations have emphasized one type at the temporary
expense of the other, but the mix has remained constant. For
example, during the 1960s U.S. policy toward Peru and Chile
was driven exclusively by imperatives of political warfare against
local forces allied to (or thought to be allied to) the Soviet Union
and Cuba. Under such circumstances it is perhaps not surprising
that during these years, the Peruvian army received extensive
counterinsurgency training and equipment, or that centrist and
conservative parties in Chile were covertly provided with financial and technical support by the U.S. embassy or the local station
of the Central Intelligence Agency.

Less predictably, however, it was during this same period
that Washington abandoned its more traditional economic
agenda (protection of investments, orthodox fiscal policies) in
favor of populist social policies intended to undercut the appeal
of the revolutionary left—including land reform, low-cost urban
housing projects, even (in the case of Chile) negotiated "buy-
outs" of the American mining companies by newly created para-
statals. U.S. authorities saw no contradiction between the two
approaches, and in fact—given the centrality of our security
concern—there probably was none. Even the Carter administration (1977–1981), which often advertised itself as having abandoned the Cold War frame of reference altogether, continued to
employ both techniques in a number of countries. Yet even in
those few (Argentina, Chile, Guatemala, El Salvador) where it
discarded military aid entirely, it was wont to argue—when
pressed by foreign policy traditionalists—that its human rights
policy made sense not only in humanitarian terms, but in
geopolitical ones as well.[2]

Evidently, throughout most of the postwar period Latin
American politicians and publicists (as well as commentators in
the United States and Europe) often objected to Washington's

subordination of its Latin American policy to the imperatives of Cold War politics. But it is difficult to imagine how it could have been otherwise. Even the greatest of world powers cannot spread themselves out evenly across the entire face of the earth. And it would have been strange indeed if, given the situation that unfolded after 1948 with the coup in Czechoslovakia, the Berlin blockade, the Chinese revolution, and the Korean War, U.S. strategic concerns in the 1950s had been centered primarily in the Western Hemisphere rather than in Western Europe and the Far East.

In any event, the Cold War was not without concrete benefits for many Latin American countries, particularly after Fidel Castro's Cuba entered the Soviet bloc in 1961. Overnight the strategic importance of the region was rediscovered, directing toward it resources and energies that would otherwise have gone elsewhere.[3] Now that the Cold War is apparently coming to an end, what organizing principle is likely to serve U.S.–Latin American cooperation as well or better?

II

The question we are really asking here is, Will there be a new hemispheric compact between the United States and Latin America, and if so, upon what will it be based? One thing is certain: such a relationship cannot be driven by economic factors alone, for Latin America's relative importance to the United States under that heading has been stagnant or declining for many years.

There is no ambiguity about the numbers. In 1965, the region represented 19 percent of all U.S. direct investment abroad; ten years later its share had dropped to 17 percent; and now (1985 data) the figure stands at 13 percent.[4] Moreover, the United States is considerably less dependent upon imports from Latin America than was formerly the case. Again, a few figures: in 1965, Latin America represented 17 percent of all our overseas purchases; in 1975, 12 percent; and now (1985), in spite of an unprecedented period of domestic U.S. expansion and record trade deficits, only 13 percent, almost exactly what it did in 1965.[5]

Moreover, the trend is not likely to reverse soon, since in most countries there has been a sharp decline in direct investment. This is a logical reaction to Latin America's populist decade, the 1970s, a period in which antibusiness and antiforeign sentiments dominated both public discourse and policy choices. In country after country—but particularly in the Andean republics—punitive nationalizations, as well as discriminatory tax and exchange regulations, were the order of the day. Today we are told things are different—and intellectually, they are. Far from regarding foreign investment as exploitive and antagonistic to the national interest, a new generation of Latin American leaders now eagerly courts it. But the damage has already been done, and foreign investment is not something that can be turned on and off like a water tap. It will take many years to lure back major American companies, once so many have relocated their operations outside the hemisphere or are planning to do so. Latin America is still seen by potential foreign investors as a risky place to make long-term commitments, and in the best of cases, this perception will take at least a generation to reverse, during which (as Latins themselves say) almost anything can happen.

Periodically Latin American publicists, American academics, or the U.S. Department of Commerce express enthusiasm over the hypothetical number of jobs that could be created in the United States, given a market of 400 million customers. The harsh truth is that the Latin American market is much less important to the United States than it used to be. And there are many indications that—with the exception of Mexico—it will be even less important in the near future. In 1965, the region purchased 14 percent of what we sold abroad; in 1975 (under the artificial stimulus of the Organization of Petroleum Exporting Countries' first oil price rise), 15 percent; today (1985), slightly less than what it took in 1965—13 percent.[6] At this point, in fact, financial services are the most important activity, though this is unlikely to remain so for long, as U.S. banks gradually write off ever larger portions of their Latin American debt and express reluctance to become involved in new lending.

In the best of cases, the Latin American market can hardly be regarded as a promising future frontier for American exporters, since in order to be customers, 400 million people have to have money to spend. Instead, most countries in the region have experienced a significant net loss of real income since 1982; governments, companies, and individuals cannot borrow as easily as they once could; and what Latin American capital exists has largely fled to safer havens in the United States, Western Europe, and the Bahamas. According to figures released in late 1989 by the Morgan Guaranty Trust Company, at the end of 1987 Mexican assets abroad amounted to $84 billion; Venezuelan assets, $58 billion; Argentine, $46 billion; and Brazilian, $31 billion.[7] This may benefit U.S. capital markets, but certainly not U.S. exporters.

The traditional security relationship has likewise lost much of its previous intensity and meaning. Even at the height of the Brezhnev Doctrine, there was no agreement among U.S. politicians, diplomats, and academics as to the overall strategic importance of Latin America to the East-West struggle, not even on the geopolitical significance of such a key venue as Panama. (The canal treaty, it cannot be recalled often enough, was ratified in the U.S. Senate by a margin of a single vote.) The recent use of military force to depose General Manuel Noriega was an unexpected episode, but it should not be allowed to confuse the longer-term trends. The real reason for "Operation Just Cause" was the presence of a residual American military community in the Zone, threatened by armed mobs—that, and the need to have a Panamanian government that would cooperate in the continuing devolution of the canal. With the consummation of the Carter-Torrijos treaties ten years hence, there will be no Americans there, no Zone, and hence no basis for U.S. concern about the internal workings of Panamanian politics, much less about the quality of the leaders Panamanians themselves may have occasion to bring forward.

In effect, if the United States could contemplate abandoning the Panama Canal at the height of the Cold War, it is difficult to see how today—when the Soviet Union finds itself barely able to project its own power into the Baltic republics—Washington can be expected to sustain an indefinite strategic interest there. Likewise, existing (or newly emerging) U.S. commitments to the government of El Salvador and the Nicaraguan opposition (now government) were made under very different geopolitical circumstances. At a minimum, they will have to be reexamined in the light of our changed international position and our diminished resource base. Probably in the best of cases both countries—as well as the Republic of Panama—can expect a final decade of assistance before they are moved to the periphery of our foreign policy interests.

Mexico is evidently a different matter, if only because it shares a 2,500-mile border with the United States. This fact, from which we can neither run nor hide, means that Mexico can always count on having its internal stability regarded in Washington (and, even more, in Texas, Arizona, New Mexico, and California) as a matter of deepest political interest. The continuing integration of the two economies into what seems to be emerging (together with Canada) as a North American common market, only underscores the fact with hard economic data. For other Latin American countries, however, whether large or small, distant or near, the relationship between their domestic politics and U.S. security will be far less clear.

Certainly, in the current international environment, characterized by an unusual degree of cordiality and even cooperation between the United States and the Soviet Union, it is difficult to say against *whom,* or against *what threats,* the Inter-American Treaty of Reciprocal Assistance (the Rio Pact of 1947) and the subsidiary institutions it has thrown off—the Inter-American Defense Board, the Inter-American Defense College, the UNITAS naval maneuvers, and the entire military education and exchange program—are directed.

Of course, all things being equal, the system could survive indefinitely on the force of inertia. But things rarely are equal, and in the particular case of Latin America, political and strategic trends within the region have been silently shifting for nearly two decades, undermining the basis of what was once a military-

cum-political alliance. Since the mid-1970s, most of the major
Latin American states have purposely reduced their dependence upon the United States for arms and training (or have been
forced to do so as the result of congressionally mandated embar-
goes). Moreover, almost every Latin American republic is currently nonaligned (and those that are not aspire to become so).
This situation arguably nullifies the mutual security commitments made under the Rio Pact and moves these countries from
the status of allies to that of neutrals at best.

In concrete political terms, no one familiar with the workings of the Council of the Organization of American States (OAS)
imagines that it would be easy for the United States to win a vote
there on any security-related matter that required the members
to take decisive action. Indeed, as the recent case of Panama
illustrates, consensus there is just as elusive where the issues are
not even security-related, involve no East-West dimension, and
require only a definition of the facts of the case. The only aspect
of the recent Panama crisis upon which most members were able
to agree—both before and after U.S. military action there—was
that the United States was somehow at fault.[8]

The emergence since 1980 of a succession of elected governments in the region—unprecedented in number—has led some
commentators to suppose that a new relationship between the
United States and Latin America might be constructed upon a
joint commitment to democratic values. Unfortunately, this argument flies in the face of an overarching need throughout the
region to defend the principle of nonintervention at the expense
of all other values. The issue is not a lack of commitment to
democracy as such—in their own countries, Latin leaders are
often eloquent and courageous champions of human rights,
political pluralism, and other civic virtues. But when it comes to
their neighbors, they reflexively opt for agnosticism ("ideological
pluralism"). The most recent example was the reluctance of the
Latin democracies to vote for a United Nations resolution con-
demning the human rights record of Castro's Cuba. This puts
the United States in the anomalous position of having to care
more about the growth of democratic institutions on a region-
wide basis than the governments and parties within it do, hardly

the basis for a new inter-American program founded on a political consensus.

III

For several years now Latin publicists and politicians (and many of their U.S. counterparts) have been advancing an alternative vision of the relationship. For them, the real issues that should dominate the hemispheric agenda are debt, drugs, ecological threats, and immigration. No doubt each of these subjects merits careful attention by policymakers concerned with the future of the entire region. The question is not, however, whether these issues are important, but whether they are likely to be perceived as important *enough* to command significant economic resources, and lead to a major deployment of policy energies in the United States. Simply put, in order for these new agendas to replace the old investments-and-security package, or the Cold War imperative, they cannot rest upon humanitarian concern alone. The benefits accruing to both North and South must be evident, direct, and—above all—compelling, in much the same way that the Alliance for Progress was seen as a necessary and mutually satisfactory response to the challenge of communism in Cuba.

Again, *in the abstract* no one can dispute that it is in the longer-term interest of the United States for all Latin American countries to prosper economically, so that people throughout the hemisphere do not feel pressured to emigrate precipitously to the United States, grow drugs, or burn down their tropical rain forests. However, the real question is not whether such a development is in our general interest, but *how much* it is in our interest. What are we prepared to pay? And can we convince ourselves that by paying it, we will get what we seek?

In the case of drugs, for example, it is self-evident that until farmers in Colombia, Bolivia, and Peru find a market for something that at least replaces the income they currently obtain from the cultivation of coca plants, they cannot be expected to cease their cooperation with the international drug cartel. The clear implication—evident in every speech on the subject by Presidents Virgilio Barco Vargas, Alan García Perez, and Jaime Paz Zamora—is that the United States is obliged to provide an artificial substitute. In one conception, we would create a kind of international version of our farm subsidy program: cultivators would be paid *not* to produce an item judged to be excessively abundant, or paid to produce something else that, presumably, we might not otherwise need. In another, the United States would simply purchase the crop from the relevant governments and destroy it.

But if the United States were willing to spend, say, $10–$20 billion a year to wean Andean farmers from the drug market, does it not stand to reason that they would have an even greater incentive to covertly remain within it, as a way of ensuring that the threat (and therefore the resource flow from the United States) did not abate? And would not such arrangements indirectly encourage nations not presently in the drug trade to move into it, as a way of extracting resources from the United States they could not otherwise obtain? Evidently the problem is how to end consumption within the United States (and probably Western Europe as well); otherwise, Latin America can always be expected to produce drugs as the only export commodity whose price and market share are firmly assured. If the United States wants to throw money at the problem, that is its business, but no one should have any illusions that this might lead to a solution.

A similar hypothetical exercise could be applied to the environmental problem. How much should Brazil be paid—either in direct appropriations or in debt forgiveness—to apply more prudent measures to the exploitation of the rain forest? Whatever figure we might arrive at would have to be continually adjusted for inflation, for rising Brazilian expectations, or to meet domestic political pressures (within that country) to find a substitute for foreign investment driven away by nationalistic economic policies.

Even if such arrangements could suddenly be agreed upon, ecological blackmail could never provide the basis for the longer-term survival of Brazil, a huge semicontinent with a population more than half that of the United States. Nor can the United States itself—which is by no means of one mind on how to divide the imperatives of growth and environmental protection at home—allow such issues to drive its relations with distant countries most Americans cannot even identify on a map.

Likewise, while the Latin American debt can hardly be regarded as helpful to the general economic prospect, in and of itself it is not—repeat, *not*—the principal cause of the current business depression in the region, nor does it necessarily limit the capacity of Latin American countries to purchase American goods and services; it is merely a convenient excuse. In the first place, debt service can hardly constitute a burden when most countries are in arrears, some (like Argentina) radically so. Moreover, other countries with an enormous debt overhang (South Korea, for example, but also Chile) sustain remarkably dynamic economies and—it follows—provide excellent markets for U.S. exports. The difference would seem to be macro-economic policies that generate business confidence and not only attract foreign capital, but keep much (or most) local capital at home.

Contrary to the traditional rhetoric of Latin American populism (and also of many "development" organizations in the United States), economic and social progress is not exclusively or even principally a quantitative matter—that is, societies do not become "developed" according to the sum total of resources injected into them (or, in the case of debt service, retained there rather than remitted abroad). Rather, they develop as a consequence of specific policies that have been proven to promote growth. The wave of market-oriented economic reforms—a Latin American version of perestroika—already afoot in Mexico and Venezuela, promised in Argentina and Brazil, and proposed by one of the leading presidential candidates in Peru, is more likely to provide new markets for the United States in the region than is debt relief plain and simple, whatever technical virtues it may or may not have at a particular moment. If the Latin American governments that have committed themselves to economic reform do not stay the course, there will be little that the West can do to help them.

IV

The evidence strongly suggests, then, that there will be no new hemispheric compact between the United States and Latin America—at least, not in the foreseeable future. This means not that the United States will have no economic or political relations with its southern neighbors in the future, but that these relations will lack an overarching ideological or strategic rationale to bridge over areas where there is no evident and immediate benefit.

The old Pan-American idea—the notion that all of the republics of the area are bound together in a kind of mystical alliance based on a supposed political, strategic, or economic community of interests—is currently on its deathbed and cannot be revived. With the exception of Mexico, our relations with individual Latin republics will depend largely upon their own economic viability and their own political choices—as well as how we respond to them. There will be no quasi-imperial (or regional) vision to render rational decisions that could not otherwise be so regarded on their own (narrowly economic) terms.[9]

Geographical propinquity alone will assure that the region does not quite fall off the map of U.S. consciousness, particularly as regards Central America and the Caribbean. But awareness of a region does not mean a willingness to become actively engaged with its problems, much less to expend resources. What is certain is that no new issue, or combination of issues, is likely to engage the United States in South America with the force of the investments-and-security package of times past.

It is a curious period we are entering now—one in which the United States, having cast aside its historic mission in the region, will in all likelihood have that mission thrown back into its face by the same people who perennially complained about its oppressive weight. However, the pattern is all but irreversible: neither our resources nor our national will nor even our national interest dictates a different course. One hopes, of course, that the Latin American nations will be able to guide their external relations in ways that satisfy their needs. But the primary responsibility for that is theirs—and theirs alone.

NOTES

1. Robert Kagan, "Latin America: There to Stay," *The National Interest*, no. 19 (Spring 1990), pp. 66–67.
2. Whether or not this was true, strictly speaking, it was at least a useful debating point, and it demonstrates once again how American foreign policy thinking about Latin America has always striven for a certain match between "realist" and "idealist" agendas.
3. The same is true of the Nicaraguan revolution of 1979, which suddenly assured Nicaragua's Central American neighbors of a windfall in U.S. financial assistance—just in time to rescue them from the consequences of their uninhibited foreign borrowing in the mid-1970s.
4. U.S. Bureau of the Census, *Statistical Abstract of the United States* (Washington, D.C.: various years).
5. Figures from Department of Trade Statistics, International Monetary Fund, *Yearbook* (Washington, D.C.: various years).
6. Ibid.
7. Matt Moffett, "Mexico's Capital Flight Still Racks Economy, Despite the Brady Plan," *Wall Street Journal,* September 25, 1989, p. 1, A10. In all likelihood these figures are low estimates; in any event, they have doubtless increased since then.
8. The time in recent memory that the OAS Council proved able to act decisively—with important strategic and political consequences—was at the end of the Nicaraguan civil war in 1979, when the member-nations (contradicting their own, most sacred doctrines of nonintervention) voted to withdraw their ambassadors from Managua, depriving the agonizing Somoza regime of international recognition. Not surprisingly, this uncharacteristically bold action was taken over the protest of the United States.
9. For example, the land reform promoted by U.S. diplomats and development specialists in El Salvador in 1979–1980 actually had the effect of disorganizing food production and promoting a rural exodus, requiring massive infusions of American food aid. However, it could be rationalized in terms of Washington's overall *political* agenda, which was to undercut local support for the Marxist FDR-FMLN guerrilla-political coalition or, at a minimum, to win support in the U.S. Congress for military aid to the government of El Salvador. In the end, the decision to become involved in the intricacies of El Salvador's economy and society cost the United States several billion dollars. In the absence of a viable security rationale, it is difficult to imagine how such a decision could be justified.

A Look at . . .

SUB-SAHARAN AFRICA

Crawford Young

The merely incredible gives way daily—in the flow of world events—to the astonishing and the unbelievable. Africa itself has witnessed in recent months some extraordinary developments: the release of Nelson Mandela, the abandonment of Marxism-Leninism by Ethiopian ruler Mengistu Haile Mariam, the peaceful transition to independence of Namibia. The erosion of the old certitudes of the Cold War as the ultimate driving force in world politics; the upsurge of democratizing impulses that threatens even the most durable of autocrats; the rearrangement of dominant forces in the global economy; the international debt crisis and its manifold ramifications: these metamorphoses well merit the designation of sea-changes. Of the major world regions, Africa[1] is perhaps the most susceptible to external forces, least able to swiftly adapt to transformations in the world economy or international politics. The implications for Africa of the profound changes occurring worldwide must be grasped in the context of equally momentous transformations taking place within Africa; I turn first to these radical alterations, especially important in Sub-Saharan Africa.

To begin with the obvious, Africa is currently locked in a far-reaching economic crisis all of its own. While this situation affects African countries unevenly, and some states remain in a reasonably healthy condition (mostly small states, such as Botswana, Rwanda, and Mauritius), the great majority of African countries experienced relative (and in a number of instances absolute) economic decline during the 1980s.[2] The African economic crisis has now been with us long enough to assume the familiarity of long usage, and perhaps to obliterate recollections of an earlier period of high optimism. The generally gloomy perspective on African development dates only from the 1980s; the 1950s were years of dramatic growth, the 1960s still looked promising, and only gradually were the omens of impending crisis recognized during the 1970s.

Africa's economic decline is not merely a temporary aberration, but is long-term: a sea-change in itself. Most states are trapped by oversize public sectors that consume public capital and generate large deficits. The major export crops have nearly all experienced prolonged price declines, with little prospect of early recovery—the coffee and cocoa markets of the late 1980s are illustrative examples. Acute and endemic foreign exchange shortages make efficient operation of the modest industrial sectors created during the previous, more prosperous postwar decades all but impossible; a veritable "deindustrialization" is now in course. A peasant sector demoralized by excessive state direct and indirect taxation and by the phalanx of poorly functioning state marketing monopolies inevitably turns to the underground economy and disengages from the state-dominated public economy.

The continent's economic crisis has many facets. Perhaps its most visible dimension is the debt imbroglio, less imposing in gross figures than that found in Latin America, but, relative to the smaller scale of the African economies, more burdensome. From a negligible figure in 1970, the total African debt has risen, by some estimates, as much as $250 billion.[3] A good part of it is simply uncollectible (Sudan's $14 billion debt, for example), but its overhang nonetheless all but cuts off those in de facto default from access to public and private credit. Despite some recent promising developments (for example, recent cancellation by France of more than $2 billion of bilateral public debts of low-income African countries), debt repayments exceeded in the late 1980s new resource inflows.[4] Heavily indebted African states were unable to secure either private bank financing or significant private investment from abroad.

The stagnation of the public economy has driven an important amount of economic activity into parallel channels. While the vigor of second economies in countries such as Zaire and Uganda has cushioned the population from the worst effects of decay in the public realm, it is difficult to see how these sectors can restore the health of the economy overall.

The crisis of the African state is also political: a widespread loss of legitimacy confronting regimes of various ideological orientations. Disaffection and alienation are rife in both rural and urban sectors. The overconsuming, underperforming state faces a gigantic challenge in recapturing the confidence of its population. Regional conflicts, especially in southern Africa and the Horn, intensified in scope during the 1980s. Somalia, Ethiopia, Sudan, Mozambique, and Angola have experienced a harvest of death and destruction no one would have forecast a decade ago. South African destabilization and aggression; the vast flow of Soviet arms into Angola and Ethiopia; the grim confluence of civil war and natural disaster in Sudan, Mozambique, Somalia, and Ethiopia: the roster of the dead, the mutilated, and the uprooted runs into many millions.[5] Further, by the late 1980s Africa and the rest of the world had learned that internal wars could persist inconclusively with no end in sight. In Eritrea, southern Sudan, Angola, Mozambique, and the western Sahara, the conclusion was inescapable: national armies, even when provided with important external aid, could not achieve military victory over regional insurgents with strong local support. This is a new development; one may recollect that the Katanga and Biafra secessions were decisively defeated in the 1960s. The Ethiopian and Sudanese conflicts also appear beyond the reach of negotiated settlement; the high-profile efforts by Jimmy Carter foundered on the intractability of the disputes. Literally millions more will perish before either of these civil wars finds resolution. These sea-changes within Africa—as unanticipated as those now transforming the global political economy, and largely unrelated to them—must remain in view when one looks at the implications of the novel patterns emerging at the world level.

The dramatic decline in Soviet-American tensions in recent years and the growing perception that the Cold War is over have already had a visible impact on African international politics. Perhaps the most fundamental change is a reduced tendency on the part of both superpowers to perceive African political developments in terms governed by their own bipolar rivalry: to suspect the machinations of the other side in political conflicts, to evaluate developments in Africa as a "zero-sum" game, to view the continent primarily as a terrain for the competitive pursuit of marginal advantage. When the intractabilities inherent in a given African conflict are added to the calculus of global strategic struggle between the superpowers, a prescription for prolonged stalemate is automatically at hand. A degree of momentum toward conflict resolution in such long-simmering disputes as those of the western Sahara, Ethiopia, Angola, and Mozambique, not to mention the Namibia settlement, indisputably derives at least in part from a lowered Cold War temperature.

In this context, superpower policy changes have been asymmetrical: Soviet behavior has changed more than has American. Moscow has clearly concluded that its expensive military supply and support commitments in Angola and Ethiopia (together an estimated $17 billion) were an endless financial drain, without any compensating hope for military triumph of these regimes over their respective insurgents. The belief, which flourished for a time in the late Brezhnev years, that a "socialist orientation" in Africa offered an alternative pathway for African states that would weaken "imperialist" positions on the continent has vanished. With respect to South Africa, Soviet policy has shifted toward favoring a peaceful, negotiated end to apartheid, and has abandoned the hope that majority rule in that country could or should occur under the banner of "socialist construction."

Whether American policy in Africa has moved beyond its instinctive disposition toward anti-Soviet reflexes is less clear, although prolonged relative inactivity by the Soviets may over time erode the tendency toward perceiving African events in global geopolitical terms. Caution is required before assuming that these changes in great power perspectives have become irreversible. There was, after all, an earlier period, in the late

1960s and early 1970s, when détente in Africa seemed already at hand. Soviet economic decline and the nationality crisis may bring conservatives back to power in Moscow, who might push African policy in a more confrontational direction. On the American side, African policy in some cases (Angola and Mozambique, in particular) remains susceptible to ideologically driven conservative pressures; this also undermines superpower détente in Africa, and complicates efforts at a cooperative resolution of these conflicts. Neither side, however, is likely henceforth to commit the scale of policy attention or material resources to African affairs that it did in earlier periods.

The shriveling credibility of Marxism-Leninism, which is an inevitable corollary to the policy retreats of perestroika and glasnost, alters the debates within Africa concerning development policy. Radical anti-imperialist populism—as political discourse and as yeast to mass ferment—is still very much alive in Africa, but the "Afro-Marxist" development pathway now seems foreclosed. (One may recollect that a decade ago a real trend toward adoption of Marxism-Leninism as regime ideology appeared to develop; the Third World Marxist-Leninist state was above all an African phenomenon.)

The political dimension of the African state crisis—weakened legitimacy of many regimes, prolonged or episodic civil strife and unrest in a number, declining capacity to assure basic social services in quite a few—leads to a growing popular cry for democratization. Most incumbent regimes are unlikely to abandon voluntarily the patrimonial autocracies they have created in order to cling to power. But the nationalist single parties (such as the former Parti Démocratique de Guinée or the Tanzanian Chama Cha Mapinduzi) and the "nation-building" technocracies of military provenance (such as the Nigerian regimes of 1966–1979 and 1983 on, or the 1969–1985 Nimeiri regime in Sudan), which once enjoyed some intellectual respectability among both African elites and overseas observers of African affairs, have unmistakably lost their standing. The African intelligentsia, across the entire ideological spectrum from classical liberals[6] to Marxists,[7] now call for democratic formulas. The former plead for constitutionalism, pluralism, and free markets; the latter argue that "bourgeois democracy" is an indispensable stage in the evolution toward a socialist future.

How the discredited patrimonial autocracy will be supplanted, however, is far less clear than the growing demand for its disappearance. For example, electoral, multiparty democracy in Sudan failed to resolve the civil war racking the country from 1986 to 1989. Similarly, many Nigerians are apprehensive about the prospects for the Third Republic, however ardently they desire its birth. Ethnic, religious, and racial cleavages are likely to find expression in party systems, and are difficult to accommodate in harmonious fashion. The effort to promote democracy in the midst of acute economic distress is historically unprecedented. Regimes of whatever nature, socialist or capitalist, autocratic or democratic, are compelled by intense international pressures (the IMF, World Bank, and Western powers) and the absence of any plausible alternative to adopt "structural adjustment" programs, which are all but impossible to make palatable to urban lower classes. The discontent these programs foster swells the disaffection toward the state that its multiple other infirmities have already created.

These frustrations will inevitably find expression in doctrines of radical protest, although what precise form these will take is uncertain. The emergence of extremist movements akin to the Peruvian Sendero Luminoso is certainly possible. In Muslim polities, fundamentalist forms of Islam may capture these social energies. Generational politics may also be expected to play an increasing role; Nigerian, Senegalese, and Algerian disorders over the past couple of years are portentous. The younger generation is the first victim of the ongoing economic crisis and of structural adjustment remedies; forced reductions in state employment rolls hit hardest at new entrants to the labor market, especially new university graduates accustomed to regard government jobs as virtually guaranteed. The marketplace, in Africa, contains no magic capable of conjuring alternative opportunities in the short-to-medium term. Youth in general, and students in particular, are the segment of society over which the state has the least leverage to constrain or to intimidate; they are not its employees and are not subject to the family responsibility pressures that induce caution among their elders.

A wild card in any African forecast is the nature and pace of change in South Africa, by far the continent's wealthiest state, and its sole truly industrial society. The startling suddenness of the collapse of communist political monopolies in parts of Eastern Europe suggests the underlying fragility to state structures that utterly lack legitimacy for most of the population. The pressures generated by the deepening international isolation of the regime, and escalating weight of mass disaffection internally, began by late 1989 to take their toll, as the Mandela release and unbanning of the African National Congress (ANC) and other antiapartheid movements suggested that a dynamic of fundamental change might be under way. The new environment of détente, and important changes in Soviet southern African policy noted earlier, had destroyed the credibility of earlier South African claims that it confronted a "total communist onslaught" that only a national security state could repel, and has altered in basic ways the international climate. The prospect of a true quickening of processes of change in South Africa—in contrast to its glacial pace over the last three decades—now appears at hand. A sudden dissolution of the Pretoria regime following Eastern European lines is unlikely; the existing government retains its legitimacy among most of the white 15 percent of the population that it represents. But the process of change may well gain its own momentum and escape the control of Pretoria authorities. There is even a more distant possibility that, at some point, there may be an abrupt acceleration of events if the enormous welled-up pressures for majority rule burst the coercive barriers that so long have contained them without a carefully negotiated formula for transition that engages the principal forces present (above all, the South African state and the ANC). The future remains inscrutable in terms of the precise mechanisms of transformation or its impact upon the sophisticated South African industrial economy. The stakes are high in finding a viable formula that averts major economic and social dislocation, not only for South Africa, but for the entire southern African region.

Overall, Africa is singularly ill positioned to benefit from whatever sea-changes are occurring in the world economy. African educational systems—everywhere in qualitative decline, even if quantitatively expanding—cannot match the Koreas or the Japans in preparing the young for a high-technology future. Except for oil, gas, and precious minerals (gold, diamonds), the primary commodities Africa produces have mediocre worldwide marketing prospects at best. The dominant current trend is deindustrialization, not the building of export industries that might find rewarding niches in world trade.

Africa, more than any other region, will desperately need economic assistance on a large scale; but the roster of potential providers is hard to identify.[8] The international financial agencies are already deeply engaged in Africa, but have yet to discover the policy formula that can bring recovery at acceptable social costs. France, a major patron in the past, now appears to be inching toward disengagement. The European Community will doubtless continue to be an important contributor, but whether the emergent mercantile powers of the Pacific Rim will be motivated to assume major responsibilities for African recovery remains problematic; neither historical ties, proximity, nor existing links of trade and economic or political interest propel them in this direction. The Middle Eastern oil exporters are unlikely to soon enjoy again the vast surpluses that made them significant players on the African scene in the 1970s. The Soviets will be forced to devote most available resources to domestic needs. The United States will be constrained by its budget deficit; the "mortgage" of 40 percent of its aid effort to Israel and Egypt; and appeals for bailouts from Eastern Europe and Latin America, both regions with stronger domestic constituencies than Africa.

The $250 billion African debt and the development impasses will undoubtedly produce consequences that the advanced industrial societies cannot ignore. Human catastrophes similar to those of the past decade will almost certainly be repeated: the drought devastation of the early 1980s in the Sahel and parts of southern Africa; the famines in Sudan, Ethiopia, and Somalia in the latter part of the decade. Normally, such disasters do wring from Western coffers significant sums in the form of refugee relief and emergency food deliveries. The high visibility of such tragedies, brought "live" into the comfortable sitting rooms of Western publics by television, do stimulate palliative measures directed at alleviating the immediate suffering. But they have not yet brought comparable responses that address the root causes of these calamities.

The cold fact is that the African development crisis has not as yet posed the same threat to Western economic stability and interests as those in Latin America and Eastern Europe. Because the African debt is owed largely to public agencies (except in South Africa), the Western banking system remains relatively indifferent to it; the major international banks show no sign of wishing to increase their activities in Africa. A downward spiral and deepening crisis in Mexico or Poland would send millions of refugees surging across European and American frontiers; to date, impoverished Africans have been contained within their own continent, although Europe may face increasing immigration pressures in this respect, from the Maghreb in particular.

In short, the sea-changes in the global political economy seem largely beneficial for the world as a whole. The new dynamic in contemporary affairs they foretell is far less encouraging for Africa. In the political realm, reduced Soviet-American tensions do hold promise for Africa, and may facilitate negotiated solutions to the regional crises and stalemated local wars that plague the continent. However, Africa economically is in no position to take advantage of the new opportunities changing global trade patterns might offer. Nor is it apparent how the redistribution of economic influence and power in the global economy will result in restored developmental momentum within Africa. Battered African economies lack the capacity to connect themselves to dynamic forces driving change at the level of the global economy—the technological and information revolutions, in particular. The struggle for Africa to avert greater marginalization will be arduous and bitter.

NOTES

1. This analysis applies primarily to Sub-Saharan Africa. The Arab tier of states on the Mediterranean shore of Africa has been much less affected by patterns of economic and political decline widespread elsewhere in Africa. South Africa is a special case, to which much of the ensuing discussion does not apply; the uncertainties in its future revolve upon its unresolved and deepening racial crisis.

2. By 1990, Sub-Saharan African incomes were expected to fall back to 1960 levels. By the mid-1980s average growth rates for the region were declining at a rate of 1 percent, or 4 percent per capita. For additional detail, see Jennifer Seymour Whitaker, *How Can Africa Survive?* (New York: Council on Foreign Relations, 1988); and Richard Sandbrook, *The Politics of Africa's Economic Stagnation* (Cambridge, Eng.: Cambridge University Press, 1985).

3. This figure includes the substantial South African, Egyptian, and Algerian debts.

4. At the present time, repayments to the International Monetary Fund (IMF) exceed IMF advances to African states by $500 million.

5. The United Nations Children's Fund estimates that at least 1.3 million people, mostly children, were killed directly or indirectly by civil strife in Angola and Mozambique from 1980 to 1988. During this period, over 11 million were displaced from their homes and lands in these two countries. In Sudan, in 1988, some 250,000 perished from war and famine in the southern region; roughly 3 million additional were forced to flee their homes. The prolonged drought in the Sahel regions in the early 1980s displaced some 10 million persons. An estimated 1 million Eritreans perished in the three-decade civil war.

6. See, for example, John A.A. Ayaode, "States without Citizens: An Emerging African Phenomenon," in Donald Rothchild and Naomi Chazan, eds., *The Precarious Balance: State and Society in Africa* (Boulder, Colo.: Westview Press, 1988), pp. 100–118; and Walter O. Oyugi, E.S. Atieno Odhiambo, Michael Chege, and Afrifa K. Gitonga, eds., *Democratic Theory and Practice in Africa* (Portsmouth, N.H.: Heinemann, 1988).

7. See, for example, Nzongola Ntalaja, address to the Annual Meeting of the African Studies Association (Chicago, November 1988); and Peter Anyang' Nyong'o, ed., *Popular Struggles for Democracy in Africa* (London: Zed Books, 1987).

8. For recent years total aid flows to Sub-Saharan Africa are estimated at roughly $13 billion annually; for details, see Robert J. Berg, "Foreign Aid in Africa: Here's the Answer—Is It Relevant to the Question?" in Robert J. Berg and Jennifer Seymour Whitaker, *Strategies for African Development* (Berkeley: University of California Press, 1985), pp. 505–543.

A Look at . . .

THE INTERNATIONAL POLITICAL ECONOMY

Miles Kahler

For much of the 1980s, absent upheavals to match the oil price shocks of the 1970s, the international political economy was overshadowed by the volatility of East-West relations. This surface calm disguised sea-changes in international economic relations, changes profound in their effects on world politics and irreversible in the medium term. Some of these changes have been glacial in pace and difficult to discern. Other events that appeared cataclysmic, such as the stock market crash of October 1987, are as difficult to assess as heat lightning in a summer sky: an illusory warning or a genuine harbinger of storms to come? International economic trends that now seem irreversible may also disappear when nations—at least larger nations—alter their economic course. Margaret Thatcher and Deng Xiaoping, for example, have drastically changed domestic economic policies and international economic orientation after decades in which both were regarded as immovable. The plight of the Organization of Petroleum Exporting Countries during the 1980s demonstrates, however, that the economic destinies of apparently powerful actors can be strongly affected by both the strategies of other nations and the behavior of international markets.

Four sea-changes in the international political economy will be discussed in the first section of this essay. The relative absence of change in the political organization of international economic relations—the dog that has not barked—will be briefly noted in the second section. Third, changes in the relationship between states and markets will be examined, particularly the intensified internationalization of financial markets and the globalization of production. Finally, an assessment will be attempted of the importance of all these changes for both the character of world politics and the future U.S. policy.

Structural Change: Shifts in Power and Place

The term "structural" is used here to signify changes in relative economic weight among the key players in the international economy and in their positions within the overlapping fields of economic relations (the trading or financial systems, for example). Two sea-changes became unmistakably clear in the 1980s—the rise of Japan and the divided economic prospects of the developing countries. The implications of two others—the leap toward further integration of the European Community and a more thoroughgoing incorporation of some centrally planned economies into the international economic order—will be fully apparent only in the next decade.

The rise of Japan has been an almost continuous process since the proclamation of the "Japanese miracle" in the early 1960s, but in its earlier manifestations, Japanese economic might expressed itself principally in a powerful export drive in manufactures. During the 1970s, that drive produced an array of trade disputes with the United States and Europe. In the decade that began with the publication of *Japan as Number One*,[1] however, Japan's economic reach expanded into high-technology industrial sectors and international finance, an expansion that fundamentally changed its bilateral relationship with the United States. As the Reagan administration's strategy of fiscal expansion produced massive American borrowing abroad, it became clear that Japan was home to the largest pool of exportable capital in the world economy. A share of that capital served to finance a yawning American payments deficit; other shares financed both a boom in foreign direct investment (in North America and Southeast Asia) and a more active stance in the debt crisis and development lending.[2]

To some—let us call them the optimists—the new financial clout of Japan, added to an existing manufacturing prowess that increasingly encroaches on U.S. high-tech preserves, is not a serious concern. This group has advanced two broad arguments. A number of commentators claim that Japan's ascendancy is transitory. Bill Emmott of *The Economist* has argued this most forcefully: Japan's savings rate and its external surpluses will erode with the aging of Japan's population and the emergence of new competitors in Asia; Japan's window of opportunity is a narrow one and may not outlast the century. According to this view, Japan will gradually come to look like other industrialized countries. A stronger yen has already increased the volume of manufactured imports; external pressures (and pressures from its own consumers) may force higher public spending, a greater attention to consumer welfare, and a weakening of powerful lobbies (such as the agricultural lobby) that would erode Japan's peculiar pattern of policy and its position in the international economy.

A second group of optimists argues that the international implications of Japan's rise have been overstated, since its "power portfolio"—heavily dependent on a cluster of export industries and its capital exports—is not diversified in the fashion of the United States. Hence, Japan will continue to need American military protection and American markets as much as the United States needs Japanese capital and technology. The result: an intensification of interdependence rather than American dependence on Japan.[3]

For many of these observers, the United States must "manage" the bilateral relationship as well as Japan's new role in the world economy until Japan's economic trajectory converges with that of other industrialized economies. Increasingly, however, a second set of arguments has been heard both in the United States and in Europe. Framed in military metaphors, such as "containment," and hedged by homilies on the importance of U.S.–Japanese ties, these new "revisionist" critics paint a more ambiguous portrait of Japanese aims and capabilities: the ambitious hegemonic power-to-be rather than the acquiescent partner. Japan not only is seen as the first plausible aspirant to that role in the economic sphere since 1945; it also is viewed as a new-model political economy, one that does *not* work like Western economies, and one that will remain closed unless more forceful pressure is exerted by its trading partners or an entirely new structure of managed trade is created.[4]

A second sea-change was less apparent to Americans in the 1980s: the widening gap in economic performance within the developing world. The 1970s seemed to herald an irreversible push toward economic and political influence on the part of the Third World as a collectivity, as well as on the part of "new influentials," such as Saudi Arabia and Brazil. The 1980s saw the deflation of those hopes with the collapse and only partial recovery of commodity (including oil) prices, the shocks of high real interest rates, and an abrupt decline in bank lending in the early 1980s. The lingering debt crisis destroyed the image of a homogeneous Third World, an image that may never have corresponded with reality. In the 1980s heavily indebted countries in Latin America and Sub-Saharan Africa experienced the worst decade in terms of economic performance since the Great Depression; the countries of Asia maintained higher growth rates and export performance. The divide is no longer between middle-income and poor developing countries (the Third and Fourth Worlds of the 1970s): India's performance in the 1980s was stronger than Peru on most measures; China's better than Brazil's.

Is this new divide the result of indebtedness, taken on in the preceding period of high commodity prices and easy credit, coupled with drastically altered world economic conditions in the early 1980s (high real interest rates, deep recession, plummeting commodity prices) that were beyond the control of developing economies? Or is indebtedness itself a principal symptom of a syndrome of national economic policies that were not successfully altered in the 1980s, an alteration made even more difficult by the burden of debt? Whatever explanation is advanced, the North-South cleavage changed in the 1980s. Conflicts continue between successful exporters, such as South Korea or Taiwan, and the industrialized countries, responding to their threatened industries. The larger debtors have repeatedly gone to the brink with their creditors, private and public. These patterns of conflict, however, rarely overlap: developing countries no longer aspire to a unified bargaining stance across issue-areas. While some newly industrializing countries (NICs) confront a transition to rich country status, other developing countries scramble to escape decades of economic stagnation and an increasingly marginal status in the world economy.

Looking to the immediate future, two sea-changes in the world economy appear likely to occur in the 1990s. The communist states were long excluded (and excluded themselves) from full participation in the institutions of international economic management. The Cold War and the organization of their economies by central planning rather than market principles made integration with the capitalist world economy difficult. Although some socialist states (notably Yugoslavia and Romania) found their way into the International Monetary Fund (IMF), the World Bank, and the General Agreement on Tariffs and Trade (GATT) after demonstrating their independence from the Soviet Union, it was not until the entry of Hungary and China into the Bretton Woods institutions in the 1980s that greater participation was clearly linked to a wider program of internal economic reforms. Now Poland has been tipped as a major recipient of IMF and World Bank lending, and the Soviet Union has made clear its own closer integration with the capitalist West.

This new wave of institutional participation and economic integration does not resemble the ties established during the last superpower thaw, the years of détente in the early 1970s. Then the communist regimes carefully controlled imports of technology and, less carefully, imports of capital to bolster an existing state-dominated mode of development. The pattern that is likely to emerge in the 1990s will couple closer integration with both domestic economic reforms, particularly decentralization, and institutional commitments that will make controlling the terms of integration more difficult and, possibly, more difficult to reverse. The current quandaries of Chinese policymakers suggest that the process may well be characterized by stops and starts, particularly when the political effects of economic liberalization become clearer. The fact that political upheaval did not bring a sharp turning away from the policies of economic openness in China suggests, however, the powerful internal allies that such a strategy can create in a relatively short period of time.

The significance of renewed momentum toward closer economic integration on the part of the European Community is less clear, and it will depend in part on the future course of events in Eastern Europe and the Soviet Union. The Single European Act will clearly have a substantial impact in the area of "negative integration": removal of remaining barriers to the free movement of goods, capital, and labor within the European Community. Its results in other spheres appear more conditional. Movement toward an economic and monetary union, surpassing the relative success of the European Monetary System, could founder on British opposition and German lack of enthusiasm. More important, dramatic changes in Eastern Europe could absorb the energies of Community members, particularly Germany, at a time when the inclusion of new members might slow the motor of integration in any case. In addition, the tug to the East could shift European attention from the international economic sphere, where Community institutions have reinforced common policies, to the political and strategic sphere, where joint positions have been harder to construct.

The Organization of International Economic Relations: The Weight of the Past

In contrast to these structural shifts in the centers of international economic power and the continuing evolution of market integration that is considered below, it is worth noting that international institution-building and institutional change have not kept pace. The international organizations that crowned the postwar international economic order remain in place; their persistence symbolizes that the international rules of the game have not collapsed during two decades of economic shock. Nevertheless, their role has been repeatedly questioned and even ignored during the past decade. Even such an apparent exception as the role played by the IMF and the World Bank in managing the debt crisis appears less exceptional in the most recent phase of the crisis, as banks and debtors have moved independently toward debt reduction. Throughout the crisis, the United States, attuned to the interests of its commercial banks, has announced the close of one phase of the international debt strategy and the opening of the next.

The GATT has served as a useful locus for agreements on trade liberalization; negotiations under its aegis have also served as a means of staving off protectionist demands in the United States and other industrialized countries. Its greatest triumph—dramatic lowering of tariffs among Europe, Japan, and the United States—had been accomplished by the end of the 1970s, however, and during the 1980s, crucial trade bargains were often struck outside the GATT. (Voluntary restraints on Japanese automobile exports to the United States were only one example.) Although the most recent trade negotiations, the Uruguay Round, have widened the trade liberalization agenda to include agriculture and services as well as strengthening the GATT, the success of the negotiations remains in doubt.

Official American attitudes toward international economic institutions are certainly warmer now than they were at the beginning of the 1980s: President Bush's proposal to use the World Bank and the IMF to assist Poland is only the latest indication of this trend. Nevertheless, the overall stance of the United States and the other major capitalist countries has been measured for two reasons: their self-proclaimed fiscal bind, which (they claim) makes it increasingly difficult to extract resources from legislatures and electorates to support international institutions, and their ideological resistance to public intervention in international markets. Thus, despite the debt trap described above, public resources have provided only a small fraction of the lending that commercial banks had formerly offered to the indebted developing economies. The creditor nations have carefully avoided establishing new international mechanisms to reverse net capital outflows from the debtor countries. The industrialized states have invested new energy in another sphere of international economic policy, economic policy coordination, since the Plaza Agreement of 1985. Those steps have not, however, been incorporated in a new institutional framework, and the involvement of existing organizations, such as the IMF, has been peripheral. This reluctance to construct new institutions or to revise existing ones is apparent across international economic relations.

The most important threat to the institutional fabric, however, is neither a scarcity of resources nor ideological skepticism. The threat arises, paradoxically, from one indicator of institutional success: the growing—and increasingly heterogeneous—membership of these organizations. Developing countries, including such long-standing holdouts as Mexico, are acceding to the GATT in increasing numbers; socialist states have gained entry to the key organizations or, like the Soviet Union, are seeking membership. Apart from the challenges to cooperative solutions that sheer numbers pose for these organizations, heterogeneity of political and economic systems calls into question postwar principles of organization, such as nondiscrimination and liberalization, in a world that is no longer dominated by mixed economies of the "Atlantic" variety. Doubts about the incorporation of Japan and the East Asian NICs were noted above; the possibilities for short-term transformation in the Council for Mutual Economic Assistance (COMECON) economies can also be viewed with skepticism. Can an international order be created with this degree of national diversity? It is a question that was originally avoided by the self-exclusion of many developing countries and the division of the world between American and Soviet blocs. In the 1990s, the question will require an answer.

The Power of States and the Force of Markets

Underlying these concerns over the repositioning of states in the international economy and the efficacy of international institutions are the ongoing integration of international markets and the changing strategies of international corporations. Integration has grown most rapidly in the financial markets, where the growth of international financial transactions has consistently outstripped the growth of world trade.[5] The level of international financial integration was clearly demonstrated in the synchronized crashes that followed Wall Street's plunge in October 1987. The interconnectedness of such markets has existed since the birth of capitalism, but the current speed of transmission, closely tied to advances in computer and telecommunications technology, and the scale of financial flows across national boundaries are clearly unprecedented and deserve the label of sea-change.

The implications of financial integration for the global economy and the international financial system are not clear: the Federal Reserve successfully reestablished financial confidence in October 1987; central bank consultation has addressed the question of an international lender of last resort. Whether such mechanisms could withstand a more severe or sustained shock is less certain. For national governments, however, the effects are not obscure: their autonomy in setting economic policies is increasingly constrained, as capital controls become less effective and financial markets read their political and economic missteps with shorter and shorter time lags. Proponents of market perfection view this as a positive development, one that will keep wayward governments on the path of policy rectitude. A less optimistic view would note the blindness of the financial markets in the years preceding the debt crisis, and their tendency to overshoot in both the optimistic and the pessimistic directions on the basis of often incomplete information.

International markets for goods were marked during the 1980s by both liberalization and greater management of trade on the part of governments responding to protectionist pressures. The early years of the decade—years of deep recession, sharp upward movements of the dollar, and an unprecedented American current account deficit—witnessed a move toward greater American and European efforts to allocate international market shares in key sectors, such as steel and autos. The often predicted collapse of the trading system did not occur, however: a threat of uncontrollable protectionist pressures in the early 1980s spurred governments to open the Uruguay Round of trade negotiations. Despite rising trade barriers in certain sectors, the growth of world trade resumed after the 1981–1982 recession, and the principal targets of protectionist measures, particularly Japan and the NICs, continued their export success. Industrialized governments also moved to lower trade barriers with some of their principal trading partners: the United States and Canada, Australia and New Zealand, the 1992 project of the European Community.

Technology had not undermined closure so clearly as in the financial markets, but governments did confront greater sophistication on the part of traders if their attempts to restrain trade distorted the market too greatly: in developing countries, whole sectors moved to the black market economy in part to evade import and export controls; in such sophisticated sectors as semiconductors, "gray markets" quickly developed to satisfy demand in the United States after the 1986 U.S.–Japan Semiconductor Agreement.

Although the postwar international economic order had always included an ideological commitment by the dominant powers to liberalization in the movement of goods and capital, the free movement of labor has remained a jealously guarded sphere of national authority. In the last decade, however, it has become increasingly clear that better international communication and burgeoning mass tourism have undermined barriers to immigration at a time when the disparities between rich and poor countries remain enormous. Even a society as hostile to immigration as Japan has found it impossible to stop illegal immigration when its own businesses collude to gain cheap labor. Outside the richest countries, brain drains and labor outflows become serious restraints on national governments, particularly in the developing world: economic downturns and political repression no longer produce only the temporarily unemployed or refugees who later return to their homes. Another option, permanent emigration, is now available, as Central America, Peru, China, and East Germany have all learned of late.

The differing pace of integration in markets for capital, goods, and labor has influenced the increasingly complex strategies of transnational corporations. The global organization of production in certain sectors, such as oil, extends back many decades; but the 1980s was the decade in which the global factory came into its own. Seeking ways to put their capital and rapidly eroding technological advantages together with low-cost labor, firms in the industrialized countries developed suppliers and production sites throughout the world. They attempted to im-

prove their competitive position through cooperative arrangements (such as licensing agreements and joint ventures) with
firms that may appear to be their rivals in other settings. The
pursuit of such strategies, by global giants as well as middling
firms, has further blurred the distinction between "home" country and "host" country. These cross-cutting corporate interests
have also complicated any definition of national economic interest. Should the United States encourage Japanese investment in
smaller, American, high-technology firms, for example? Are
American corporations in Japan part of the U.S. economy situated abroad, or are they essentially Japanese firms? Such a web
of private connections at first appears to create important pressures for liberalization in government policies: the complexity of
relations among firms makes efforts at international restriction
less likely to be effective or beneficial. On the other hand, nationalist political responses to these new relationships—particularly
foreign investment—could provoke a backlash that will create
renewed pressure for controls.

Sea-Changes and the Transformation of World Politics

That this intensified if uneven integration of markets in capital,
goods, and labor could be reversed by some future shock—major
financial crisis, global economic depression, or war—is a possibility that has haunted liberal memories since the end of World
War II. A more pertinent question is whether such dis-integra-
tion could arise from the actions of governments, perhaps
through unwitting exercises in economic brinksmanship that
end up unraveling, in a perverse game of tit for tat, the fabric of
economic openness. Few governments are willing to argue any
longer for the benefits of economic closure, whatever their skepticism about the stability of markets or the effects of external
liberalization on more vulnerable groups or sectors. Governments will certainly continue to shape the rules of the game to
protect the interests of politically powerful and less mobile sectors of the economy. Calculated measures in favor of dis-integra-
tion, however, seem unlikely.

   If the configurations described persist, some might be
tempted to argue that they will constitute a sea-change in the

very character of world politics, profound enough to contribute to an "end of history." Such predictions would have seemed outlandish at the beginning of the 1980s, when the newest chapter of the Cold War intensified concerns over military dangers. Today, however, one may well ask whether relations among states are not characterized by a permanent shift toward goals of economic welfare and a concomitant rise in the importance of economic resources and economic instruments in interstate competition. Such a change is linked not only to those international economic developments already mentioned, but also to reduction in superpower rivalry and widespread, if not yet universal, internal political liberalization. Foreign policy elites may not yet be ready to accept arguments made by Paul Kennedy (among others) regarding the inherent liabilities of imperial policies, but they can hardly see any gains accruing from traditional military competition in an era when governments, in order to remain in power, must respond to their populations' outspoken desires for economic well-being.

Arguments in favor of such a benign transformation in the character of world politics can be challenged on at least three grounds. First, even if "welfarist" concerns come to dominate the domestic politics of most societies, they might produce more, rather than less, international conflict. If elites depend more on economic performance for their internal hold on power, redistributional questions may loom larger than ever in the international arena. This domestic political dynamic, coupled with the internationalization of national economies, may cause some states to define their security requirements more broadly rather than less: Japanese semiconductors may be added to Persian Gulf oil as critical constituents of national economic well-being and security. Second, elites are rarely sensitive politically to a general notion of economic welfare. Rather, they will make efforts to satisfy the economic demands of certain constituencies within their societies instead of others, thereby maintaining distributional conflicts between classes and groups. Those internal conflicts may then drive states in the direction of more conflictual foreign policies. Finally, and most important, people are not interested only in issues affecting their material well-being: nationalism and religion have resurfaced as explosive issues and major concerns in the wake of the political liberalization that we are seeing—most dramatically in Eastern Europe—and may be reflected in the international behavior of states as well.

Thus, without lapsing into a Spenglerian pessimism that risks becoming as fashionable as the most recent hype over the new era of good feelings, we should see changes in the international economy not as producing an inevitable resolution to age-old problems of interstate conflict, but as intimately tied to that conflict, as they have been since the birth of capitalism. The ever changing economic fortunes of nation-states affect their strategic position as well as their perception of national security. Internationalized though they may be, markets will continue to confront fragmented political authority. Whatever the sea-changes in the international economy, they will take place within these deeply embedded features of international relations, for they have not yet transformed them.

International Economic Change and American Policy

The balance between persistence and change in the international economy confronts the United States with particular challenges. Both the goals that the United States has pursued since 1945 and the instruments that it has employed to reach those goals may be called into question. One preeminent national aim has been a liberal world economy, in which any government controls and interventions that affect the free movement of goods and capital are reduced. This goal has always been qualified: the United States not only has imposed such controls itself (whether as instruments of national strategy or as responses to domestic demands), it also has recognized that completely liberalized markets might be politically insupportable.

The goal of a liberal world economy is now questioned for two reasons. First, those who view Japan and the NICs through revisionist eyes argue that the United States has become a liberal dupe in a world that does not operate according to neoclassical economic principles. As economic exchanges with the socialist economies grow, such complaints are likely to surge. Such criticisms could lead policy in several directions: protectionism, industrial policy, or reciprocal liberalization with "like-minded" countries (for example, the free trade agreement with Canada).

The second reason for viewing liberalization more skeptically derives from the reconsideration of market deregulation that is now under way. The infallible wisdom of markets, even markets untouched by political manipulation or monopolistic behavior, is less likely to be taken for granted in the future. An economic shock (a second, more severe financial crash, for example) would only add support to such criticisms.

A global rather than a regionalized world economy has been a second overarching goal of the United States; this goal has been closely related to the multilateral structure of international economic institutions and such norms as nondiscrimination in trade. Since the economic shocks of the 1970s, some observers have predicted a world economy divided into regional blocs; some of the sea-changes described above—the consolidation of Europe and the rise of Japan—may point in that direction. The United States has endorsed certain regional groupings, particularly the European Economic Community, for their value in offsetting Soviet power. If the Soviet military threat fades and regionalization takes a form that appears damaging to American economic interests, that support may disappear. The United States may need to specify its economic interests in either a global or a regionalized economic order on purely economic grounds.

In advancing its goals in the international economic arena, the United States also faces choices concerning the instruments that it employs. The role of collaboration among governments (within or outside established international institutions) must be assessed as an alternative to either unilateral measures by the United States to impose its policy preferences (for example, threats of trade sanctions to open markets) or the avoidance of political intervention in international markets. It seems unlikely that either the immiseration of parts of the world or the integration of the socialist economies can be dealt with in the absence of sustained cooperation on the part of the major industrialized countries. Throughout the 1980s, the United States was skeptical of international institutions that were often portrayed as either bloated bureaucracies or unwanted restraints on American action. A reassessment has already begun: unilateral American action is likely to be less effective, and the workings of an untrammeled market may be less desirable than innovation (or renovation) of mechanisms for international collaboration.

In any collaborative initiatives that are undertaken, the United States faces a final choice—the claims of leadership that it will make and the price that it is willing to pay for those claims. Japan has now become the largest donor of foreign aid. The Bush administration has signaled its willingness to have the European Community lead in organizing economic assistance for Eastern Europe. Our fiscal deadlock has made it difficult for the United States to lead on issues of international economic importance. In a regionalized world economy, demands would not be so great: each major actor—Japan, Europe, the United States—would tend its own backyard. If such a fragmented world is not the future that we desire, then the United States will need economic instruments for a world in which military instruments may become increasingly unsuited. If the threat of Soviet military power recedes, then a central question will be what price the United States and its taxpayers are willing to pay in order to possess those instruments and, with them, a central role in sustaining an altered international economic order.

NOTES

1. Ezra Vogel, *Japan as Number One* (Cambridge, Mass.: Harvard University Press, 1979).
2. Economist Lawrence Krause has summarized some of the latest indicators of Japan's economic power: "When measured in a common currency, Japanese per capita income is already larger than in the United States, and the rising yen is increasing the gap. . . . Japan is the largest creditor nation in the world. Seven of the eight largest commercial banks in the world are Japanese. Three of the five largest insurance companies are Japanese, including the largest (Nippon Life). The largest brokerage firm is Japanese (Nomura). . . . In 1987, the total value of equities in the Tokyo market exceeded that in New York, even before the crash, and the drop was larger in New York than in Tokyo." See his "Changing America and the Economy of the Pacific Basin," in Robert A. Scalapino et al., eds., *Pacific-Asian Economic Policies and Regional Interdependence* (Berkeley, Calif.: Institute of East Asian studies, 1988), pp. 48–49.
3. For example, see Joseph S. Nye, Jr., "Understating U.S. Strength," *Foreign Policy*, no. 72 (Fall 1988), pp. 118–125; and Samuel P. Huntington, "The

U.S.—Decline or Renewal?" *Foreign Affairs*, vol. 67, no. 2 (Winter 1988/89), pp. 90–92.

4. Although the diagnoses and prescriptions of these observers differ considerably, the Japanese have singled out a "Gang of Four" who espouse this more pessimistic view: James Fallows, Chalmers Johnson, Clyde Prestowitz, and Karel van Wolferen. For an excellent summary, see Chalmers Johnson, "Rethinking Japanese Politics: A Godfather Reports," *Freedom at Issue* (November-December 1989), pp. 5–11.

5. Ralph Bryant, *International Financial Intermediation* (Washington, D.C.: Brookings Institution, 1987).

A Look at . . .

THE FUTURE OF CAPITALISM

Robert L. Heilbroner

The emergence of capitalism as the uncontested system of world economic order is arguably the most important event of modern economic history. It may well be that capitalism has always been such a dominant world system—certainly it was self-consciously so during the nineteenth century—but this has not been the general perception in our times. However mistakenly, some form of planned socialist economy has been widely seen as the direction in which economic organization has been drifting, more rapidly in the underdeveloped areas, more gradually in the developed ones, but with ineluctable tread in all. The virtual collapse of centrally planned socialism has cleared away all such anticipations. The shape of things to come will be determined by the dynamics of world capitalism alone—an awareness that conjures up in some minds Pogo's famous statement that we have met the enemy and they are us.

The reason for this unease lies, of course, in the widespread view of capitalism as characterized by self-induced dysfunctions, whether in the form of Marx's economic "contradictions," such as its bouts of depression or inflation, or as the sociological deterioration expected by Schumpeter, evidenced in a loss of managerial élan and self-confidence. The purpose of this essay is to reflect on the cogency of these misgivings, now elevated to newly appreciated importance by the disappearance of socialism as a moving force on the historical stage, and to speculate on possibilities for the future of a capitalist world order.

110

II

We should begin by noting that the emergence of such an order has two distinct meanings. One of them, to which I shall devote this section, is that the leading force in global economic affairs will henceforth be provided entirely by a family of nations with common structural characteristics.

What are those characteristics? I do not think there will be much quarrel that three elements demarcate this sociopolitical order from others. The first of these is the need to accumulate capital—a requirement whose vital importance has been acknowledged since Adam Smith's day. Accumulation is vital because it fulfills both an economic and a political necessity for the continuance of capitalism. The economic function is to provide the material and financial basis by which employment is sustained, economic growth facilitated, and—not least—profits secured. Less commonly recognized is the political function served by capital accumulation. This is the continued legitimization of what I have called the "regimatic principle" of capital, the core of beliefs and social institutions that embodies its historic mission. From this viewpoint, accumulation is to capitalism what the expansion of territory was to earlier empires or the winning of converts to theological ones.

The second attribute of capitalism needs less explication. It is the presence of the market as the principal means of coordinating economic activity. Here I need only caution that no capitalist economy is coordinated by market relations alone. As Adam Smith was the first to make explicit, a substructure of governmental allocation is as ubiquitous as it is indispensable. Nevertheless, the key role of market allocation unquestionably characterizes the capitalist economic order.

Third, I single out the existence of two realms of authority in capitalism, the political counterpart of its system of dual allocation. One of these realms, the state, carries out the traditional prerogatives and duties of political power—the waging of war, the enforcement of law and order, the conduct of ceremony. Of central importance for our purposes, however, the state in a capitalist order is no longer entrusted with a function it performed in precapitalist stratified orders—namely, the direct supervision of the general activities of production and distribution. Under capitalism those activities became the province of a new realm of social authority—the world of business, which supplies the missing economic functions of the state, but without its coercive prerogatives. Only two further observations are needed here. First, the two realms become the basis for capitalist democracy, insofar as they create a social space from which state coercion is largely excluded. Second, the relationship of the two realms, at once mutually dependent and mutually rivalrous, sets the stage for a political tension also characteristic of the capitalist order.

III

This much too compressed excursion now enables us to return to our original question—namely, what can be ventured as to the prospects for world capitalism seen as a congeries of systems all possessing these core attributes? This formidable question can be made more manageable by breaking it into two:

1. Can we generalize as to the economic dynamics of the family of capitalisms over the coming few decades? I shall risk the prognosis that we can. I anticipate that world capitalisms (in the plural) are likely to manifest the same kinds of perturbation, within roughly the same range of amplitude, as we have witnessed since 1945. The prognosis proceeds from the problems associated with each of the three constitutive elements of the order: demand saturation as the self-created difficulty of accumulation, instability as that of market allocation, and government-business divergences of interest as that of the bifurcation of authority. My crucial assertion is that none of these problems will worsen to such a degree as to disrupt the uneven but politically adequate growth of the past half-century.

This is, I need hardly say, an assertion that cannot be demonstrated. Nonetheless, it seems more realistic than its contrary—namely, that demand saturation, market instability, and interrealm tension are headed for new levels of disorder. Such a pessimistic outlook must ignore the extraordinary range of scientific and technical advance, the increasing ability of capitalisms to prevent market disorders from spreading in an uncontrolled fashion, and the development of "corporatist" structures of public-private coordination in many, if not all, capitalisms.

2. *Does the failure of centrally planned socialism change the outlook for world capitalism?* I will argue that it does not. Admittedly, there will be short-term gains. The failure of the socialist alternative bolsters the political and ideological security of capitalism. In addition, there will almost certainly be a diminution of arms spending, which, while removing the stimulus of "military Keynesianism," opens the way for a much needed transfer of resources into public investment. Finally, there may be important new investment opportunities within the former planned economies.

Despite these favorable short-term changes, I would argue that none of them affects capitalism's long-term economic trajectory. This is because the problems of saturation, instability, and interrealm tension are rooted in the nature of the system, and will not be removed or fundamentally altered by the "disappearance" of socialism.

From this analysis it follows that the outlook for world capitalism—always implying a family of structurally related regimes—will vary from one national entity to the next. As in the past, differing institutional configurations will cope with the self-generated problems of the system with differing degrees of effectiveness. All capitalisms will be impelled to accumulate capital, but their business realms will do so with different time horizons and thresholds of acceptable performance. All these business realms, in turn, will display the inherent instabilities of market systems, but these will be countered with varying degrees of success through regulation or other corrective actions of the state. Similarly, all public realms will seek to coordinate political and economic objectives, but they will do so in the widely varying fashions of Sweden and the Union of South Africa, Japanese capitalism and the capitalism of the United States.

The prospect for world capitalism thus appears as a kind of evolutionary process for a social genus whose species are capable of striking differentiation. This leads to the obvious final question: Can one generalize with regard to the configuration best suited for success? I do not think so. Arguments over dirigisme versus laissez-faire, demand management versus supply-side economics, free trade versus protectionism, do not point with irrefutable cogency to an optimal configuration even for an abstractly conceived system. Much less so do they serve as a guide for a concretely realized capitalist nation. As in all evolutionary processes, the outlook is essentially unpredictable, however much we should like to argue for the superior chances of a configuration that reflects our particular preferences.

IV

I do not think, however, that this rather bland prognosis exhausts what can be said with respect to capitalism's prospects. For there remains another perspective that greatly alters the prospective dynamics of the system—this time conceptualized not as a family of structurally related national entities, but as a supranational structure of capital itself in a "pure" (i.e., depoliticized) form.

Such a supranational aspect of capital is visible as far back as the accumulation process itself. Accumulation naturally lends itself to what the economic historian Immanuel Wallerstein calls "chains of commodities" that can stretch over widely separated regions or nations.[1] The ancient caravan routes of merchants are an instance of depoliticized capital accumulation in embryo; in modern capitalism, this process reaches a new level of development with the multinational corporation, the principal vehicle by which capital is accumulated without regard to national identity. A second aspect of supranational capitalism appears in the denationalization of money and credit—again, visible as early as the banking networks of the Renaissance, but attaining new importance in the immense volume and speed of modern global credit.

At a less dramatic but no less important level, the internationaliz-ation of production inputs, including managerial skills and tech-nical know-how, has again freed the process of accumulation from its earlier national embeddedness and created a new scope for supranational operation.

I am far from believing that capitalism could exist without a national basis for its transnational operations. Nevertheless, there is no doubt that these operations today not only differ in many ways from those of national capitalism, but threaten it in vital respects. The most important of these threats is the capa-bility of supranational capitalism to rearrange the global division and distribution of political and economic power. The transfer of centrality from the Atlantic to the Pacific basin in scarcely 30 years is a dramatic example of the power of modern suprana-tional capital to rearrange the economic geography of the world. And beyond the rise of the Pacific Rim lies the possibility of an even more dislocating transfer of centrality to other regions of the former "periphery," India and Brazil as possible candidates.

Such core-periphery rearrangements can be seismic in their impact—more disruptive by far than any of the dysfunctions of national capitalisms. Supranational capitalism is disruptive be-cause it raises the dynamics of accumulation, markets, and bifur-cated authority to a level at which the "logic" of economic processes, freed of considerations of political territory, national interests, or cultural coherence, becomes pitted against the logic of traditional capitalism in which the economic realm is con-strained by its political twin.

It is difficult to see the outcome of this contest of forces. On the one hand, shifts in the global location of economic power are likely to continue in the near-term future because there is little that the older centers can do to inhibit these supranational dynamics. The prospect therefore arises of a flourishing world of corporate enterprise arched over a depressed world of na-tional economies. On the other hand, nation-states cannot be expected to acquiesce passively in the erosion of their sovereign powers, and have the capacity to control the operations of supra-national capital inside their own borders. Ironically, then, the rise of "pure" economic forces in shaping the international economic prospects of nations is likely to strengthen the assertion of political resistance to this subservience, especially within the older, and perhaps now more vulnerable, central nations. As I have said, I do not think the outcome of this contest can be foretold, although it seems an inescapable conclusion that its severity will increase.

V

But a second aspect of world capitalism remains to be examined—an aspect that is likely to overwhelm both the national and the transnational consequences of supranational capitalism. This is the looming confrontation of capitalist dynamics with the limits of ecological tolerance.

The magnitude, irreversibility, and potentially disastrous aspects of this challenge are by now familiar. In broad outline, the challenge emerges from a prospective rise in global mean temperatures of between 1.5 and 4.5 degrees Celsius over the next half-century. This rise is mainly the consequence of the steady addition of carbon dioxide to the ecosphere, where it catalyzes the atmosphere into a "greenhouse" that traps heat. There is disagreement as to the expected magnitude or speed of arrival of the greenhouse effect, but not as to its ultimate seriousness. If the present rate of increase of carbon emissions is not reduced, the effect could assume life-threatening proportions beginning in about a century. The near-term effects—mainly severe droughts—are likely to appear much sooner.

These environmental disturbances are, of course the supreme challenge of the heat pollution problem, but they are not the immediate issue posed by the ecological threat. That issue concerns the rate at which we can reduce the carbon emissions at the center of the heat problem. That reduction, in turn, can be attained only by a large-scale abandonment of fossil fuels. Until a safe alternative energy source is developed, the use of gas, oil, and coal must be gradually, but in the end drastically, curtailed. In turn, this curtailment would entail a substantial reduction of industrial output and energy consumption. Such a reduction would threaten the historic thrust of all modern socioeconomic orders, and of capitalism in particular.

Is this portentous scenario unavoidable? The answer depends in the first instance on the resources and effort devoted to alternative fuels—solar and geothermal energy, in particular; nuclear energy as a desperate last resort—and to the degree to which capitalist social orders are prepared to alter their pollution-generating mode of material life. (Each year the average automobile throws its own weight in carbon emissions into the air.) These adjustments are unquestionably within the existing technical capacity of modern society. The challenge is whether capitalist societies will develop the political will to make them. Here the obstacles derive in part from adversely affected business interests, and in part from the resistance of the consuming public itself. It would be foolhardy to underrate the power of these counterforces.

Even this, however, is not a full measure of the difficulty of the problem. One could imagine that the necessary adjustments might be made within capitalist economies of high internal discipline and moral consciousness, such as Sweden. But it is in the nature of the ecological threat that it respects no national boundaries. The greenhouse effect must be tamed for the entire world or for none of it. All advanced capitalisms must therefore bring the heat problem under control together, for the Western nations are responsible for 75 percent of all carbon emissions. It need hardly be said that the task of international cooperation on such a scale poses issues of vastly greater difficulty than those of economic control within any single nation. In addition to—or perhaps more accurately, as part of—those difficulties, the imposition of an ecological standstill agreement would perpetuate interregional inequalities, creating other problems of unprecedented magnitude and potential consequence. The prospects for an orderly and rational resolution of these problems are small. One must therefore anticipate that many crucial adjustments, such as the recent Montreal Convention to ban the chlorofluorocarbons that now threaten the ozone layer, will take place as defensive reactions to limited disasters. Drought is a very likely candidate for such future limited disasters, although we cannot foretell what responses they might evoke.

To speak of the outlook for capitalism under these conditions may appear to trivialize the problem. But the framework of our analysis enables us to sharpen and make more imaginable some of the actual challenges to be faced. To begin, it is clear that industrial pollution cannot be permitted to continue for more than a few decades at most. This means that the industrial (capitalist) West must shift to a pollution-free energy technology. Such a shift may be triggered by limited disasters, but its actual implementation will require a very large degree of government intervention.

Second, it is apparent that government supervision cannot be limited to energy technology alone. All industrial processes must be monitored for ecological safety. The guidance of economic activity by considerations of profit alone becomes too hazardous to allow.

Third, it follows that the allocational role accorded to the market is certain to be drastically reduced. The market can serve an allocational role only if prices are adjusted to reflect the costs of ecological damage. Such an adjustment cannot arise spontaneously from private motives of supply and demand, but must be imposed on prices by "ecology taxes."

Thus the radical changes in the world's social and natural environment imply radical changes in the setting within which economic activity must be carried on. Can capitalism absorb such drastic institutional restructurings? In particular, can the two realms of power, on which capitalist democracy has been based, survive the expansion of the public realm in both intracapitalist and intercapitalist relations?

It is a sobering outlook, but not one that is beyond remedy, incompatible with the structural elements of capitalism. Economic activity can retain its expansive thrust as long as this thrust is directed toward ecologically safe pursuits. I have already said that economic activity could be guided by a market mechanism of incentive and competition, provided that prices are adjusted to reflect ecological sensitivities. Within these narrowed limits, economic activity could still constitute a realm largely screened off from state power.

Is such a radically constrained system capitalism? I would think it might retain the name if it so desired, although such a capitalism would no doubt be as distinct from the present configuration of institutions and ideologies as welfare capitalism is from its industrial predecessor, or industrial capitalism from its mercantile beginnings. Like its predecessors, though, it might have a good run for its money.

NOTE

1. Immanuel Wallerstein, *Historical Capitalism* (London: Routledge, Chapman & Hall, Inc., 1983) pp. 29–31.

A Look at . . .

SCIENCE AND TECHNOLOGY

Kenneth H. Keller

Extraordinarily rapid growth in scientific knowledge in the latter part of the twentieth century, coupled with technological innovation and expansion, is having a profound influence on our lives. One manifestation of that influence is the effect of certain scientific and technological trends on American foreign policy, (a) constraining, (b) enabling, or (c) forcing new choices in the positions that the U.S. government can take in promoting its global interests.

Science and technology (S&T) affect society at several levels. New technologies and products can ease or burden our individual and collective lives. Technological advances have been a cornerstone in national security planning and military strategy, particularly since World War II. S&T developments are central factors in determining our national economic competitiveness. Beyond these direct influences, scientific and technological development can have a profound effect on the values, institutions, and patterns of decision making of the society as a whole. To understand the influence of S&T on society generally and on American foreign policy in particular, it is necessary to consider the *processes* of scientific and technological development as well as its *products,* paying particular attention to the complex interaction of technical, social, and cultural factors that affect and are affected by them.

II

In terms of impact on foreign policy concerns over the next decade, the trends in the following S&T areas appear to be of singular importance: biosciences; materials science; information technologies; "big" science; and large-scale technology.[1]

Biosciences. In the first half of the twentieth century, physics occupied the most prominent position among the sciences, leading the way in increasing our understanding of nature through the development of atomic theory, quantum theory, and particle physics. Its power lay not only in the extraordinary novelty of the ideas it presented, which altered our views on the nature of matter and energy, but also in the applicability of those ideas, which form the basis of most of today's technology.

It now appears that the biosciences have displaced physics in that leading role. Molecular biology and cellular biology, in particular, but ecology as well, have taken biology beyond its descriptive phase into the development of powerful models and experimental techniques that are helping us to understand the most fundamental of life processes. This, in turn, is allowing us to create and alter life-forms, blurring the distinction between "natural" and "synthetic," and raising important and difficult issues *with international implications* concerning property rights and the appropriate limits, if any, on "interfering" with nature. The consequences are already manifest in the debate among developed nations about patenting life-forms, a debate that may cast a new light on the question of how a nation's natural resources should be treated in international commerce in comparison with the treatment of materials created through biosynthetic means.[2]

As physics did at an earlier time, the biosciences emerge as important because of their technological potential. As our basic scientific understanding has increased, we have been able to link the various fields in which biology is applied, from agriculture to medicine, benefiting from the cross-fertilization of research and development between historically distinct disciplines, and making extraordinarily rapid advances in each of them. Our ability to tinker with the machinery of life is allowing us to create disease- and weather-resistant plants, to program bacteria to clean up pollutants or to manufacture rare chemicals, and to custom-design drugs to combat disease.

What distinguishes these technological developments from the earlier ones that grew out of physics is their intimate connection to agriculture and health, areas of great political sensitivity and social importance. In this respect, international technology transfer in the biological fields is a matter not simply of sharing the benefits or luxuries of a consumer society, but of sharing the means of survival. As a result, strong humanitarian considerations affect (and sometimes dominate) technology transfer policy development. Furthermore, as sophisticated technology collides with varying cultural norms in the application of biology, the issues in trade and technology exchange negotiations are made more complicated. Some examples:

- In development aid, the United States has been attempting to shift to programs that stimulate and rely on market mechanisms. However, where the solution to specific Third World health problems involves high-cost, high-technology medical therapies, which developing countries are unlikely to be able to afford, straightforward market approaches will not work and alternative ways will have to be found to make such therapies available if humanitarian goals are to be achieved.

- It is unlikely that a multilateral framework such as the General Agreement on Tariffs and Trade will be suitable for negotiating trade and technology agreements where biotechnology is involved, since noneconomic issues quite specific to each trading partner are likely to be as important as economic ones (limits on genetic alteration of plants and people, standards for drug testing, protection of individuals participating as subjects in clinical investigations).

- The increasing technological sophistication of agricultural research is requiring greater use of American university equipment and facilities in support of international aid programs. This is creating domestic political problems because of the strong tradition of regional "ownership" of these facilities. Indeed, university research to improve Third World food production is already under attack as a misuse of public funds and a threat to domestic farmers.

Materials Science. Materials science is a field linking advances in solid-state physics—research aimed at fundamental understanding of the behavior of condensed matter—to the development of materials with a desired, often unusual, set of properties. It is included here because of its vast array of applications and the many ways in which it can reduce the resource and energy dependence of the United States and thus improve the nation's economic competitiveness. Some examples:

- Advances in information technologies depend on the development of new materials: semiconductors for chips; orientable surfaces for magnetic storage of information; fiber optics for fast communication links.

- The development of new materials ranging from superconductors to high-strength, lightweight construction materials is a key element in improving the efficiency with which the United States uses energy. Increased efficiency is allowing us to control, and may soon allow us to reduce, our total energy consumption without paying a significant domestic political price. Not only would this reduce our energy dependence, but it would strengthen our presently weak negotiating position (as the nation with the highest per capita energy use in the world) in seeking to limit the worldwide growth in energy use that is necessary to deal with the global greenhouse gas problem.

- Much as the development of synthetic rubber altered the course of World War II, our growing ability to design materials with highly specialized properties from readily available raw stock is likely to alter our strategic materials stockpiling needs in ways that should increase our autonomy. Thus, electrically conductive polymers and ceramics may well become a practical replacement for copper wire; new catalyst materials will decrease our dependence on sources of platinum and other noble metals; nonferrous construction materials should reduce our dependence on steel.

Information Technologies. Information technology, which includes the gathering (through sensors, imaging techniques, telephotography), processing and storage (in computers), and transmission (via communications networks, broadcasting) of information, has, since World War II, affected our lives and our society more intimately and more ubiquitously than any other field of science or technology.

While one cannot discount the developments in nuclear technology, materials science, and chemistry, information technology has been the bedrock of national defense for the past half-century. Command, control, communications, and intelligence (C^3I), the bases for military strategy and tactics, all now depend on new developments in information technology. In the bipolar world in which we have lived since World War II, U.S. leadership in this area has given this country a military advantage that has more than compensated for the USSR's greater size—as measured in terms of geography, total military personnel, and sheer rocket power.

Information technology will obviously continue to play an important role in national security affairs in the next decade, even as U.S. military strategy is altered by declining East-West tensions. However, the nature of its influence appears to be shifting as a consequence of two new trends. First, leadership in some areas of computer-related technology is diffusing to other nations, so the United States cannot expect to retain the same technology-based military advantage in the future that it has had up until now. Indeed, as some Japanese spokesmen have commented, even without a substantial military structure, the Japanese could exercise a significant (though not unchallengeable) influence on the global strategic balance by the export policies they adopt for their electronic components.

Second, as the size and complexity of weapon systems grows, their error-free command and control become ever more demanding and difficult to accomplish. The redundancy (and cost) necessary to assure acceptable performance increases many times over, and, as was manifest in the recent Strategic Defense Initiative debate, it is not even certain that such control will be within our technical capacity in the foreseeable future.

On the other hand, the quite different performance requirements of intelligence and information-gathering systems appear much more technically feasible; and, indeed, they are quite likely to continue to improve during this decade. Satellite observation, remote chemical and physical analyses, vibration sensing equipment, and computer processing of information all increase our ability to obtain earlier warnings of attack and to verify arms treaties. Thus, it appears that S&T developments may be a significant stimulus to further arms reduction by the superpowers in the coming decade.

Four other aspects of information technology's influence are also worthy of note. First, our prodigious ability to gather information not only is forcing a review of the legal and practical meaning of the notion of individual privacy, but will require a similar review of the "privacy" of nations. Second, the existence of inexpensive, multiple, and worldwide networks for communicating information has shifted power from governments to individuals and given major impetus, at a practical level, to the heretofore rather abstract notion of a "linked" world. Third, the availability of supercomputers—and the likelihood that they will continue to improve in calculational speed—goes beyond merely allowing us to do more of the same in computing; we can now envision a time (probably closer at hand than energy generation by controlled fusion, for example) when any problem that can be *conceived of* as amenable to calculation will be doable at acceptable cost and in a reasonable period of time. Thus, there has been an enhanced interest in pushing back the limits of what we can conceive to be reducible to calculational terms. Artificial intelligence and the new, popular field known as chaos theory are two manifestations of this phenomenon. Fourth, we are being forced to shift our conceptual framework concerning information. We are now so inundated with information that our problem is dealing with it rather than collecting it: sorting, absorbing, understanding, avoiding.

On the national level, the issue is illustrated in the concern over the influence of polling in elections; in the instabilities caused by computer-initiated stock trading; in the extraordinary power of the electronic media to convey information through visual images in a way that is *both* effective and *distorting*. On the international level, we see it in the concern of Canada and European Community nations to control the influx of American television programming at least in part so as to preserve national cultural identity; in the fear of misinformation in media advertising by multinational companies (as in the case of cigarette ads in less developed countries or Nestle's promotion of infant formula); in international instabilities in stock-trading and currency exchange mechanisms; in the assignment and preservation of intellectual property rights.

Big Science. In many scientific research projects, the costs of equipment and its operation and maintenance now far exceed the annual salaries of the scientists involved in the project. It is not unusual for the equipment necessary to support the work of a single scientist to cost in the range of $1–$2 million. In some megaprojects—the superconducting supercollider (SSC) and the human genome project are two examples—the total equipment costs are in the $4–$8 *billion* range.

The effects of this economic reality are profound. First, the need to share equipment (as well as the increasing importance of multidisciplinary efforts—research requiring the joint participation of scientists with several areas of specialization) is causing a shift from research projects conceived and carried out by individual investigators to group activities. This may reduce innovation by narrowing the variety of research approaches and the greater risk-taking associated with individual projects. Second, since the equipment used in research is now the *product* of high technology, the sequential nature of research and technology is being importantly altered by a feedback loop (the availability of technology to allow further advances in science). This gives new importance to the quality of a nation's infrastructure for research, making it significantly more difficult to create oases of good research in the technological deserts of underdeveloped countries and, therefore, tending to widen the gap between developed and developing nations. Third, megascience has now reached a scale that is beyond the capacity of even a nation like the United States to support independently. For example, the annual budget of the National Science Foundation is about $2 billion, a fraction of the cost of the SSC project alone. This means that international, cooperative scientific research is becoming ever more critical and that we must deal with the issues of national security, competitiveness, and pride that make such cooperation difficult.

Large-Scale Technology. While the proponents of what is called appropriate technology would argue that technological clever-ness (or sophistication) need not be of enormous scale, at least two factors have led inexorably toward larger and larger produc-tion in applying technology. First, our level of comfort—our standard of living, our "wealth"—is itself a quantitative concept, most often correlated with measures of productivity such as gross national product (GNP), and one that encourages in-creased production. Second, many technology-based systems are cost-effective only when the scale of production is large, thus justifying the use of capital-intensive, integrated production facilities—that is, large-scale technology.

As technological systems become more integrated, more sophisticated, and larger in scale, technological development becomes more complex, dependent on research in a number of disparate areas so that the development process does not follow sequentially and obviously from a well-defined set of research projects. Development of a particular product or technology depends on research in many disciplines, and research in a particular discipline feeds a number of technological develop-ments.[3] Not only is the progression from research idea to techno-logical application no longer linear, but it occurs much more rapidly than it has in the past.[4]

Under these new circumstances, the traditional American separation of basic researchers (usually at universities) from appliers (usually in industry) hurts both scientific *and* technolog-ical development and can be a considerable handicap to the United States in terms of international competitiveness, partic-ularly with respect to a country that has encouraged much closer relationships between university and industrial scientists, like Japan. A closer university-industry association in the United

States could ameliorate that situation and would also be valuable in helping to reduce the likelihood and danger of rapid professional obsolescence, which the accelerated rate of S&T evolution can produce.

III

These significant recent trends in S&T are giving rise to the following four phenomena:

1. Increasing limitations on the exercise of national sovereignty. There are now practical limitations on the ability of a nation to exercise governing authority over its territory and people, as well as strong reasons for limiting the assertion of its autonomy and the exercise of its authority.

The limitations arise in several ways. While information technology vastly increases the power of a government to monitor its people, the government's control over the distribution of information is largely gone. Information may still represent power, but it is now shared. The ease of person-to-person communication also makes it increasingly impractical for nations to try to control the international diffusion of technological information as a means of improving their competitive position. Further, it is counterproductive to attempt such control because of the interdependence of (developed) nations in scientific research and the need for openness within societies for technology to keep competitive in an environment characterized by a very short time scale for development.

Geographic boundaries are becoming less meaningful as improved remote sensing allows any nation to "see" anything going on in the open within another's borders. Moreover, the autonomy to make decisions within those borders—on such issues as trade barriers, energy policy, or pollution standards—is seriously reduced by the increasing interdependence of nations brought about by the need for international markets in an S&T–driven economy, as well as by the constraints of a shared global environment.

Also, the increased worldwide distribution of information has led to a heightened awareness in less developed countries of how the "other half" lives, and to a heightened desire to share that life-style and standard of living. As a practical matter, developed nations cannot ignore those aspirations. Thus, they do not have as wide a range of options in industrial policy, economic development policy, or technology transfer and developmental aid as their national autonomy once suggested.

2. *Approaching limits on the capacity of the earth to sustain civilization.* In its more modest rendition, this is basically a question of the finiteness of "spaceship earth." The more radical notion is the comprehensive, ecological, quasi-organic "Gaia hypothesis." The root causes are clear enough: the combination of rapidly increasing populations and intensified technology.

Technology, through the improvements it has brought about in food supply, shelter, and the reduction of disease, has made human population growth possible. Since 1800, world population has grown from 1 billion to 5 billion. At the same time, technology has expanded to an even greater extent. Unfortunately, the obverse of technology's salutary influence is its impact on the environment, which is at the very least to temporarily disrupt the ecological balance and, in some circumstances, to damage it "permanently." Since this negative impact is roughly proportional to both the number of people and the level of technology available to each of them, the very factors that facilitate population growth magnify its negative effects.

By the end of the twenty-first century, world population will probably have doubled from its present 5 billion to 10 billion. The growth will occur almost entirely in developing countries (4 percent annually is the present growth rate in Kenya, for example), facilitated by technological advances that have already occurred. But technological adaptation and productivity must continue to increase in these countries if their GNP is to increase and their quality of life is to improve; and that will further challenge the global ecological balance.

There is no way to gauge what the absolute limits to world population are, which makes it too easy to dismiss the issue as a whole. However, the hard evidence—as represented by widespread poverty, resource and energy limitations, global warming, ozone depletion, acid rain, deforestation, and reductions in biodiversity—provides a sobering indication that we are getting there, wherever "there" may be.

The challenges for multilateral negotiation created by this situation are daunting. First, no nation can find solutions to these problems on its own; indeed, a nation may worsen its negotiating position by taking early, unilateral action. Second, the wide variation in energy use and waste production among and between developed and developing nations makes it difficult to devise an equitable basis for dividing up responsibility for correcting the problems. Third, the cost to different nations of accepting a set of environmentally related limitations (preserving forests, reducing carbon dioxide emissions, eliminating chlorofluorocarbon use, desulfurizing coal) will differ widely depending on their state of development, their sources of energy, or their raw material resources. Fourth, the differential production costs from country to country created by unequal (even though equitable) environmental restrictions will affect international market competitiveness, introducing the need to modify free trade agreements in order to achieve fair markets.

While each of these issues presents special difficulties, it is the degree of linkage between them that will place the greatest burden on multilateral negotiating structures. Energy policy cannot be separated from environmental policy; national technological choices will have to be considered appropriate matters for international negotiation; and future trade treaties will have to reflect global pollution agreements.

3. Uncertain control in a technology-based society. This is a question that now extends to many areas beyond the traditional military ones. Technological leverage is a liability as well as a boon. In the nuclear energy field, the nature of the technology magnifies the effect of human error in accidents like those at Three Mile Island or Chernobyl and renders us susceptible to acts of terrorism through the theft of fissionable material. A new term, "computer virus," has been invented to describe software programs that can (by design or by accident) disrupt and destroy whole national networks and data banks. Oil spills have always been a problem, but the advent of huge tankers, such as the *Exxon Valdez,* has made those spills significantly more damaging.

The complexity of large-scale technological development gives rise to a second aspect of control uncertainty. Where the links between basic research and technological breakthrough are many—and somewhat unpredictable—it is difficult to be overly prescriptive in planning development strategy. In these circumstances, the American approach to federal support of technology—given mission goals such as the development of the liquid metal breeder reactor (Clinch River), the manned space station, or the (proposed) high-definition TV development—appears less attractive than, say, the German strategy of building a flexible technological infrastructure with a strong emphasis on retraining capacity, which makes it possible to incorporate newly available technologies very quickly as they emerge.

Moreover, the difficulty in anticipating the areas in which technological breakthroughs will occur, the end of the American monopoly on technological leadership, and the easy movement of technical information between nations limit the value of strategic industry identification or the COCOM (Coordinating Committee on Export Controls) treaty as a facet of national security policy. It is likely that new approaches to both will be necessary in this decade.

We face additional difficulties in fully assessing and understanding how new advances in technology affect flora, fauna (including people), and the environment. Our ability to manipulate nature provides us with great power in fighting disease and physical disability, but the implementation of technology often takes place so rapidly that we do not have the time to fully understand its effects. In medicine, for example, we encounter problems with drug side effects, coronary bypass procedures, dialysis, artificial hearts. With respect to the environment, our ability to affect our ecological niche, discussed earlier, is accompanied by an inability to assess the consequences of ecological change. In contrast to similar problems experienced in the past, certain situations we now face have negative effects that may be irreversible if we do not act to correct them; thus, we act before we can be sure that we understand the situation prompting the action. This presents us with a major political as well as a scientific challenge. We must negotiate limits that may require nations to curtail their development (and require individuals to pay the price in restricted wealth and standards of living) without having the compelling argument of scientific certainty to justify the action or to give precise guidance on how far we must go.[5]

4. Popular involvement in S&T decision making. While the availability of information networks generally strengthens democratic structures, it also diminishes the reliance on elected representatives and technical experts to make decisions on the behalf of the public at large. As people gain more information through the media, and political leaders are forced to react to that reality, it is the forum of public opinion rather than the ministerial negotiating table that often controls the resolution of issues. (It is no accident that the banners carried by demonstrators in Tiananmen Square were written in English.) The problem arises when the information distribution system, instead of reflecting the complexity of real world problems, reduces them to simplistic terms. In so doing, rather than stimulating useful popular participation in a debate concerning important world issues, the system blocks proper consideration of those real issues by *either* the public *or* its representatives, forcing instead a different, often trivial, debate.

Information availability and the effects of S&T on everyday life have had a particularly strong influence in increasing public awareness of S&T issues throughout the world. In America, this greater public involvement has produced some positive results: for example, public pressure forced those who propose to undertake developments that might affect the environment to prepare technically based environmental impact statements before proceeding with their projects. However, in other areas the public has become involved in determining the direction of technological change at a level that previously was viewed as the province of experts only.

Thus, while most scientific experts would agree that our space program could be carried out more cost-effectively if we did *not* try to place a man in space, abandoning that goal would be unacceptable to the public. On the other hand, while scientists agree on the value of fetal tissue research, political pressures have put a halt to it. Similarly, because of domestic political considerations, the United States has of late fallen seriously behind other developed nations in birth control research, limiting this country's effectiveness in aiding international population control efforts. Moreover, our decisions on whether or not (or how fast) to proceed with complicated technologies, like SDI, are now determined—by and large—politically rather than scientifically.

These worrisome trends suggest that, in the future, we will require much greater attention to the *quality* of the information available to the electorate, so that public judgments achieve a higher level of sophistication. While the media have an obvious role to play in such an effort, the foreign policy and scientific establishments must become increasingly aware of the pressing need for improved public education on these issues.

In any event, the major technological developments arising out of advances in the biological sciences over the next few decades are likely to intensify the effect of public opinion on scientific decision making because we will be forced to develop regulatory policies concerning research and its application in areas in which people have strong religious and cultural convictions. For example, genetic manipulation carries with it the burden of the history of eugenics; abortion technology (and life-extending technologies) gives people a measure of control over life and death. Fetal screening, the movement of pharmaceuticals across national borders, and the access the wealthy clientele of one country have to the limited pool of transplantable organs in another country are typical examples of the kinds of issues we will have to confront.

IV

Taken together, these four phenomena give added impetus to the shift so obviously occurring from a bipolar to a multipolar world in which North-South tensions are constantly increasing. Information technologies have hampered ideological control by governments, and the need for technological investment has raised the opportunity costs of military budgets; both these factors have led to diminished East-West polarities. Shared technological leadership and interdependence help reinforce the notion of multiple power foci. At the same time, the growing gap between North and South in the rate of technological development, the increasing aspirations of the have-nots, and the additional interdependence created both by global environmental stresses and by national economies oriented to world markets all contribute to escalating North-South frictions.

These frictions are reflected most dramatically in the Third World debt problem and in the issue of global warming. Since environmental problems have arisen largely because of the cumulative effects of development in the North, the assertion made by developing nations that they are *owed* economic and technological recompense is gaining credibility, leading to a linkage of the debt and global-warming problems. The linkage of debt and environment—to which must be added the larger issues of energy needs and economic competitiveness—as well as the shift from superpower bipolarity to multipolarity, suggests that the practical resolution of these growing international problems will require multilateral approaches and that we will find ourselves pressed to devise orderly ways of coupling issues that have historically been negotiated separately.

The transfer of technological equipment and know-how to Third World countries will clearly play an increasingly important role in relieving some of these North-South tensions, but achieving that transfer is not without problems. For example, through advances in technology, facilities and equipment are now available to produce energy more efficiently and cleanly than ever before. However, the capital cost of replacing less efficient, but still functional energy-generating plants in the United States or other developed countries would be enormous: far more than the cost of installing those plants in developing countries as their need for energy increases. Since energy conservation and pollution control are global problems, the latter approach is an economically more practical one and would be equally effective in helping to solve our shared problems. The question is whether we have the political resolve to allow and support the transfer to Third World countries of technology even more sophisticated than that in use in our own country.

Beyond the political obstacles, there are grave practical difficulties in transferring technology. The absence of a suitable sociotechnical infrastructure makes it exceedingly hard for a developing country to absorb sophisticated new technology. The physical components of that infrastructure can be provided, at least in principle; the human resources present a knottier problem. Clearly, education and training must be an increasingly prominent part of American foreign aid programs. However, where it was once reasonable to train students from the Third World by having them enroll in American universities, as technical knowledge has expanded, science and engineering curricula at U.S. universities, particularly at the graduate level, have become increasingly sophisticated. Thus students from developing countries are less prepared to undertake studies in the United States and less likely to receive the kind of education that would serve the needs of their own countries. There is no evidence that we have yet begun to address this issue in formulating our Third World development policy.

The need for multilateral cooperation in big science and large-scale technology, and the practical limitations on controlling the flow of information, pose for the United States the difficult challenge of maintaining economic competitiveness without having a strong proprietary position or a commanding lead with respect to scientific knowledge. The solution would appear to lie in learning to take earlier and better advantage of basic knowledge wherever it is developed. As a policy matter, this will require that we press for all nations to maintain total openness in basic scientific research and to provide unrestricted opportunities to each other to license technology. However, these policies will do us little good unless we improve our efficiency in adopting new technology throughout our domestic industries, and also increase the number of American scientists and engineers who can function in foreign cultures, thereby establishing the working-level contacts necessary for successful technology transfer. In other words, we need to focus on the innovative steps that follow research and scientific discovery, while at the government level we promote international cooperation, coordination, and funding to ensure that scientific progress continues.

V

In sum, the effect of scientific and technological trends on American foreign policy is growing and will continue to do so. Moreover, understanding the relationship between the two can no longer be a peripheral activity for U.S. policymakers.

In the shorthand of the field of science, technology, and public policy, the approach I have taken is referred to as science for policy—the impact of the former on the latter. The reverse— policy for science—could, in principle, be ignored. The shortcomings of choosing that option are fairly obvious. If S&T *will* affect our foreign policy options, and can affect them for good *or* bad, we have a strong motivation to devise policies that orient the development of science and technology in a way that will serve our national interests. I think it is a fair assessment to say that, at this moment, the United States has no meaningful, conscious, or connected set of policies with respect to any of the issues discussed here.

NOTES

1. The first three are particular fields of S&T in which there has been a remarkable growth in knowledge and influence; the last two describe the significantly changing characteristics of the processes of S&T. They are not listed in order of importance.
2. For example, if life-forms can be patented, is a nation entitled to license and collect royalties on the use of germ plasma removed from its territory by a company in the course of developing a genetically engineered wheat seed?
3. In these circumstances, any attempt to retard one kind of technological development by restraining research runs the risk of hindering development in a number of other areas. Conversely, any attempt to be overly focused in scientific research to give priority and stimulus to a particular development effort runs the risk of neglecting an apparently unrelated area of research that may actually hold the key to a breakthrough.
4. For example, it took about 40 years for the concept of the interconvertibility of mass and energy through fission to move from basic scientific discovery to useful application in the generation of electric power. Today, the infrastructure of technology and the rapidity of the diffusion of

information have significantly shortened that time frame, and technological application is often almost contemporaneous with the basic research (as noted earlier, giving impetus to continued progress in the research, thus further accelerating the entire process).

5. We have long dealt with risk and uncertainty in military and political matters. The challenge now is to learn how to deal with scientific uncertainty with the same sophistication. At the moment we are more likely to shape the latter into a convenient political certainty (a tack taken, for example, by those who assert with confidence that there is no evidence that automobile industry emissions are responsible for acidifying Canadian lakes) or to discount scientists as incompetent or useless because they cannot provide definitive answers to certain questions or they modify their answers as further research provides improved understanding (cold fusion, cholesterol, earthquake prediction).

A Look at . . .

THE ENVIRONMENTAL CRISIS

Roger D. Stone

Even without considering the growing problem of atmospheric pollution, the multiple environmental pressures on the surface of the planet constitute a crisis. Desertification worldwide proceeds at the rate of an Ireland (6 million hectares) a year, with devastating consequences for affected farmers and pastoralists. While human populations and food security problems grow rapidly, soil erosion and depletion are causing rain-fed croplands to become ever less productive. Tropical deforestation has reached the point where many once heavily wooded countries (the Philippines, for example) have practically no forest left. The assault is not only causing accelerating losses in biological diversity but also weakening already fragile economies. Before the turn of the century, the World Bank has reported, the number of developing countries that are exporters of forest products will fall from 33 to fewer than 10, and the net export value drop from $7 billion in the late 1980s to less than $2 billion.[1]

A senior World Bank economist attributes 25,000 deaths a day to the direct and indirect effects of water shortages (caused largely by deforestation) and acute water pollution.[2] The increasing scarcity of fuelwood affects 1.5 billion people.[3] While 2 billion people depend on seafood as their principal source of protein, severe downturns have occurred in many inshore fisheries. Oil spills, toxic pollution from agricultural chemicals or poorly managed waste disposal, industrial disasters such as Bhopal and Chernobyl, the environmental tragedy of Eastern Europe—all form part of the deepening imprint of human misuse upon the earth's surface.

The newer issues of air and atmospheric pollution provide further cause for concern. Acid rain kills trees and fish. Stratospheric ozone, essential to life on earth because it absorbs most of the sun's dangerous ultraviolet radiation, is being rapidly depleted. The continuing atmospheric buildup of carbon dioxide and other gases contributing to the greenhouse effect, with carbon dioxide concentrations already at a level 20–25 percent higher than at any time in the last 160,000 years,[4] carries with it a long list of imprecisely defined consequences. One is global warming, which, all else being equal, is the scientifically assured accompaniment to the buildup of the greenhouse gases. As the earth warms, it is also highly probable that the sea level will continue to rise because of a combination of thermal expansion of ocean water and glacial melting. According to the National Academy of Sciences,[5] average global temperatures could increase by 1.5–4.5 degrees Celsius by 2030 as a result of a doubling of greenhouse gases from preindustrial carbon dioxide levels. The warming could, the World Meteorological Organization (WMO) has estimated, raise the global sea level 40–120 centimeters by as early as 2050.[6]

Broad uncertainties that will occupy scientists, and complicate matters for decision makers until well into the coming century, accompany these forecasts. Climate models produced by even the most powerful supercomputers can make only rough estimates of the trend's effects on small regions. Refinement can only be gradual even if prodigious sums are spent. Dozens of complex reactions, called feedback mechanisms, could result in substantial divergence, either way, from aggregate computer forecasts. The interaction between the atmosphere and the oceans, which function as a "sink" for about 60 times more carbon dioxide than the atmosphere contains, remains far from fully understood. Increased cloud cover might dampen the impact of warming on the earth's surface.

Warming within the forecast range would, scientists have calculated, have some advantages. Agricultural prospects in Siberia and Canada would improve. Rice yields might increase in growing areas high enough to avoid saltwater intrusion from rising seas. Among less encouraging scenarios are major losses in biological diversity, disruptions in world agriculture and trade leading to food scarcity, further poverty and heightened Third World tensions, flooding of low-lying areas, the spread of parasitic disease, and additional damage to already weakened forest areas. The World Bank, pointing to "risks which could be menacing, cumulative, and irreversible," has referred to the situation as "potentially catastrophic."[7] Even if the threat turns out to be less than that, there is little doubt that an already serious problem will worsen quickly unless sharp corrective measures are taken.

II

For the United States and other industrial powers, the destabilizing consequences of environmental stress upon developing nations pose new political and security threats. Ongoing strife in El Salvador reflects a dismal history of land and resource utilization, as well as more recent political tensions. Egypt attempts to feed ever more people on the basis of a small and fragile supply of arable land. The region's next war, its foreign minister predicted in 1985, will be waged "over the waters of the Nile, not over politics."[8] As a widening circle of nations gains access to nuclear weapons, the possibility is ever increasing that the use of such weapons in local environmental wars could give ominous new meaning to the word "tinderbox." In 1989, well before fast-changing events in the Soviet Union and Eastern Europe provided compelling new reasons for broad shifts in thought and action, both *Foreign Affairs* and *Foreign Policy* ran articles arguing that heightened environmental pressures had outmoded customary Cold War notions of global security.

U.S. economic interests are increasingly tied by trade and investment patterns to the stability and progress of developing nations.[9] A wide range of U.S. exports to them, currently about 40 percent of the total, is expected to maintain a healthy growth rate if the vulnerable South can somehow afford to buy what we produce. Private U.S. investment, particularly bank lending, has increased far faster in the Third World than it has in industrial nations. While U.S. banks have edged away from the brink of the debt crisis by increasing loan-loss reserves, their welfare and that of debtor nations of the South remain more closely entwined than either side would prefer.

Tight links also connect the level of pressure on U.S. borders to environmental well-being in developing nations. Haiti is one among many nations in the Caribbean, Central America, and Asia where environmental ailments have helped to swell the ranks of illegal immigrants to the United States and place ever greater demands on domestic public services. These effects are already being felt. The Census Bureau reports that from 1980 to 1989 the Hispanic population of the United States has risen by 39 percent; half of the increase is due to legal and illegal immigration.[10] The more severe the world's environmental crisis becomes, the more likely it is that growing numbers of environmental refugees will seek entry into the United States.

In most developing countries environmental deterioration is a direct consequence of poverty. It accounts for most local forms of resource misuse and for a large share of all tropical deforestation. But if poor countries[11] occupy most of the space on earth and house 80 percent of its people, the affluent nations do the lion's share of the environmental damage. Of all the carbon dioxide that enters the atmosphere to become the principal greenhouse agent, only 20 percent is caused by tropical deforestation. The remainder comes from the combustion of fossil fuels to supply energy, whose consumption is overwhelmingly a Northern habit. The Group of Seven industrial nations contribute 42 percent of all carbon dioxide emissions from fossil fuels; the United States, with only 5 percent of the world's population, accounts for 22 percent. The average Third World citizen consumes only one-tenth of the energy used by the average American. Usage of chlorofluorocarbons (CFCs), a class of greenhouse gases that also causes ozone depletion, is similarly attributable to Northern behavior. Any global cleanup effort must, therefore, integrally involve the industrial as well as the developing world.

Individual nations can help in significant ways—by maintaining or increasing their support for international organizations with environmental responsibilities, for instance. But none acting alone can bring about more than a marginal improvement in overall levels of pollution. Were the United States to hold carbon dioxide emissions constant at the 1985 level while the rest of the world maintained current trends, according to a recent Department of Energy study, the world's overall carbon dioxide output would be reduced, over the next 20 years, by only 6 percent.[12] The much-criticized, and indeed tragic, cutting and burning of Brazil's Amazonian forests accounts only for some 4 percent of the atmospheric carbon input. Regions can develop mutual objectives and work together toward their achievement. Controls established through the Regional Seas Program, administered by the United Nations Environment Program (UNEP), apply to the flow of toxic and nutrient pollution into coastal seas and landlocked water bodies, such as the Mediterranean. Such is the nature of many current environmental abuses, however, that curbing them will often require global commitments of unprecedented magnitude.

III

Polls do not necessarily reveal how people would react to future environmental control policies that might immediately affect their pocketbooks or constrain their behavior. Nor even do all opinion surveys indicate new public commitments to "green" values. Surveyed by Louis Harris and Associates for UNEP in 1989, 58 percent of Brazilians felt that "life in this country is so difficult that the environment is not a top concern."[13] Still, from the many nations where green politics is flowering to rural India, where angry citizens frequently demonstrate against a proposed large dam whose construction would cause environmental damage, indications abound of expressed citizen determination to halt environmental decay. The turnout for Earth Day 1990 in the United States underscored the resurgence of the environment as a paramount concern. Some 90 percent of Mexicans also queried by the Harris firm favor a healthier environment even if achieving it means accepting a lower standard of living.[14] Leaders representing many segments of society are issuing ever shriller calls for action. The final report of a multidisciplinary Columbia University American Assembly held in April 1990 urges the United States and other nations to subscribe to specific goals to curb global warming.[15] A similar appeal marked the conclusion of an international meeting of parliamentarians convened in Washington that same month. Top-level members of the multinational InterAction Council, gathered in Montreal in 1989 to discuss "ecology and energy options," issued a report calling on all nations to "adopt the stabilization of the composition of the atmosphere as an imperative universal goal."[16] What is required, said Dr. Soejatmoko, the late Indonesian scholar and diplomat, at a conference in 1989, is a "new outburst of institutional creativity" as intense as that which followed World War II.[17]

Movement in this direction has long since begun. In 1987, 24 key nations signed the benchmark Montreal Protocol, limiting usage of CFCs and other ozone-damaging substances. The agreement, subsequently strengthened, represents what the chief U.S. negotiator, Richard Benedick, has called "the type of global diplomacy that must be practiced in the future to assure the health of the planet."[18] Even in this specific sector, unexpected difficulties inhibit overall progress: though harmless to the ozone layer, some of the new chemical substitutes for CFCs also contribute to greenhouse warming. Dealing with the greenhouse question on a global scale is infinitely more complex. But work is under way in this far broader arena as well. Under the auspices of UNEP and WMO, the Intergovernmental Panel on Climate Change (IPCC) is holding preliminary discussions toward assembling a "framework convention" to govern global climate change. Some nations hope that this compact will be ready for adoption at the United Nations "Stockholm plus 20" Conference on Environment and Development, scheduled to take place in Brazil in June 1992.

Strong recommendations favoring ecologically sustainable growth were contained in *Our Common Future,* the comprehensive 1987 report of former Norwegian Prime Minister Gro Harlem Brundtland's World Commission on Environment and Development.[19] Following these dicta and looking forward to 1992, op-ed and conference hall orators now often advocate sweeping changes in North-South relationships in order to achieve better management of no less than the entire global commons. As their portion of a new "global bargain," industrial nations would reduce their contributions to atmospheric pollution by enough to offset the growing amounts that the South will need to emit in order to maintain adequate growth, and thus stabilize the overall greenhouse budget or, at least, reduce the buildup rate.[20] Radical redefinitions of costs, benefits, and what constitutes "real" economic progress would guide Northern initiatives to underwrite Southern growth in innovative ways involving debt reduction, more favorable trade arrangements, and greatly magnified and improved forms of development assistance. The South, in return, would reduce tropical deforestation and other environmentally degrading practices, emphasize sustainable forms of development, and lower population growth rates.

Despite the reality that the planet is already committed to further climate change because of past and present practices,[21] agreement on such arrangements could sharply modify the ultimate magnitude of the change. According to former U.S. Environmental Protection Agency (EPA) Administrator William D. Ruckelshaus, a 2 percent annual increase in energy efficiency, not inconsistent with strong economic growth, would hold the average global temperature to within 1 degree Celsius of present levels.[22] People and institutions would gain time to adjust to altered conditions. On the ground, a major shift would take place away from unsustainable resource use and toward more equitable global income distribution as well as greater ecological stability.

Since substantial North-South financial transfers are involved, the proposal faces obstacles similar to those that inhibited the new international economic order (NIEO) initiatives of the 1970s, even though the North now stands to lose far more if the South fails to move forward. Already, Washington has balked at a proposal to supply direct cash transfers to help developing countries make the transition away from CFCs. Many observers, skeptical about the prospects for the 1992 meeting or any similar broad approach, feel that a patchwork of bilateral and regional arrangements is far more likely to emerge than is a single global deal. Other suggestions include strengthening UNEP, providing an environmental role for the United Nations Security Council, creating a monitoring mechanism on the model of the General Agreement on Tariffs and Trade to help manage the global commons, and negotiating a Law of the Atmosphere as a counterpart to the Law of the Sea.

IV

Political and governmental enthusiasm about all this is not equally distributed. Western European leaders, eyeing the growing power of local green movements and the promise of new markets for environmental technologies in Eastern Europe and the Soviet Union, have flocked under the banner. While Britain remains slower to control most forms of pollution than her neighbor nations, Mrs. Thatcher has become a conspicuous convert to the environmental cause. Even the governments of Spain and Italy, long the nemesis of tidier Northern European regimes, have come to express new determination. Actions often back up the words. Although Western Europe still trails the United States in certain areas of pollution control (use of leaded gasoline and of catalytic converters in cars, for example), it has surpassed us in most. In the Netherlands, the National Environmental Policy Plan (NMP), endorsed by all political parties, calls for a comprehensive and very costly attack on pollution to make the domestic environment "manageable" by 2010. Switzerland, which is banning all plastic and aluminum beverage containers, already recycles 80 percent of its glass. In 1989 Chancellor Helmut Kohl told William K. Reilly, the current EPA administrator, that West Germany viewed carbon dioxide emissions stabilization by 2000—and a 20 percent *reduction* by 2005—as technically and economically feasible goals.

At a November 1989 gathering of environment ministers in the Netherlands to discuss government responses to global climate change, Japan was 1 of 3 nations among some 70 represented to oppose a resolution obliging signatories to stabilize greenhouse emissions by 2000.[23] Japan has a domestic environment that is cleaner than most, in part because it has laid off so much degradation on supplier nations. While it remains 70 percent forested, Japan has long been the principal purchaser of hardwoods from the denuded Philippines. A Japanese response to the quest for new global arrangements is, however, in progress. The government's new package of $2.65 billion in environmental aid to developing nations is by far the largest of its sort ever to be created.[24]

Despite the possibly beneficial effect of global warming on the Soviet Union's frozen tundra, and the inability of the technology-shy USSR economy to make rapid adjustments to new conditions, Soviet leaders have repeatedly (if also more cautiously than most) stated their willingness to join a global effort to tackle the problems of atmospheric pollution. In the summer of 1989, at a session organized by actor Robert Redford's Institute for Resource Management in collaboration with the USSR Academy of Sciences, top Soviet scientists joined U.S. counterparts in urging both governments to avert catastrophe by forming an "environmental security alliance."

Forty years of Stalinism in Eastern Europe resulted in inefficient economies and in pollution so rampant that the environment is sometimes cited as a leading reason for the 1989–1990 uprisings. These nations' turn to the West for ideas, money, and technical assistance to curb their pollution has quickly won a positive response from the United States and elsewhere. The new freedoms in the region offer the West expanding opportunities to apply market-oriented solutions to environmental problems. It will often be more cost-effective to invest in simple antipollution measures in Eastern Europe than to try to squeeze one last tenth of a percent of purity from an already pristine Swedish smokestack.

In the South, some leaders still contend that the North has added the environment to family planning as a device to retain competitive advantages. Ignoring evidence of the growing importance of sustainability to the health of their nations' economies, some Third World spokesmen continue to insist that addressing environmental issues remains an unaffordable luxury. "As long as the poverty gap exists," said Dr. Soejatmoko, "it will be impossible, in my view, to develop a global management structure that will enable us to deal effectively with the threats to the global commons."[25] At the same time, bitter lessons learned have prompted other developing-country governments to begin to change their tune. While deforestation worked as an economic strategy in the fertile United States and in Western Europe, it tends to produce at best a short-term return in forested tropical lowlands where barren soil, not rich humus, tends to lie beneath the towering trees. Nepal, Indonesia, Thailand, Costa Rica, and Zambia rank among the Third World countries where ecological considerations are helping to shape development planning and where measures to control destructive practices have been installed. In nations such as these, it should be added, leaders fear that environmental aid they might have received will now be inequitably diverted to far better-off Eastern Europe.

Brazil, which at the 1972 United Nations Stockholm Conference on the Human Environment astonished many delegates by expressing willingness to import pollution to create new jobs, and then did so with shocking consequences, provides a turnaround example. In 1988 President José Sarney won nationalist plaudits by chiding the world for interfering in the Amazon. Later he surprised foreign observers by launching efforts to arrest Amazonian devastation and a mounting torrent of toxic substances in industrial areas. Fernando Collor de Mello, Sarney's successor who was inaugurated president in March 1990, reinforced the shift by expressing his eagerness to work with other nations to stabilize the basin and announcing the appointment of two deeply committed environmentalists to key government positions. While antienvironmental sentiments continue to run deep within both Brazil's military and its professional diplomatic corps, and the Harris poll's revelation of popular disregard suggests political obstacles in the way of a substantive policy overhaul, Collor's initial moves at least bode well for Brazil's comportment in the key role of host for the 1992 conference.

V

Up to the late 1970s the world looked to the United States for leadership in environmental affairs. If not the designer of the original and pivotal Stockholm conference, the United States played a powerful activist role there. Early in the 1970s the United States also enacted the Clean Air Act, the Clean Water Act, and several other innovative pieces of environmental legislation. Our brisk response to the oil price hikes was to reduce the "energy intensity" of a growing domestic product by 23 percent between 1973 and 1985.[26]

Though momentum waned during the Reagan era, George Bush in his 1988 campaign managed to preempt the environmental issue in several thoughtful speeches, as well as with the Boston Harbor rhetoric. At the mid-1989 Paris summit he outgreened other Group of Seven leaders, who left their environment ministers behind, by including EPA Administrator Reilly as a principal member of his delegation. Though the resulting communiqué (and many subsequent White House declarations) fell short of the commitment to specific emissions reduction targets that some had hoped for, its environmental section expressed a tone of urgency that was lacking elsewhere in the document. U.S. insistence had much to do with this outcome.

After Paris, consistently favorable overall poll ratings for Bush lessened his political need to diverge any further than necessary from established positions. On environmental matters, the "environmental president" has emphasized talk. The United States supports the IPCC process, has suggested an acceleration of the movement toward negotiations for a framework convention on global warming, and, as Bush told Montanans in the fall of 1989, is pledged to "take the lead internationally" on environmental issues.[27] But U.S. caution in refusing to target emissions goals disappoints other nations that are more eager to press on boldly (recklessly, some would argue) even without precise scientific information or a firm grasp of costs and how they can be met. Bush had little to offer either to an IPCC panel that met in Washington in early 1990 or to frustrated European participants in a subsequent international climate change conference at the White House. More positive, though still lacking in bite, was a well-crafted speech by Secretary of State James Baker, in February 1990, in which he pledged "the greening of our foreign policy" and the full integration of environmental concerns into all aspects of it.[28]

The United States will not easily establish credibility in the field of global environmental leadership without setting a better example at home. The executive branch has worked hard to achieve improvements in the Clean Air Act. It has stated that it would "not oppose" the elevation of the EPA administrator to cabinet rank. It has also manifested little interest in taking the harder steps: establishing a full-fledged energy policy for the nation, applying taxes or other control mechanisms on greenhouse emissions that could bring new bursts of efficiency, separating the global population question from the domestic abortion debate. While many nations are already adopting unilateral measures to stabilize or reduce the levels of their atmospheric pollution, the United States compounds the problem by increasing carbon dioxide emissions at an annual rate of 4 percent.[29] Uneconomic harvesting of Alaska's Tongass National Forest and other federally owned timberlands undercuts U.S. leverage on the tropical deforestation issue.

Budget limitations and the sheer costs involved in retooling for environmental stability are obstacles to which the administration often points. It is far easier for a politician to give a speech or draft a bill, officials point out, than for the executive branch to maneuver a program through the Washington maze to successful implementation. Some who counsel the White House[30] rank prominently among those who believe that effective countermeasures to atmospheric pollution can be designed only after more precise climate change data become available. Among those who no longer doubt that global warming is at hand are some who also feel that its effects can be offset, at least in large part, by means of adaptations and technological innovations rather than through preventive measures or sacrifices. Summing up, EPA Administrator Reilly advocates a "no regrets" stance in which, in a reverse twist of the Brundtland Commission's definition of sustainability, the United States would "act toward the future in such a way that you will have no cause to regret the past."[31]

Environmental degradation continues, meanwhile. Time is short. Delay increases the magnitude of the corrections required and therefore their cost. Applied judiciously at this timely moment, the combination of U.S. antipollution technologies, multinational management skills, and Japanese capital could result in dramatic accomplishment. The end of Cold War confrontation could become the outset of a new epoch of environmental cooperation. Most nations seem ready to pursue this agenda even if hardships and incalculable costs are involved. As the world fastens upon what Sir Crispin Tickell, Britain's ambassador to the United Nations, calls the "hard, biting realities" of the matter, many eyes are fixed on Washington for signs of more than a nibble.

NOTES

1. Jeremy J. Warford, *Environment, Growth, and Development* (Washington, D.C.: World Bank, 1987).
2. Ibid.
3. James Gustave Speth, "Environmental Security for the 1990s—In Six Not-So-Easy Steps," *Issues and Ideas,* World Resources Institute, January 1990.
4. Mark C. Trexler, Irving M. Mintzer, and William R. Moomaw, "Global Warming: An Assessment of its Scientific Basis, Its Likely Impacts, and Potential Response Strategies" (Paper prepared for the EPA Workshop on the Economics of Sustainable Development, Washington, D.C., January 1990).
5. National Academy of Sciences, *Changing Climate* (Washington, D.C.: National Academy Press, 1983).
6. World Meteorological Organization, "Developing Policies for Responding to Climate Change," *World Climate Program Impact Studies,* WMO/TD, no. 225 (1988).
7. Erik Arrhenius and Thomas Waltz, *The Greenhouse Effect: Implications for Economic Development* (Washington, D.C.: World Bank, 1989).
8. As cited in Norman Myers, *Not Far Afield: U.S. Interests and the Global Environment* (Washington, D.C.: World Resources Institute, 1987).
9. See ibid.
10. U.S. Census Bureau, Department of Commerce, "U.S. Population Estimates, by Age, Sex, Race, and Hispanic Origin, 1989," *Current Population Reports,* Series P25, no. 1057 (March 1990).
11. Those classified in the World Bank's 1989 *World Development Report* as having per capita gross national products of $6,000 or less.
12. Rae Edwards et al., "Analysis of U.S. CO2," 1987. (Unpublished.)

13. Shane Cave, "Brazil Speaks," *Our Planet,* United Nations Environment Program, vol. 1, no. 4 (1989), p. 11.

14. Cited in "Environment Poll—Public Alarm," *Development Forum* (July/August 1989), p. 1.

15. Leonard Silk, "A Global Program for the Environment," *The New York Times,* April 27, 1990, p. D2.

16. Report of the InterAction Council, Montreal, Canada, April 29–30, 1989.

17. Speech before the Aspen Institute Forum on Global Climate, Aspen, Colorado, July 5–7, 1989.

18. "The Ozone Protocol: A New Global Diplomacy," *Conservation Foundation Letter,* no. 4 (1989).

19. World Commission on Environment and Development, *Our Common Future* (New York: Oxford University Press, 1987).

20. A particularly difficult challenge will be for China and India, which both possess abundant stocks of "dirty" coal, to achieve adequate growth while also doing their part to achieve global emissions stability. Western help with the introduction of expensive "clean coal" technologies, and the installation of nuclear generating power, will probably be required.

21. The WMO estimates 0.7–2.0 degrees Celsius over preindustrial levels.

22. William D. Ruckelshaus, "Toward a Sustainable World," *Scientific American* (September 1989), p. 170.

23. The other two opponents were the Soviet Union and the United States.

24. The U.S. Agency for International Development, in contrast, supplies about $300 million a year in development assistance projects (for example, forestry) that may be considered environmental.

25. Speech before the Aspen Institute Forum on Global Climate.

26. William D. Ruckelshaus, "Toward a Sustainable World," pp. 166–174.

27. Speech at the State Capital in Helena, Montana, September 18, 1989.

28. Speech before the National Governor's Association, Washington, D.C., February 26, 1990.

29. William K. Reilly, testimony before the U.S. Senate Foreign Relations Committee, November 20, 1989.

30. Notably, the Council of Economic Advisers.

31. A phrase used in his speech at the New York Botanical Garden, January 17, 1990.

A Look at . . .

DEMOCRACY RESURGENT?

Tony Smith

At least since the time of Woodrow Wilson, there have been American leaders who have held that a global order composed of democratic states, joined together in what Wilson called "a covenant of cooperation," would be the best conceivable guarantee of world peace and of the protection of American national interests abroad. It was in this spirit that Wilson pledged the United States to back constitutional democracy in Latin America as early as 1913 (subsequently sending the marines to Mexico, the Dominican Republic, Haiti, and Nicaragua), waged war in Europe in 1917–1918 to "make the world safe for democracy," and fought for American membership in the League of Nations. Later, Franklin Delano Roosevelt echoed some of these themes with his call for the Four Freedoms, the Atlantic Charter, plans for the United Nations, and the Bretton Woods system, just as the first task of the American forces occupying Japan and Germany in 1945 was to democratize them. John F. Kennedy's Alliance for Progress, Jimmy Carter's human rights campaign, Ronald Reagan's National Endowment for Democracy—all of these initiatives, and many more, have depended on the conviction that American interests would be better secured in a world where democracy was expanding.

Yet ever since the days of Wilson, this ambition to make the world safe for democracy has been blocked by two major obstacles. First, democratic government has seemed irrelevant to the part of the world that has still been largely agrarian, and where for historical reasons the commanding heights have been held politically by forces that have seen nothing to gain from converting to the liberal democratic faith. Just as Wilson's convictions proved unable—by themselves—to convert the Dominican Republic in 1916–1924, or Poland in the interwar years, to democracy, so other peoples—from the Islamic to the communist world—have seemed recalcitrant thereafter. Second, the program to promote democracy has lacked a clearly articulated defense. Why should such a world order succeed in securing American national interests? Was not most of this talk about democracy hollow and platitudinous, making American conduct appear so self-righteous that it often proved self-defeating? Had not Wilson's own failures served as just warning about taking such talk too seriously?

Yet as we can see about us on every side, everyone today claims to be a democrat: the students in Beijing, Rangoon, and Seoul; Mikhail Gorbachev, the ethnic movements, the ecologists, and Solidarity in Eastern Europe; the Aquino and Bhutto governments; the antiapartheid forces; the military regime in Nigeria, and the military successors to Duvalier in Haiti and Stroessner in Paraguay; the Catholic church (though less so when it comes to its own internal organization), as well as Islamic leaders from Libya to Iran. For most of this century, faith in the future expansion of democracy seemed exceedingly naive. To many people democracy appeared unable to provide the national unity and direction of its totalitarian rivals; its strong leanings to materialism, individualism, proceduralism (that is, the elaborate set of rules and institutions needed to make it function); its very tolerance of its harshest critics seemed to deprive it of the toughness necessary to survive in a Hobbesian world of belligerent, ideologically driven states. But with the defeat of European fascism in 1945, and with the devastating weaknesses of communism being acknowledged now in Eastern Europe, the Soviet Union, and even China, the real strengths of democracy could once again be vaunted. However varied the forms of government may be that rightly call themselves democratic, their ability to accommodate class and ethnic diversity through complex institutional forms means that, as the end of the twentieth century approaches, democracy—as a system of governance—remains unparalleled in its political flexibility, stability, and legitimacy even if one refuses to accept Francis Fukuyama's hyperbolic statement that we shall soon see "the universalization of Western liberal democracy as the final form of human government."[1]

Democracy's most obvious characteristics are guaranteed free, competitive elections to all major offices of political power on the basis of a universal suffrage that accepts such a procedure as creating a legitimate source of authority. Underlying this representative political system is an autonomous civil society, where individuals join together voluntarily into groups with self-designed purposes, and where these groups, in turn, collaborate with each other through the mechanism of political parties whose final ambition is to contest elections and to gain power. Because these arrangements are largely political and—despite social welfare provisions—not egalitarian, since private property remains basically intact, it is "liberal" and not "social" democracy of which we are speaking.

II

The principal reason for the triumph of democratic government is that, in the Western world and Japan, it has provided for relative economic prosperity, political stability, and mutually beneficial relations with fellow democracies.

By any historical standard, the degree of economic growth in the capitalist world since 1945 has been unprecedented. The nineteenth-century Pax Britannica diffused the know-how of the Industrial Revolution over the entire globe and so produced what, from roughly 1815 to 1914, was the greatest increase in material output the world had seen. But the pace of growth under the Pax Americana during the second half of the twentieth century has been greater still.

The interconnection between democracy and capitalism is a subject of immense complexity. Suffice it to say that, while a market economy is no guarantee of democracy (think, for example, of Taiwan, South Korea, or Singapore), all modern democracies are fundamentally market economies. A principal reason for this phenomenon is that the market has deliberately limited the powers of government, depriving it of formidable mechanisms of direct control over society. At the same time, this arrangement has helped to strengthen civil society, serving as the most important guarantee of its autonomy from the state.

As capitalism has suited democracy, so democracy has suited capitalism. Thus, as the level of economic activity has increased—producing higher levels of education and urbanization, and a more specialized and interdependent division of labor—the political realm has had to become more decentralized, a function perfectly suited to democracy, with its twin virtues of accountability and flexibility (the latter permitting an openness to change that enhances the system's vitality).

Yet the stability of the democratic political order is in good measure independent of the success of capitalism and provides yet another explanation for the fact that the "democratic era" is now upon us. In this century, democratic government has become more robust than it ever was in the nineteenth, demonstrating—in the West and in Japan—its ability to accommodate both class and ethnic tensions while providing an enduring, popularly accepted framework for legitimate rule, thus neutralizing serious challenges to its authority from traditional religious or military quarters. Whatever its problems, the modern welfare state has provided both freedom and justice to society at large on an unprecedented scale.

A third extraordinary accomplishment of the liberal democratic world has been the ability of its member-states to collaborate with one another on a range of international issues in a manner that has helped preserve the world's peace while also promoting domestic harmony and prosperity. To a certain extent, this development has reflected the hegemonic role played globally by the United States since World War II; but the character of this American-inspired political and economic "system" has depended greatly on the democratic character of the other nations participating in it. The North Atlantic Treaty Organization, for one, has no rival in the annals of modern history as a successful, long-term, multilateral security pact. So, too, no precedent exists for the accomplishments of the Organization for

Economic Cooperation and Development or the various related "international regimes" born of the Bretton Woods system after 1945. Here again, cooperation has depended on voluntary participation where core procedures are safeguarded by the political culture of democratic states, whose lifeblood is diplomatic negotiation and realistic compromises aimed toward a peaceful resolution of conflict. Yet in the days to come, it may be the bringing together of the European Community as an increasingly supranational, confederal union of democratic peoples that will provide the most astonishing proof of the pacific potential of such systems. And should the Soviet Union move successfully toward genuine democratic government, who can predict what kinds of success Gorbachev's notion of a "common European house" might yet attain?

To be sure, the virtues of democracy are relative, not absolute; its cardinal advantage is the shortcomings of other forms of governance in providing economic prosperity, civil order, and international cooperation—a lesson summed up in Churchill's famous observation that democracy is the worst form of government . . . except for any imaginable alternative.

III

It thus appears that the current era represents the closest the United States has ever come to seeing the international system reflect its own traditional foreign policy agenda: a world order opposed to imperialism and composed of independent, self-determining states bound together by institutions promoting free trade, collective security, and the promotion of common political objectives—including basic human rights.

But will current trends actually serve American national interests in any but the most obvious way—that of reducing even further the military threat still posed by a highly armed Soviet Union? Does democracy abroad really matter?

This type of question was first raised by Immanuel Kant in the late eighteenth century (and more lately was addressed by the young American political theorist Michael Doyle): might an international system dominated by democratic states herald a different kind of world order from any that has existed previously and help inaugurate the reign of what Kant called "perpetual peace" based on a "pacific union" of republican states that would serve the common good by observing certain disinterested rules of ethical fairness (what Kant described as "categorical imperatives")?[2] Certainly this was Woodrow Wilson's own hope in pursuing his efforts to expand the range of democratic cooperation internationally as the Great War came to a close. Has the time come to retire the dictum normally attributed to Lord Palmerston to the effect that a nation has only permanent interests, not permanent friends, and assert instead that the world's democracies do find themselves with an unprecedented opportunity to cooperate as "permanent friends" in order that their common interests be most propitiously advanced through an international order where the old dictates of self-serving realpolitik are progressively abandoned?

Three reasons argue that such might indeed be the case, all drawing on ideas contained, at least in embryo, in Kant's famous text of 1795. The first is that a democratic state is likely to be inherently more pacific than one ruled by a military aristocracy or any other form of ruling elite, where those who make the decisions are different from those charged with the onerous duty of executing them. When the people rule, they are by definition prescribing a policy that they themselves must carry out, and it is logical to assume that they would surely think carefully before consigning themselves to the hell of war. In this century, Joseph Schumpeter was to add to Kant's thesis by arguing that capitalism is an inherently pacific system, where individuals have materialistic preoccupations and are bent on success in entrepreneurial terms in ways that fundamentally contradict devotion to the martial arts.[3] To the extent that we see an "international bourgeoisie," enriched by a liberal world economic system, providing the major dynamic for a cooperative world order, Schumpeter's assumptions now carry even greater force. It could be argued, then, that a democratic society operating under a market economy has a strong predisposition toward peace.

A second factor by which democratic states contribute to a pacific international order is through a mutual respect that their principles of incorporation enjoin them to observe. To be sure, serious conflicts of interest may arise among them, and democratic states are not incapable of waging aggressive wars. But as Doyle has pointed out, for over a century and a half there has been no case of war breaking out between democratically constituted states. Moreover, the post-1945, U.S.–led, liberal international economic order, whatever its problems, has allowed the elaboration of a system of global trade, investment, and finance that has done far more to create solidarity and a harmony of interests among the advanced capitalist, democratic nations than to breed distrust and conflict among their peoples.

Accordingly, the third major contribution of democratic, capitalist states to a peaceful world order is to be found in the progress they have achieved in promoting international cooperation. To be sure, the overriding reality of world politics is the existence of sovereign states. But the variety of international "regimes" that nowadays facilitates international economic transactions; the stability of security arrangements among the major democratic powers, and the progress made by the European Community (on the march once again, more than 30 years after the Treaty of Rome) indicate the ability of capitalist democracies to cooperate in terms of both collective security and mutual economic interest in ways truly without historical precedent.

IV

The importance of maintaining a liberal international economic order cannot be overemphasized, for it is largely under its auspices that the advanced democracies have enjoyed prosperity and have experimented in a wide variety of increasingly institutionalized cooperative endeavors with great promise for the future.

That said, several caveats are in order. First, individual states will continue to insist that trading and finance practices allow for orderly transitions in employment and investment. If high levels of protectionism must be avoided, it is nonetheless unrealistic to suppose that workers and business investors should be exposed to the full force of global free trade.

Second, for reasons of national security, states may legitimately insist on sheltering certain enterprises from foreign purchase or competition.

Third, for ethical reasons, or in order to pressure other countries to join the democratic ranks, the liberal international economic system may decide to remain relatively closed to hostile or undemocratic countries.[4]

Fourth, it should respect the efforts of certain countries to integrate their economies more closely through forms of preferential treatment where this policy contributes to democratic political union, as in the manner of the European Community.

A final consideration is in order here: namely, that the current success of the democratic movement should not be taken for granted. There is little reason to believe (as Fukuyama apparently does) that those nations that do not imitate the liberal democratic model are fated to historical oblivion. Nor can the presently functioning democracies themselves be confident that such critical issues as the international control of the environment, the future character of Japanese trading practices, or the growing fear among some Europeans of the resurgence of German power will be successfully handled. On a more mundane level, there could be a temptation to take the evolving international economic or security systems for granted now that the external threat of Soviet expansionism has diminished, thus trivializing the important work of international agencies such as the General Agreement on Tariffs and Trade, whose staffs might accordingly lose a sense of direction and purpose. If one of the virtues of democracy is its openness (allowing thereby for a flexible accommodation to social forces and thus to change), this very virtue may ultimately contribute to its weakening. It takes no Solzhenitsyn to point out that democratic openness can degenerate into narrow self-interest, mindless consumerism, and boredom—weaknesses that sap the sense of collective identity and worth, and are apt to stimulate the growth of such antidemocratic forces as are invariably harbored in an open society.

NOTES

1. Francis Fukuyama, "The End of History?" *The National Interest*, no. 16 (Summer 1989), pp. 3–18. An excellent critique of Fukuyama is Samuel P. Huntington, "No Exit: The Error of Endism," *The National Interest*, no. 17 (Fall 1989), pp. 3–11.
2. Michael Doyle, "Kant, Liberal Legacies, and Foreign Affairs, Part 2," *Philosophy and Public Affairs*, vol. 12, no. 4 (Fall 1983), pp. 323–353; and Immanuel Kant, "Perpetual Peace," in Carl J. Friedrich, ed., *The Philosophy of Kant: Immanuel Kant's Moral and Political Writings* (New York: The Modern Library, 1949), pp. 430–476.
3. Joseph Schumpeter, *Imperialism and Social Classes* (New York: Augustus M. Kelley, Inc., 1951).
4. The West's Control Commission, assuring that militarily sensitive technology not reach potentially hostile hands, and the Sullivan Principles, assuring that American corporations helped erode apartheid practices, are models of the kinds of restrictions on trade and investment that the liberal democracies should continue to support. By contrast, the insistence of the European Community that Greece, Spain, and Portugal be demonstrably democratic before becoming Community members serves as a striking example of how economic clout can be used politically.

PART TWO:

Reconsiderations

Reconsiderations

WINDS OF CHANGE

William H. McNeill

Human affairs never stand still for long. Innumerable small, everyday, and almost unnoticed changes have a way of undermining existing patterns of behavior and belief until a single individual's actions or a single public event may suddenly trigger rapid and far-reaching alterations in the public life of millions or, in our day, hundreds of millions of people. The Oath of the Tennis Court was such an event in 1789; Lenin was such a triggerman in 1917; and now, 200 years after the French Revolution, Mikhail Gorbachev has initiated changes that may well turn out to be comparably important, even though they have not yet provoked much revolutionary violence.

The wearing out of Stalinism as a system of belief and as a way of managing the Soviet economy seems definitive. But what will replace it remains profoundly uncertain. The upsurge of nationalist demands for effective self-determination may presage disruption of the Russian empire—one of two imperial structures that survived World Wars I and II. (The other surviving empire, that of China, does not seem in much danger, owing to weaker mobilization of political consciousness among its various subject peoples, and to the overwhelming numerical preponderance of ethnic Chinese within the imperial frontiers.) But whatever happens among the various subject and associated peoples of the USSR or to East European satellite regimes, events in the Russian heartlands of the Soviet Union are likely to remain decisive. The Great Russians of old Muscovy were the principal support of czarism as they were of Leninism and of

Stalinism. Their reactions to the upheavals Gorbachev has provoked are likely to matter as much as in 1917, or at other times of
crisis in Russian history.

Looking backward is, in fact, a useful way to try to assess
contemporary probabilities and possibilities in Eastern Europe.
Parallels between the current situation and the disarray precipi-
tated by czardom's failures in the Crimean War (1854–1856)
seem especially striking and are worth pondering.

Imperial Russia emerged from Napoleonic wars as the
strongest military power of Europe. As a result, Russia enjoyed
hegemony over eastern and central Europe during the ensuing
decades, where a rather tattered Hapsburg Empire was Russia's
principal rival and rather reluctant ally. Stalin's expansion into
Eastern Europe after World War II divided Europe with the
aptly nicknamed Iron Curtain. Thereafter, ideological hostility
delimited Stalin's sphere of influence far more precisely
than occurred between 1815 and 1856, when a vaguer distrust
nonetheless did limit the czars' westward reach.

Despite this difference, the way the rest of Europe found
itself poised between Russia's starkly militarized land power to
the east and an offshore naval-commercial-industrial great
power to the west (Great Britain in the nineteenth century; the
United States of America in the twentieth) is amazingly similar.
So is the fact that during the more or less peaceful decades that
followed the end of cataclysmic warfare, the unstable West,
wedded to market economics, clearly outstripped Russia, where
the economy (and society generally) responded mostly to political command, both in czarist times and in the socialist era
inaugurated in 1917.

Finally, in both instances, failure in war was the clinching
experience that compelled Russia's rulers to face up to their
backwardness. Russians were shocked in 1854–1856, when the
army that had defeated Napoleon proved incapable of defending the Crimea against amphibious attack by a comparatively
small and ill-managed expeditionary force from France and
Great Britain. The inability of the Red Army that had defeated
Hitler to pacify Afghanistan in the 1980s was comparably de-
moralizing, if only because the antagonists appeared to be so

unequal. Once again, as in 1856, past efforts to overtake the West had fallen short. Long-standing defects in Russian society and economy had to be faced anew.

Thus we see a remarkably repetitive rhythm in modern Russian history. Twice the Russians responded to revolution from above by building a new military and industrial establishment along the most advanced Western lines. Peter the Great carried through the first of these frantic efforts to catch up, between 1689 and 1725; Stalin presided over the second, between 1928 and 1953. Twice the Russians reaped the reward of catching up, or nearly catching up, with the West, by becoming the greatest military power on the continent of Europe. And twice they fell behind again because Western nations devised new forms of economic management and introduced new weapons of war that the Russians found difficult or impossible to equal.

In the nineteenth century, finding an effective response to falling behind proved exceedingly difficult. Accordingly, between 1856 and 1917 Russia labored through a prolonged period of indecision and divided councils. Some urged change along Western lines, and on the whole they prevailed. Thus, the first great reform, the abolition of serfdom in 1861, was aimed at bringing Russian law and society abreast of European standards of personal freedom and careers open to talent. But when new industries and technologies began to stream into Russia, with the construction of railroads and the opening of mines and steel mills (often financed by foreign capital), a contrary reaction gained momentum. Self-styled Slavophiles wished vehemently to avoid the evils of European society and hoped to preserve authentic Russian culture and Orthodox solidarity by turning their backs upon the West.

In particular, Slavophiles wished to maintain the rural institution of the mir, whose most distinctive characteristic was periodic redistribution of land, so as to match each family's holdings to its labor power, thus guaranteeing close equality of circumstance among the inhabitants of each village. The peasant majority of old Russia clearly agreed with Slavophile intellectuals in thinking that whereas this was just and right, allowing unscrupulous individuals to enrich themselves by buying and selling in the marketplace, as Westernizers wished to do, was nothing more nor less than a license to cheat.

Incidentally, Russian anti-Semitism assumed its inflamed intensity largely because Jews pioneered and profited from the extension of market relationships into the countryside. Identification of chaffering over prices with Jewishness made it hard for Russians to embark wholeheartedly on market behavior. Buying and selling for personal gain involved too much betrayal of village custom, human solidarity, and authentic Russianness. But this left local commerce and moneylending to Jews, and exposed them to a virulent popular hostility that still endures.

The charm of Bolshevism as it developed in Russia after 1903 was that Lenin and his followers combined a distinctively Western "scientific" ideology in the form of revolutionary Marxism with emphatic espousal of equality and justice—the goals of socialism—which appeared to ordinary peasants as a restatement of traditional village ideals. Marxist criticisms of capitalism and the exploitation of the proletariat also resonated with Slavophile distaste for the West and its corrupt, self-seeking ways. By thus straddling the two camps into which Russian opinion had so long been divided, Lenin and his followers were able to consolidate their power and, under Stalin, launched themselves upon a new effort to match and overtake the West.

Just as Peter the Great had recruited an elite of miscellaneous origins to carry out his reforms, Lenin and Stalin, too, recruited a new party elite to manage Russian society and government. Many of them (and sympathizers in other lands) devoutly believed that by following the precepts of scientific socialism as set forth by Marx and Lenin, and by faithfully adhering to the party line as defined by Stalin, Russia could and would surpass Western accomplishments. But by the 1980s that hope had worn out. All too obviously, Russia still lagged behind.

More important for most Russians, the revolution had been betrayed. Social equality, demanded both by socialist ideals and by a deep-rooted Russian sense of justice derived from the practices of the mir, was systematically flouted everywhere. Scarce goods and other privileges were reserved for high-ranking party members and government officials. In effect, the new ruling class behaved as selfishly and unjustly as the nobles who served Peter and his successors had done under the czars. And in the eyes of most Russians, including many of the privileged classes, the resulting inequity compromised the regime's legitimacy both before 1917 and again in our own time.

But what to do about it remains just as uncertain as when Slavophiles and Westernizers disputed over what ought to be done about Russia's backwardness in the second half of the nineteenth century. Some sort of standoff between those who want to borrow from the West (or from Japan!) and those who wish to hold fast to Russian (and socialist) differences from the West seems inescapable; but how the balance may fluctuate between rival recipes for the future, no one can tell. The only certainty is that profound ambivalence toward foreign models of social management will prevail, even among those who opt most emphatically for one or the other course.

Ambivalence of this kind is age-old in Russia. Ever since their conversion to Orthodox Christianity in the tenth century, it has been the Russians' fate to coexist with a civilization more skilled and therefore richer and more powerful than anything attained within Russian borders. Russia's modern greatness rests on the fact that twice the country's rulers deliberately tried to overcome backwardness by hectic, heroic action. They met with considerable success, but ironically their very success, by lopsidedly emphasizing military power and relying on the command principle for energizing innovation, differentiated Russian society more sharply from the looser social structure of the leading countries of western Europe. Dependence on orders from above also tended to inhibit the sort of spontaneous innovation needed to sustain creativity. Bureaucratic lethargy and inefficiency were therefore free to take their toll, assuring the eventual renewal of Russian backwardness. Much of what is happening in Russia today, therefore, looks very like a reenactment of what happened after 1856, when the czar's government found itself lagging behind France and England so conspicuously that something had to be done, even though effective consensus about what to do was never achieved.

Nonetheless, the current situation of the Soviet Union differs from that of late-nineteenth-century Russia in three important respects.

First of all, the "dark and deaf" peasantry that constituted an overwhelming majority of the Russian population before 1917 no longer undergirds urban society. Millions emigrated from the countryside to provide unskilled labor for the Five-Year Plans. Those left behind live under new circumstances, too, thanks to modern communications that have penetrated the villages of Russia. As a result, the sharp gap that once prevailed between what rural folk knew and experienced and what urban populations knew and experienced has been drastically reduced. This constitutes the most fundamental social and political change wrought by the technological transformations of the twentieth century, and its consequences within the Soviet Union are only part of a much wider global phenomenon, to which we will return.

But for Gorbachev and his successors, the awakening of the populace means that they face a more difficult task than Lenin or Peter ever did, because common folk—peasants and ex-peasants who have moved into cities—are now in a position to make their wishes felt far more effectively than ever before. In 1917 Lenin promised land for the peasants and won their tacit support by doing so. This was probably decisive for the Bolsheviks' eventual success in retaining power in Russia, but it did not require Lenin to do anything for the peasant majority in the villages. Instead, demobilized soldiers and other peasants distributed their landlords' acres among themselves without outside help and continued to cultivate the land as they had done before, insofar as the civil disorders of the revolutionary era allowed.

Far from aiding and abetting the peasant majority, Bolshevik policy soon turned emphatically against the interests of the peasantry, and in 1928, when collectivization began, Stalin took back all that the peasants had acquired after 1917, as well as the share of the land they had been given at the time of the abolition of serfdom in 1861. He did so in order to be able to requisition grain from the villages to feed the expanded work force needed for the new dams and factories of the first Five-

Year Plan. The crass inequity of such a policy was justified by promises of future benefits; in fact, within a few years, tractors and other farm machinery lightened rural tasks considerably. But this in itself did nothing to elevate rural levels of consumption, which remained abysmally low.

Instead, the quite real industrial and military achievements of the Five-Year Plans continued to depend on a ruthless exploitation of the rural population. Rural opposition remained ineffective, very largely because the urban careers that multiplied around all the new mines and factories drew potential malcontents away from the fields. Indeed, the hope of building socialism and of attaining an improved, expanded way of life attracted ambitious young people into cities so rapidly that Russia soon ceased to be preponderantly rural. As a result, only about one-third of the population remain in agriculture today, whereas something like four-fifths were peasant cultivators in 1914.

Russian society is therefore no longer composed predominantly of isolated villages, completely unable to defend themselves against urban predation. Nevertheless, children and grandchildren of peasants constitute a majority of the Russian public. Undoubtedly, old rural attitudes, combining outward deference and an often grudging obedience to superiors, did not decay all at once. Nevertheless, expectations are now far higher, patience is less. Information about conditions of life in other lands has spread throughout Russia. Demands for freedom and justice, together with longings for greater material comfort and more equitable distribution of goods, are strong and insistent.

It is no longer feasible to postpone the realization of revolutionary goals until after the enemies of socialism have disappeared from the face of the earth. Worldwide socialist brotherhood, as Lenin envisioned it, seems wildly improbable after 40 post–World War II years during which capitalist countries have prospered as never before and, instead of collapsing because of the inner contradictions of class war, have clearly outstripped the Soviet Union because of greater social efficiency.

The sort of high-handed treatment that Russia's rulers felt obliged to impose on the Russian people in the past will therefore be difficult to replicate in the future, and will surely become impossible if official policy involves continued exploitation and oppression of the majority, as was the case under the czars and Stalin alike. This means that the old way of catching up by reallocating manpower and other resources through government decree and administrative fiat seems foreclosed, or nearly so. The reason is simple: Any really large-scale reallocation will hurt vested interests and arouse politically effective opposition of a sort that was weak and ineffectual when it was merely peasant interests that had to be overridden.

A second important difference between conditions of the 1990s and earlier times is demographic. What has withered away in Russia is not the state, as predicted by Marx, but the abundance of manpower that once sustained both Petrine and Stalinist reforms. As long as millions of peasants could be drawn from the countryside and put to work in new industrial enterprises without noticeably reducing rural productivity, even the crude and wasteful methods of command worked wonders. This was possible because before 1917 untapped natural resources abounded in the Soviet Union, and at the same time the rural population was systematically underemployed. Throughout the winter months there was little or nothing to be done in the fields, so even wasteful use of manpower in factories and on building sites constituted net gain of labor efficiency.

But this style of profitable shift of manpower from farm to factory could continue only as long as the remaining rural work force could feed the entire population. Under Peter, natural increase in the villages made that possible. Under Stalin, natural increase faded, but the delivery of new farm machinery to the collective farms nevertheless allowed a shrinking rural work force to supply food for the whole population, urban and rural alike. That ceased to be the case about 30 years ago, when, as we all know, the Soviet government began to experience food shortages, at first only in bad harvest years, and then with increasing frequency. Harvest shortfall reflected the fact that rural manpower (and machinery) was in short supply, given the existing inefficiency with which it was used. Birthrates had plummeted after World War II throughout European Russia. Wartime losses were therefore hard to replace, especially in the poverty-stricken villages and collective farms.

The demographic transformation of rural Russia means that the old path to enhanced wealth and power that first Peter and then Stalin followed is foreclosed in still another way. Reserves of underused labor and of unused natural resources are seriously depleted. The only ethnic groups that continue to produce a rural surplus of population are dubiously loyal to the regime, having a Muslim heritage and a lively tradition of hostility to the Russians. Socialist ideals, secularism, and expanded urban careers have not induced Muslims to merge into an undifferentiated Soviet citizenry, as the Bolsheviks once hoped and believed would happen. Instead, mutual distrust permeates relationships between Russians and Muslims, and, of course, the war in Afghanistan exacerbated the uneasiness. As a result, the growing rural population of the Central Asian republics does not constitute as valuable a resource for Russian planners as would otherwise be the case. Instead, it may become an embarrassment if heightened Islamic consciousness ever seeps across the borders of the Soviet republics of Central Asia from neighboring Iran and Afghanistan.

How to reconcile future increases of efficiency with Russian traditions of management by political command remains an unresolved question. If an effective answer continues to elude the managers of Soviet society, catching up with the West will remain an impossible dream, and some other justification for the regime will have to be discovered. Under such circumstances, demoralization of the managerial elites coinciding with tumultuous popular demands for radical improvement of living conditions and for national self-determination might well invite revolutionary change again, as in 1917.

This brings me to *the third important difference* in the contemporary situation of Russia that distinguishes it from anything experienced in the nineteenth century. Revolution of the old-fashioned kind that occurred in France in 1789, in Russia in 1917, and in China as recently as 1949 has become all but inconceivable today. However nasty, political violence and local disorders, extending over months and even years, were tolerable for most people as long as they lived in villages and raised the food they consumed. But a flow-through economy and society cannot endure disruption of exchanges, even for short periods of time; and despite all the defects of its system of distribution, the USSR has become such a society.

A persistent paradox of all human achievement is that gains in wealth and power always involve increased vulnerability to breakdown simply because all such gains involve deliberate alterations in preexisting "natural" relationships. This was evident among farmers from the beginning of agriculture. Crop failure often occurred, and so did life-threatening losses of harvested crops to marauding plunderers. These were risks that hunting bands never faced. But subsistence farmers' vulnerability to sudden loss of livelihood is far smaller than the vulnerability urban populations face when political or natural disaster interrupts the flow of goods and services upon which they depend for daily sustenance. Stocks on hand can never be enough for more than a few weeks or months.

Hence it is not surprising that frantic efforts to feed the cities were a prominent feature of both the French and the Russian revolutions; and such efforts succeeded, in spite of all difficulties, because village routines persisted. These routines required harvested grain to be stored in peasant barns, where raiding parties from the cities could lay hands on it. But in a world where the grain harvest depends on delivery of fuel for tractors from refineries located many miles away, urban levels of vulnerability embrace the rural sector of society too. There is no longer any base level at which accustomed routines of life can persist, producing food in accustomed fashion, even when political disorder interrupts the smooth delivery of supplies from a distance.

Thus the increased efficiency achieved in Russia (and many other parts of the world) by shifting from subsistence farming to a machine-based style of agriculture involves an enormous enhancement of risk should breakdown in the flow-through economy occur. Further increases in economic efficiency, if they are ever achieved, will simply increase vulnerability to breakdown. Indeed, a good part of existing Soviet inefficiency (compared with Western "just in time" delivery) is a form of insurance against the minor interruptions in the flow of goods and services that characterize the system. Soviet factory managers like to maintain large stocks of raw materials on hand to cushion themselves against irregularities in supply; they like to hoard manpower as well, so as to be able to minimize emergencies by improvising repairs or substituting manual work for the output of a broken-down machine.

Eliminating most of these safeguards is the price of further advances in efficiency in a society where massive underemployment and untapped natural resources no longer coexist. Yet, by a cruel irony, reducing these inefficiencies might well put the stability of the command economy as a whole very much at risk. Deprived of existing cushions in the form of hoarded manpower and stocks of raw materials, significant interruption of deliveries to any segment of the economy might spread rapidly throughout the system and create a paralyzing gridlock.

The problem is not unique to the USSR, of course, but centralized political management of economic exchanges in the Soviet Union minimizes alternate (i.e., market) sources of supply more rigorously than elsewhere. Nonetheless, market systems like that of the United States are vulnerable to large-scale disorder as well. The simple fact is that old-fashioned, survivable political revolution can occur only in predominantly peasant lands. No one really knows what prolonged disruption of a modern, flow-through society would entail. Mass starvation in a matter of weeks would be a first stage, and unless relieved from outside, as happened after World War II in the worst devastated countries, famine might soon destroy most of the population.

On the other hand, if catastrophe really loomed, pressure to accept the dictates of a single leader and knit the pieces of a shattered economy together again as quickly as possible would become enormous. Everything would then depend on what sort of leadership emerged. Possibilities for sudden, sharp turns inhere in such a situation, and should be expected whenever existing daily routines show signs of faltering. Recent events in Eastern Europe illustrate the remarkable volatility that results; and, of course, if one new leader and ideal fails to restore (or maintain) equilibrium, someone else is almost sure to take power and try a different tack.

Appeals to ancient solidarities and traditional, national faiths are likely to prove especially attractive in such circumstances. Hence it is not fantastic to suppose that Holy Orthodox Russia might emerge anew from the tribulations of the twentieth century; and such a government, seeking authentic purity and orthodoxy, might deliberately spurn the entanglements of empire, just as the Ottoman Turks did after World War I. A ferociously secular, fully militarized, and defensively aggressive police state is perhaps just as likely. No one can tell ahead of time; but it seems sure that in Russia and throughout the socialist world we should expect sudden surprises, not just in 1990 but for some time to come.

Nevertheless, the travail of the USSR and its satellites ought not to be counted as a clear and definitive victory for the United States and the American way of life. Freedom has not definitively triumphed, nor has history achieved its appointed end, despite recent assertions to that effect. It is entirely unlikely that the American style of more or less managed market economy and its accompanying political system will ever take root and flourish in Russia. Even heartfelt efforts at imitating a foreign model run into difficulties when what is borrowed has to fit into a very different social and psychological setting. In such circumstances, even when things look the same, they do not work in the same way. Moreover, efforts at imitation are sure to encounter widespread resistance, since deliberate and admitted borrowing from a rival would be humiliating. (Think how hard it is for us in the United States to conceive of deliberately remodeling our conduct along Japanese lines! Instead, we indignantly ask the Japanese to conform to our ideas of how to manage their economy.)

A fundamental obstacle to the effective reorganization of Russia on American or Western lines is the fact that most Russians are convinced that anyone who enriches himself by buying and selling cheats his customers by setting prices too high. Justice therefore requires price regulation and confiscatory taxation of such ill-gotten gains. This makes the growth of a market system for distributing goods politically precarious—persistently and inescapably so. In other words, the old ideal of equity, once sustained by periodic reapportionment of fields in the village mir, is still very much alive in Russian consciousness. Overt repudiation of that ideal seems improbable, however difficult it may be to apply it to the complexities of a modern, flow-through economy.

II

Another reason for not congratulating ourselves on having won the Cold War is that American society is also in difficulty. Our competitiveness on the world market has decayed. New firms, especially along the Pacific Rim, have left Americans and Europeans far behind, owing to cheapness and, often, to the quality of their output. The resulting shift in economic primacy is still in its infancy and may not endure. On the other hand, if China's enormous bulk should ever begin to attain efficient modernity, it is hard to doubt that the Far East would reassert a world primacy like that it enjoyed between 1000 and 1450, before Western Europe usurped that role. This sort of seismic shift in the locus of world leadership—economic, cultural, and political—occurred from time to time in the deeper past and may be under way again. Even without so drastic a change in the world distribution of wealth and power, an indefinite continuation of the post–World War II alignment that so enormously exaggerated the hegemony of the United States and of the Soviet Union, each within its own sphere, is utterly improbable. The only question is when and how suddenly new balances will assert themselves, and in what way they will do so.

Clear signs of trouble in American society and economy are not far to seek. The persistent trade deficit and the unwillingness of our political leaders to balance government income and outgo by raising taxes or lowering expenditures are outward indicators of deep-seated ills. Drug addiction and crime are probably more important symptoms. Ethnic frictions, creeping bureaucratization (private as well as public), and the theatricalization of politics and society perhaps count as additional indicators of social malfunctioning.

Reflecting on recent changes in the United States brings personal bias and individual taste mercilessly into the open, for of course no one knows for sure what the costs and implications of contemporary behavior will turn out to be. Nonetheless, some recent developments that have come to the fore since World War II seem dangerous to me, if only because their long-range implications seem calculated to put all but unbearable strains on our society and polity in time to come.

The first of these is the glorification of instant gratification of personal impulse as the presumed path to happiness and success. Among the young, the gratification sought is often, perhaps always, sexual—if not consummated physiologically, then by association, connotation, transference. Pop music is the primary medium delivering this message; but movies, TV, and other mass media crowd close behind. Such an ideal is essentially adolescent, and its principal defect is that it undermines human solidarities by putting personal wishes and demands ahead of any sort of obligation to others. No society can survive on such a basis, and insofar as individuals adhere to such a pattern of conduct, they disrupt or at least fail to assist in public action aimed at achieving the common good.

A second, related difficulty is the decay of the old-fashioned way of nurturing the young within the bosom of the family. Women who leave home to work for pay obviously have less time and energy for looking after their children than was true when nearly all the work women did was unpaid and domestic. The massive withdrawal of female labor power from the home and family and its transfer to office and factory in the United States and other Western countries since World War II closely resembles the shift from field to factory that took place in Russia after 1928. In both cases, new machinery allowed a diminished work force to achieve the same, or almost the same, output. In Russia, tractors allowed cultivation to continue as before, while millions migrated to town. In the West, household appliances played the role of tractors in Russia. Housekeeping became a part-time job, and women could therefore enter the monetized workplace and, with some help from their husbands, still keep house in their spare time. Men had done the same thing before them, wherever subsistence farming and artisanal production in the home de-cayed as a way of life. In both cases, the increases in labor efficiency that monetization involved were presumably more or less equivalent.

Yet there was a catch to women's liberation. A large part of traditional household drudgery consisted of child care and su-pervision. But unlike other household tasks, the nurturing of children can be neither mechanized nor performed on a part-time basis. As contacts with parents diminish, other stimuli and experiences take over the nurturing function, shaping the young differently. Just how differently depends on what such experi-ences are, and on who sets the fashions of what to admire and what to avoid. Even if young children are carefully supervised by professionally trained personnel in preschool settings, it seems safe to assume that peer group behavior takes primary place in a child's consciousness when he or she has no contact with parents during the working day.

It also seems safe to suppose that peer group behavior is profoundly affected by words and images on TV. Continuity of values and behavior across generations is hard to sustain under such circumstances. Consequently, as the post–World War II baby boom generation came of age, a path opened for the almost uninhibited expression of adolescent sexuality, selfishness, and shortsightedness that now dominates the popular culture of the United States.

It is remarkable that this popular culture is (with weaponry) the most successful American export, presumably because the decay of generational continuities in the United States is a little ahead of parallel processes in other countries. Our precosity in this respect presumably reflects the immigrant experience, which required newcomers to give up their ancestral language and modify outward behavior so as to blend into the American melting pot. New identities, variously out of harmony with early experience within the innermost sanctum of the family, were shallowly rooted and therefore open to further change. Indeed, repudiating the ways of the older generation became something of an American tradition.

The impact of American TV programs on viewers in foreign countries is one of the great conundrums of our time. In some lands, American TV may not affect behavior much, being so far removed from actual social practices and expectations that no one dares or cares to act upon such a model. In some countries, it has generated emphatic rejection, as in Iran. Elsewhere (in Greece, for instance), American TV, along with other factors (like the forced displacement of women and children from villages during the Greek civil war of 1946–1949), abruptly eroded generational ties, creating a discontinuity far sharper than anything that has happened in the United States.

Ironically, the extraordinary diffusion of American pop culture to the world at large coincides with a problem of cultural reproduction at home that seems quite as serious as our failure to maintain competitive advantages in industrial production. The two are, of course, related, for the quality of the labor force has much to do with efficiency of output, and recruits to the labor force who have embraced an ideal of instant gratification are likely to resist the discipline of work.

The process of cultural reproduction in the United States is complicated by the fact that since World War II, the ideal of assimilation to a predominantly Yankee (or at least WASPish) style of Americanism has been supplanted by the ideal of cultural pluralism. Instead of mimicking the ways of the first comers, some (not all!) ethnic strands in the American population are now expected to cherish their own cultural heritages and take pride in being different. According to this ideal, tolerance of differences is the American way, and the resulting mutual respect among divergent groups maintains social harmony.

This is, indeed, a generous ideal and not to be lightly discarded. It is, however, difficult to maintain when parental contact with children diminishes and the young are left to interact among themselves without much adult instruction in any particular ethnic heritage. Churches used to provide extrafamilial institutional frames for such transmission, and still do; but their influence, like the influence of parents, has diminished among most Americans.

In addition, there are real problems of equity when some ethnic groups do better than others in exploiting possibilities for social mobility in American society. Those who lag behind feel discriminated against, and they may in fact be severely handicapped by some misfit between their cultural heritage and the requirements for getting ahead in an urban job market where the very meaning of work, whether skilled or unskilled, has undergone enormous alteration and no longer refers primarily to muscular exertion. How mutual respect and tolerance of diversity will fare under these circumstances remains to be seen. No one should assume that the hopes and assumptions upon which recent American public discourse has been predicated are securely rooted in the actual behavior and feelings of the American population as a whole, or in all of its parts.

How to maintain spontaneous commonality in view of the actual diversity of American society is all the more delicate because of differential birthrates among different ethnic groups. As in Russia and Europe generally, the white population of the United States in not reproducing itself biologically. Total population continues to grow because millions of immigrants, mostly from Latin America and the Caribbean, fill lowly jobs that native-born Americans have learned to scorn; and, at least to begin with, their birthrates remain about as high as they are in the societies from which they came. If existing rates of birth and migration continue unchanged, Americans of European descent will soon become a minority in the country as a whole, and if Spanish-speaking immigrants retain their language and culture, the United States will swiftly become more Latino than Yankee. But to assume that existing rates of population change will remain as they are is a sure way to err. Human behavior is nothing if not changeable, and in our era of mass communication and pop culture, sexual behavior is particularly volatile.

Nevertheless, whatever the path toward the future may turn out to be, existing differentials in birthrates are bound to put strain on existing ethnic and cultural relationships as newcomers multiply their numbers and learn to exert an increasing weight within American society. In particular, the place of the black population in our cities is problematic. Will blacks rise on the backs of the newcomers, in the way successive waves of immigrants from Europe did, distributing themselves more or less evenly among the ranks of American society? Or will newcomers outstrip them, as recent Asian immigrants clearly are doing. And if a poor and defiant black population remains confined to urban ghettos indefinitely into the future, what sort of mutual respect and tolerance is likely to prevail in American society as a whole?

No one knows the answer; but it seems clear enough that strains within American society have already called into question the tacit agreement arrived at in the 1950s about the role of government in redistributing economic resources among the citizenry. During that decade, the primacy of defense spending over other forms of governmental redistribution of income came on stream as a feature of peacetime policy. Welfare and social security payments, together with guaranteed price supports for farmers, date back to the Depression years of the 1930s; but these programs benefited minorities at the expense of the majority of the citizenry. For that reason they could never command universal support and attain as massive a scale as defense expenditures soon did.

Military outlay, after all, could plausibly claim to serve the common good. As a result, special interests seeking contracts for new weapons met no concerted opposition, and military expenditure ballooned enormously. Governmental purchases of arms, in fact, became a stabilizing flywheel for the American economy, being more or less immune to the business cycle, since political, not financial, calculations governed the demand and production of weaponry.

In effect, therefore, the arms race with the Soviet Union after World War II allowed diluted forms of deliberate management of the American economy, which had worked wonders between 1941 and 1945, to continue indefinitely in peacetime. It is worth remembering that only when arms production got into gear on the eve of World War II did the Depression of the 1930s finally give way to full employment. During World War II, acute shortages required rationing and other forms of high-handed and unpopular political intervention in the marketplace; but in the postwar period, milder forms of political management, centering on arms expenditure and the deliberate manipulation of tax and interest rates, sufficed to sustain a long period of prosperity.

Rising standards of living for most of the population meant that no one complained very much about continued welfare expenditures, or bothered about subsidies for farmers. This contributed to the smoothness with which the American economy functioned after 1950, although the evened-out flow of goods and services within the borders of the United States depended mainly on defense expenditures. Conceivably, as in Japan and Germany, where weapons production remained unimportant, a different basis for American prosperity could have been devised. But, in fact, it was the arms race with the Russians that provided the principal stimulus for what has turned out to be remarkably effective political management of the economy throughout the past four decades.

If that rivalry should falter, the United States will face awkward choices. What, if anything, ought to replace the billions expended for weapons since 1950? How can resources be reallocated without creating massive unemployment and local disruption? Worthwhile goals are easy to imagine, but attaining anything like a political consensus for expenditures that overtly benefit some segments of society more than others (as, of course, defense expenditures have done covertly) will be very difficult.

Thus, for example, breaking up the ghetto culture of defiance that unfits so many black youths for peaceable participation in civil society may be eminently desirable. A general repair of our system for nurturing the young would be even more useful. But, to be effective, such programs would have to trample on existing interests, alter habits, change outlooks. Where would political support for such deliberate social engineering conceivably come from? And what about the unexpected side effects and undesirable consequences that will result even from well-thought-out programs for social change? Much the same objection hampers ecological reform. Unexpected side effects and hidden costs that haunt existing industrial processes will surely arise if and when policies designed to protect the environment from further pollution come into force.

The simple fact is that the more we tinker with human behavior and seek to manage it in accordance with some deliberate goal, the more we entangle ourselves in processes we do not fully understand. Yet when governmental intervention in the exchange of goods and services already affects everyone's daily life, there really is no choice. Decisions have to be made and policies implemented—somehow. The situation we face in the United States as the Cold War winds down and the arms race peters out—if that does turn out to be the path into the future— is that some new balance among all the special interests and social groupings of American society will have to be contrived. That calls for the sort of political process that went into the redefinition of the role of the federal government after World War II. Debate then centered upon what the United States ought to do overseas to "contain communism." The domestic impact of rearmament and foreign aid was not at issue, and the question was, in fact, almost entirely overlooked. But this time, unless some new foreign danger raises its head, American politicians and the public will have to think about what ought to happen at home.

This promises to be far more difficult than the postwar debate, since, like the Russians, no one really knows what to do or how resources ought to be reallocated. Struggles for governmental favors among ethnic groups, age cohorts, protectionists, environmentalists, and other special interests will be hard to compromise as long as a plausible vision of the common good remains stubbornly elusive. Reversion to an unregulated market would introduce its own forms of inequity, simply because some persons and groups are more adept at taking advantage of market opportunities than others. Moreover, once the feasibility of massive and deliberate governmental redistribution of economic resources has been discovered (and that discovery is a matter of our own century), it is hard to imagine that groups disadvantaged by the market will not demand help—and since they constitute a majority, in a democracy they are likely to get it.

The United States does have a constitutional commitment to individual freedom and a tradition of openness to newcomers that may suffice to keep the political process from ugly deadlock among competing groups. Maybe we will manage to maintain our liberal political tradition, even if group rivalries intensify as the tacit compromise of the 1950s that gave priority to defense expenditures wears out. But finding a new consensus will certainly be difficult and may even imperil constitutional procedures, if social confrontations multiply or if the economy falters.

Under the circumstances, an obvious temptation is to maintain arms expenditures more or less at existing levels. It is conceivable that developments in Russia will make such a policy attractive, for the Russians face a far greater problem of shifting resources from armament production than we do, and if public disorder were to threaten the Soviet Union, a return to militarism, with or without the front dressing of Marxist ideology, might well occur. Under such circumstances, it is easy to imagine heartfelt sighs of relief from both governments at being spared the hard choices needed to make a successful retreat from the arms race.

Yet such a policy would exacerbate existing internal difficulties in both countries and make efficient production of real wealth harder to attain. We can probably afford it, at least for a while; the Russians could do so only at great sacrifice and would need to find a fierce and really believable enemy to justify the price their people would have to pay. But deliberate cultivation of intensified hostility so as to justify the arms race is a risky business in our atomic age. And when global communication has penetrated as deeply into private homes as is now the case, can enmity remain intense enough to sustain the arms race and platonic enough to keep the peace?

Obviously, Gorbachev and his supporters in Russia decided that this balancing feat was becoming impossible. Their opening to the West, and the positive responses elicited so far, surely make return to Cold War strategy difficult. But no one knows for sure whether intensified militarization will not seem preferable to facing the difficulties of finding a new domestic balance among competing interests and groups within the USSR. We in the United States face a parallel dilemma. The upshot will depend on the interplay of policies and personalities, not merely within the two superpowers, but around the world. In addition, the acts, hopes, and fears of millions of common people will affect the outcome. So will chance timing of events. As usual, the future remains unknown and unknowable, even though we can be sure that we are living through a time when radical shifts in political alignments both at home and abroad are possible and perhaps inevitable.

III

In reflecting on the winds of change that are blowing so forcefully around us as the decade of the 1990s begins, it is worth reminding ourselves that the rivalry of the two superpowers and their domestic distresses do not exhaust the complexity of world affairs. National policy, even for such giant states as the USSR and the United States, has to take account of the rest of the world, where mounting signs of global disequilibrium make indefinite preservation of the post–World War II balances improbable, to say the least, though exactly how disturbances in the rest of the world may impinge upon the two superpowers is as impossible to foresee as is the internal dynamic of their respective paths to the future.

Still, one can say something about what is happening globally. Not surprisingly, the same factors that have been altering political realities and alignments within the borders of the United States and the Soviet Union have upset older social balances throughout the rest of the world as well. The fundamental fact is that demographic surges (and declines), together with more powerful communication nets, are changing human life and experience in every part of the earth, and at a very rapid pace.

In recent decades, rich, urbanized lands are everywhere seeing birthrates fall below replacement levels. This is a very recent phenomenon, or more accurately, it has only recently manifested itself among entire nations. Since civilization began, town dwellers have seldom or perhaps never reproduced themselves; but in the European past, migrants from the nearby countryside, who shared much the same cultural identity, compensated for urban die-off, thus allowing a single people and culture to maintain itself for centuries in the same geographic area. Only since World War II have entire nations in Europe, Japan, and lands of European settlement overseas become so urbanized and rich that they have ceased to reproduce themselves.

Under such circumstances, if society is to maintain itself, recruits must cross cultural boundaries to take on lowly jobs that the native-born disdain, thus creating ethnically and culturally plural societies. In Europe, the principal alien immigrants are Muslims: Turks in Germany, Algerians in France, Pakistanis and other "New Commonwealth" immigrants in Great Britain, together with Turks and Iranians from Central Asia in the Soviet Union. In the United States, Caribbean and Latino immigrants from the south play an analogous role; in Australia, it is a mixed assemblage of Asians; and in South Africa, of course, it is black Africans who work at jobs the white inhabitants disdain.

Japan remains exceptional, since so far it has refused to accept immigrants, preferring instead to establish new factories on foreign soil. But the decline of the Japanese work force has barely begun to assert itself, and if existing demographic trends continue (as always, an implausible hypothesis), even xenophobic Japan may decide to admit foreign workers, as other countries with declining native-born populations are doing.

It is worth pointing out that national unity within defined territorial boundaries was not the norm of civilized societies in times past. Large imperial states, especially in the Middle East and India, were polyethnic. Normally, rulers came from the steppes of Eurasia, where warlike tribes cultivated the military virtues with unusual single-mindedness. Their subjects were of diverse ethnicity; and special occupations were often monopolized, or nearly monopolized, by a particular people. Cities therefore housed multiple ethnic and occupational groups, commonly living apart from one another in separate quarters. Within such cities, religious and other cultural institutions sustained ethnic divergences indefinitely, since the ideal of assimilation to a single norm was completely absent before European ideals of nationalism began to spread abroad after 1789.[1]

In effect, ethnic homogeneity appears as a characteristic of barbarian communities, not of civilized society; and the peculiarity of western Europe and of Japan is that when these remote regions of the Eurasian continent eventually did become civilized, the local demographic situation was such that enough rural recruits were available close at hand to maintain ethnic homogeneity in spite of urban die-off. Consequently, European and Japanese cities did not need to recruit slaves and strangers from afar, as was the case in the Middle East and India. Accordingly, what had been a barbarian ideal of ethnic and cultural homogeneity could be and was combined with occupational diversity of urban, civilized society, beginning around 1000 A.D.

Political benefits turned out to be substantial. Starting with the French *levée en masse* of 1793, modern European governments were able to demand military participation from the entire population in a way that was entirely impossible for the ethnically and occupationally laminated societies of Asia. (China was intermediate in this respect. Until after 1368, when the Ming dynasty came to power, ethnic pluralism prevailed in Chinese cities as elsewhere in the Eurasian world; under the Manchus [1644–1912], government was at least partly in the hands of foreigners from the steppe. But under the Ming and Manchus, xenophobia and rural demographic growth combined to make Chinese cities more ethnically uniform than before.)

The recent emergence of polyethnicity and cultural pluralism in European and American society therefore looks like a return to a civilized norm of the deeper past. But that raises troublesome questions, for democratic politics and liberal economics did not prevail in former times. Maintaining the sort of basic consensus required for effective and democratic public action obviously becomes more difficult if society divides into distinct and separate ethnic and cultural blocs. The capacity to mobilize the whole, or very nearly the whole, of society for war and other common enterprises was at the heart of Europe's recent superiority over other states and peoples. This will become much more problematic, perhaps impossible, if cultural diversity produces enduring cross-purposes and political deadlocks of the sort that characterized the imperial polyethnic states of Eurasia's past. Yet this is what continuation of existing demographic trends in the rich and urbanized countries may provoke if immigrant populations refuse or are not permitted to assimilate to the national norm.

The phenomenon of population decline among Americans of European descent has attracted remarkably little attention in the United States so far, even in regions and cities where whites have become a minority. Quite appropriately, we are much more aware of the galloping population growth that, on a global basis, far outweighs the still incipient demographic decay of the rich and urbanized peoples of the world.

This growth is a rural phenomenon. Until very recently it prevailed in Europe and the lands of European settlement overseas, and in fact sustained more dramatic growth of those populations than anything experienced by the rest of the world until after World War II. Demographic balances between European and non-European peoples have therefore shifted very sharply indeed in recent decades, but political consequences, whatever they may be, have not yet become very noticeable.

Nonetheless, in seeking to understand the course of public events, it is well to have a clear notion of how the demographic upheaval of modern times got started. It dates back to the century between 1750 and 1850, when peasant populations began to increase systematically all around the world. Reasons for this remarkable change in human affairs are debatable, but everyone agrees that the most important proximate change was the fading away of lethal epidemic disease. This, in turn, may have been due to intensified communications, making formerly epidemic infections endemic among an ever larger portion of the human population of the earth, until only small children remained at risk of the major disease killers of former ages.

An important result of such a change in the incidence of infection was that death rates decreased.[2] Disease was not everything, of course, and other factors always affected human numbers. Food supply, for instance, and legal systems that defined rights to the harvest always mattered.[3]

Improvements in preventive medicine are another obvious factor promoting population growth.[4] Lastly, public order and its lack always affected human populations. Where governments provide effective public relief services in times of crop failure, for instance, the vagaries of the weather lose much of their importance for human life, even in poor and overcrowded lands. When, instead, armed bands roam the landscape and get the food they need by robbing those who have labored to produce the crop, prolonged disorder can result in radical depopulation, even in places otherwise favorable to agriculture.

Suffice it to say, therefore, that changes in the incidence of infectious disease, combined with intensified food production, public health measures, and an improved level of public order, provoked the modern growth of human numbers. This growth constitutes a remarkable horizon in the history of humanity, and it involves no less extraordinary risk for many of the other species with which we share the earth. Indeed, from the point of view of most other creatures, human beings must be classed as an epidemic disease that underwent a particularly lethal mutation after 1750. Everywhere, growing human populations persist in altering the face of the earth to suit themselves, using an ever more powerful technology to cut down forests, divert watercourses, plant fields, dig mines, and in still other ways alter natural environments beyond recognition.

By thus making more room for ourselves in the earth's ecosystem, human ingenuity and organized effort have allowed more and more people to find enough to eat and procreate. Prophecies of disaster have so far proven false even though many millions of people live near the edge of hunger in all the poorer parts of the earth. But hunger stalked human populations throughout history, so this, in itself, is nothing new. What is new is the scale of the human assault on other forms of life, and the disturbances of atmospheric and oceanic balances that human activity has begun to make, not merely locally but also globally. Just what the consequences may be no one knows. They may turn out to be drastic.

At least we are wise enough by now to know that the flows of matter and energy that sustain daily life are inextricably embedded in the earth's ecosystem, and all our skill cannot escape the limits that simple fact imposes. Nevertheless, technical possibilities for wresting still more food and energy from the earth are far from being exhausted, and it seems likely that the modern surge in human numbers will be checked by social and political changes long before absolute ecological limits are approached.

The reason for making such an assertion is this: Human populations resist immiseration and will go to great lengths to avoid obvious lowering of their accustomed standards of living. Long before increasing poverty reaches the level of consumption required for bodily sustenance, people take action of one sort or another to avoid further impoverishment. Sometimes peaceable migration or change of occupation suffices to relieve the problem for individuals and families. When that fails, collective violence normally results. The political history of the world since 1750 reflects this fact, for it was rural discontent arising from overcrowding on the land that provided the background for crowd action and revolutionary upheaval in France in 1789, in Russia in 1917, in China in 1949, and more recently in such places as El Salvador, Peru, Lebanon, and Iran.

Moreover, resistance to immiseration has become far more vigorous in recent decades because new forms of communication have penetrated even remote villages, thanks to the flexibility of radio and TV broadcasting. Subsistence farmers, who in a previous generation encountered outsiders only rarely and as strangers, find a new world opening before them when radio and TV programs begin to flood into the village square or even into their homes. This has now happened to most of the population of the earth. Entrancing visions of the possible swim into peasants' consciousness when radio and TV expose them to urban talk and to urban scenes. Pushed by intensifying land shortages at home in the village and pulled by the charm of urban comforts as revealed to them by the new communications, peasant populations are ready, as never before, to claim the rights of full citizenship and equality of circumstances with privileged urban dwellers.

This, it seems to me, is the most critical axis of world affairs in our time. Since civilization began, the gap between town and country has been fundamental. The rural majority produced more food than it consumed, and surrendered the surplus to its social superiors in the form of rents and taxes, thus provisioning the town dwellers, who for millennia gave little or nothing back in return, unless one counts a somewhat uncertain protection against rival human predators. Even when economic exchanges between town and village began to modify the stark exploitation of the countryside that prevailed in the earliest phases of civilized history, rural folk long remained economically disadvantaged and politically passive. (It is worth remembering, for instance, that farm laborers got the right to vote in Great Britain as recently as 1884.)

Desperate peasant rebellions did sometimes occur, usually when crowded conditions on the land made it impossible to persist with existing patterns of rural life while also paying traditional rents and taxes. A few peasant-based rebellions even attained political power. (The most recent was the Algerian victory over the French in 1962.) But peasant rebellions took power only by betraying whatever egalitarian ideals they had initially espoused in order to create a professionalized armed force and a tax system to support it. Whether the rebels won or lost, effective pacification commonly set in only after local violence had brought resources and rural numbers back to a balance that permitted the survivors to pay rents and taxes and still have enough left over for their own traditional and customary needs.

The issue in our world today is whether rural aspirations for equality with urban folk and for active citizenship will conform to the patterns of peasant rebellion from the past, or not. Modern communications make it hard to imagine that a great gap between town and country can be maintained indefinitely into the future. Rural folk are unlikely to accept their disadvantaged status passively as in times past, particularly when growing numbers make continuation of traditional village routines impractical because there is no longer enough land to support the rising generation in the old way.

In most of the Third World, this kind of pressure on traditional behavior looms close ahead, if it has not already reached critical levels. To be sure, improvements in technique can stave off immiseration for a while. But there are limits to what new crops, fertilizers, and pesticides can do in crowded countrysides, especially when entitlements to the increased harvests are not equally distributed among the population as a whole, or even within the village itself. When successful, agricultural improvements avert crisis for a generation or so. But if population growth continues, that merely postpones collision between still greater numbers and available plots of land, and makes the crisis that much more massive and intractable when it comes.

Whenever the old ways fail to produce traditional and expected results, breakdown of what is perceived to be right and just makes resort to political violence along the lines of traditional peasant rebellion easy to organize. Ideological flags to justify armed rebellion are everywhere ready at hand. Religious, Marxist, and nationalist programs compete and blend into various combinations of the three. But generous revolutionary ideals have a nasty way of inviting betrayal. The plain fact is that a numerous, poverty-stricken, and angry peasantry, inspired by revolutionary ideals, is almost impossible to fold into democratic politics, and dictatorship, of whatever kind, must depend on some sort of elite, whose efforts to maintain its power and enforce public peace and order are sure to alienate the poor. Leveling down is easier than raising the majority to new levels of skill, wealth, and political participation. But that, too, disappoints the hope of betterment that burns so bright among the world's disadvantaged rural majority.

Emigration to richer lands offers an alternative for some villagers. Millions have already come to the United States and to Western Europe; and their remittances back home help to cushion local difficulties in many Latin American, Caribbean, and Muslim villages. But the hardships migrants face, and the dislike they arouse because of their different appearance and behavior, make emigration a political risk for both parties, and, in any event, demographers unanimously agree that migration on a scale sufficient to relieve rural overcrowding among the four-fifths of humankind that now confront it is simply inconceivable.

IV

Behind the turbulence of our age lies another intractable problem. We face a gap between the scale of political management by separate, sovereign national units and the exchanges that flow so swiftly around the globe. Information flows are especially pervasive. As I have already emphasized, by penetrating everywhere, modern communications alter prevailing patterns of conduct, expectation, and behavior. Indeed, one can argue that the central disturber of our age is the communications revolution, in the sense that it is this that directly affects human consciousness, arousing new hopes and fears, and provoking new sorts of behavior.

It is worth reminding ourselves of how recently a truly global system of communications arose. Sailing ships took months to carry news across oceanic distances; the telegraph inaugurated instantaneous communications a little more than a century ago. Telephone, radio, and TV crowded close behind, attaining global scope and penetration of nearly all populated landscapes in the decades after World War II. Most recently of all, computer hookups and satellite communications systems have magnified the carrying capacity of the global communications system enormously. Instantaneous data flows are matched by almost instantaneous capital flows, and by accelerated export of technology, wherever market calculations suggest that the best conditions for cheap and reliable production prevail.

Instantaneous communications of such power enhance the possibilities of management and control at a distance, as international business firms and governments have long since discovered. Indeed, another way of thinking about recent social transformations is to focus upon the race between the expanding scale of deliberate control, on the one hand, and the even more rapidly expanding scale of communications nets and human responses to the messages such nets convey, on the other.

With every improvement of communications technology, the scale of human interaction expanded and intensified. Efforts to manage and control the processes so unleashed inevitably lagged behind. Yet in the recent past, a series of breakthroughs abruptly expanded the scale of control and each such breakthrough brought vast rewards of wealth and power to those who succeeded in pioneering the new ways of management. Thus, after the crash of 1873, large manufacturing corporations arose, mainly in the United States and Germany, capable of controlling production processes from the extraction of raw materials to the distribution of finished products among individual consumers. Enormous savings became possible when economies of scale and carefully orchestrated flows of energy, materials, and labor minimized waste and delay along the way. Moreover, the new giant corporations were usually able to foresee and control the prices at which they bought and sold, since most of those with whom they dealt were not organized on any comparable scale and had the choice only of accepting terms the corporation offered or refusing to deal at all. Managed prices thus matched the managed flow of materials, energy, and labor to assure handsome profits that kept the whole enterprise going.

By the 1930s, however, integrated corporations and managed prices had become so thick on the ground in the American and German economies that some of the initial advantages of corporate organization disappeared. In particular, when financial panic occurred in 1929, corporations' efforts to protect themselves by maintaining prices and cutting back on production backfired disastrously. Dismissed workers could not buy very much, and diminished demand had the effect of deepening and prolonging the Depression until even the best-managed great corporations began to feel threatened.

Resolution of the resulting deadlock took place when first the German and then the American government started rearmament and, once war began, learned to manage the entire nation as a firm whose aim was to maximize the war effort. The Germans relied largely on booty, compulsion, and improvisation; but in the United States, improvisation was soon supplemented by new macroeconomic concepts implemented with the help of statistics that allowed national managers to monitor material and financial flows and so achieve desired results with truly remarkable precision.

In a far less precise fashion, transnational management was also experimented with during World War II. Thus, for example, millions of slave laborers were imported to staff German war factories, and the raw materials and food supplies of the entire Continent were ruthlessly (and sometimes irrationally) allocated for the support of the German war effort insofar as administrative efficiency and transport permitted. The major Allied powers of World War II also experimented with transnational management through lend-lease and strategic consultation, but administrative integration of the Allied war effort remained far weaker than within the Germans' *Festung Europa*. As for Japan's Co-Prosperity Sphere, it remained more a creature of propaganda than a reality because transport soon became critically short.

The net effect of the World War II−style of nationwide management was to expand the scale of production enormously, and, as we have seen, a modified form of national management persisted in the United States and other leading industrial nations after the war.

By far the most interesting postwar experiment in widening the scale of deliberate management beyond the national frame arose from the ruins of the Nazi war economy in Europe. After cringing beneath the *Diktat* of jackbooted conquerors between 1940 and 1945, Western Europeans responded to the gentler hegemony of the United States and qualified for Marshall Plan aid by embarking upon a policy of consultative cooperation across national frontiers, beginning in 1947. The European Economic Community, which eventually emerged from these efforts, has proved so vigorous that most barriers to economic exchanges are scheduled to disappear in 1992. How gracefully twelve supposedly sovereign governments will submit to a single set of rules for their respective national economies remains to be seen, although the post−World War II record of international cooperation and coordination in Western Europe, and the prosperity that has prevailed there since the 1950s, augur well for the future.

The European Economic Community, nevertheless, owes much of its past success to the fact that separate and individual European nations felt themselves dwarfed by the emergence of the two superpowers and, more recently, by Japan. By combining resources, Europeans could meet Americans, Russians, and Japanese on even terms, or even hope to outstrip them. In effect, therefore, the postwar world has been dominated by a handful of industrialized powers, each responding to its own system of large-scale internal management. And just as big private corporations were once in a position to dictate terms of their exchanges with ill-organized consumers and small businessmen, so in recent decades the best-organized political economies have been in a position to dictate terms of trade to the less well-organized peoples of the Third World.

It is arguable that the result is to increase market risks confronting the poor and ill-organized peoples of the earth. Efforts to concert financial policy among the principal trading nations with respect to loans and aid to the so-called developing nations may ease the difficulty, or may exacerbate it, since what benefits the rich may not always benefit the poor. All depends on how broadly the key managers—political as well as economic— envision costs and benefits.

Clearly, what is needed is a global effort at ecologically and politically sustainable development. Somehow, worldwide management of capital flows, migration flows, pollution, energy use, and exchange of goods needs to become explicit—and efficient as well. In all such exchanges, the needs and interests of the senders and of the receivers must be balanced against each other, relying upon a combination of market pricing and deliberate acts of policy to adjust the terms of trade. That is to say, the scale of management needs to become global to catch up with the actual interdependence that modern communications have in fact inaugurated.

Easy to say; hard, perhaps impossible, to accomplish. But the same might have been said in 1870 about the possibility of managing an entire industrial process from extraction of raw materials to the marketing of finished goods, and the same most certainly was said in the early 1930s, when effective nationwide economic management was only a socialist dream. The reality of our actual interdependence may eventually come home to all the peoples of the earth so forcibly that efforts to minimize risk and expand the range of deliberate control will prevail over all the obstacles that now make such a world system hard to imagine.

Recourse to world government, exercising mandatory and presumably dictatorial power over all of humankind, is anything but attractive to anyone who is heir to the liberal tradition. Recent difficulties in Russia surely suggest that such a regime might be more of a problem than a solution to the disparities that currently distract global society. Piecemeal coordination and negotiation among existing states and transnational organizations, private as well as public, is clearly more promising. People can learn to take account of a widening circle of interests and consequences of their actions if all the parties affected by a given policy are able to make their wishes known.

On the other hand, there are and always will be divergent interests. Policies that benefit some and hurt others will be hard to enforce, even if some urgent global need or a clear majority of the human race may seem to require such an action. Politics has always turned on exactly this question, and if the theater of politics becomes increasingly international and global, as seems likely, one can perhaps suppose that the same sort of compromises, evasions, deceits, and half-truths that dominate public life within the national frame will continue to operate within the expanded horizon of transnational interests and concerns.

Real disaster, if it occurs, will teach its own lessons, as the wars and depressions of our century assuredly have done. Conversely, behavior that gets results most people like will tend to spread and multiply. That is how human societies have always conducted their affairs—avoiding what hurts and seeking what satisfies human needs, wishes, and hopes. No doubt, mistakes always outnumber effective solutions to new problems, but sooner or later, when mistaken behavior becomes too costly, people correct their mistakes, or at least try to. That is what seems to be happening in the Soviet Union and Eastern Europe right now. American mistakes are less obvious, and we are correspondingly sluggish in seeking to correct them.

Two such mistakes, I suggest, are the halfheartedness of official response to ecological problems and a military policy preoccupied with preparing for high-tech international war when low-grade local violence—both at home and abroad—is a more likely occasion for American military action. But our most important mistake, it seems to me, is that our public discourse has neglected demographics almost completely, even though population changes within our country and abroad seem likely to present the most acute problems we will face as a nation in the next 50 years or more.

The increasingly obvious failure of our system of child nurture is perhaps the most critical expression of the demographic changes sweeping across our country, and it surely deserves to be addressed in wider terms than the existing "war on drugs" and "Just say no." Thoroughgoing monetization of nurturing is probably inescapable in an urbanized and thoroughly monetized society such as ours. We cannot expect to halt the decay of civil society until we recognize this necessity and allocate the sums needed to assure effective transmission of adult habits and values to the young. Paying mothers to stay home and look after their children is an obvious possibility. How to assess the quality of child care such salaried mothers actually delivered to their young would present obvious difficulties; but ways of checking up and of teaching mothers how to earn their salaries might be discoverable, if we really decided that reorganization of existing patterns of nurturing is necessary.

Action abroad to help other countries absorb the shock of population growth is no less critical. Dissemination of agricultural improvements can help for a time, but in Third World countries, where pressure of population threatens the existing social order, parallel efforts to disseminate methods of birth control are just as necessary. Wherever local governments are prepared to cooperate, international efforts ought to concentrate on hastening both these changes. A few examples of actual success in containing population growth and raising standards of rural productivity, if these goals can, in fact, be achieved, are then likely to prove highly contagious, for no one really wants to perpetuate poverty and civil unrest, which are the only alternatives. The United States ought therefore to devote all the influence it has, both in the United Nations and in the various countries of the Third World, to advancing both agricultural improvement and population control.

Migration flows that reflect rural overcrowding present critical questions as well. Perhaps there is such a thing as an optimal rate of migration both for receiving and for sending societies. If so, no one knows what it is; and what is optimal for the sender is unlikely to be optimal for the receiver. In countries with rapidly growing populations, massive concentration of discontented rural emigrants in capital cities creates a volatile crowd that is sure to have decisive political importance in revolutionary and quasi-revolutionary situations. A policy of keeping surplus hands back on the farm has seldom been attempted and is very difficult to enforce. (As far as I know, the People's Republic of China is the only country in which this has been tried, but with what success no one, I think, can tell. Official statistics are certainly no guide to the truth; and risks endured in getting to Hong Kong show that the Chinese, when they hear of a chance to better their lot, are as ready to disregard the law as any other human population.)

Prohibitions of international migration are also difficult to enforce, even though the principle of territorial sovereignty gives each national government full liberty to define who shall and shall not be allowed to come into the country legally. American experience with illegal aliens shows how hard it is to enforce rules that run against the interest and wishes of millions of people. Foreseeable demographic changes in Mexico and other Latin American and Caribbean countries make it equally obvious that additional millions are likely to wish to come to the United States in the next few decades. Only some sort of catastrophic economic depression that made it impossible for immigrants to find jobs would be capable of stopping the flow. Severe police measures might check but could scarcely halt it completely.

This, I think, is symptomatic of the limits of policy. People resist official acts that run counter to their wishes and interests, and are clever at deceiving constituted authority that seeks to prevent them from doing what they want to do. Given the ease with which people now can travel across long distances, and the even greater ease with which information about living conditions in far places spreads across political borders, I suspect that migration, legal and illegal, will increase in scale until such time as differences in living standards diminish so as to make migration less attractive. On the world scene, this requires closing the age-old gap between village and city—a daunting task indeed. It also requires alteration of the family patterns that sustain the extraordinary rate of rural increase that prevails today.

All the same, governmental policy can affect the pace and scale of migration, and if the United States really wishes to diminish illegal immigration, surely the most efficient way to achieve that end is to penalize employers for hiring illegal aliens so severely that the practice would grind to a halt. That, of course, would enhance wage differentials between Mexico and adjacent parts of the United States, and intensify the motivation for deceiving and bribing officials charged with enforcing the law. It would also raise the price of vegetables and other farm products on the American market, and encourage imports.

Whether such costs are worth paying in order to protect Anglo predominance within the borders of the United States is not a trivial question. Ethnic pluralism is sure to lead to internal tensions, especially when class and occupational stratification coincide with ethnic demarcation lines, as will be the case for some time to come in the southwestern United States. It takes time for the descendants of peasant migrants to acquire the skills that might allow them to distribute themselves across the social spectrum of the United States, or any other urban society. Immigrants who hold fast to their native language and culture cannot easily interpenetrate the host society, and, when immigration assumes a certain mass and rate, the motivation for learning the host country's language and coming to terms with the culture of the environing society diminishes sharply.

This, it seems to me, is the crucial question for Latino immigrants in the United States. If they maintain their separateness in matters of language and culture, American society will swiftly polarize between Anglo and Latino communities, with

Anglos all too clearly on top. This is a recipe for civil unrest and would put enormous strain on democratic institutions.

Educational policy, immigration policy, and the way Caribbean and Latin American societies move either toward greater poverty or toward closer parity with the conditions of life within the United States will govern the way the situation evolves. Two goals of policy emerge: one is to do all we can to hasten the demographic and economic transformation of the lands of emigration so that motives for coming to the United States will fade; the second is to do all we can to hasten the assimilation of recent immigrants into the American mainstream, inviting them, in effect, to distribute themselves up and down the social ladder instead of huddling into a subordinated community of their own.

Of course, they, and we, together with the hard-pressed populations of other peasant and ex-peasant countries, may merely proceed to make new mistakes. Nevertheless, over the long run, people have always preferred wealth and power to their opposites, and, when choice becomes apparent, the great majority of human beings have always been ready and eager to accept whatever social arrangements seemed able to bring them greater wealth and power. In making such choices, foresight is persistently defective. Unexpected side effects and unforeseen costs always arise, creating new situations that require new decisions and further choices. That is the stuff and substance of recorded history; but despite all the blind alleys and cruel disasters that have beset humankind across the centuries, it still remains true that our predecessors did succeed in cumulatively increasing the wealth and power at their disposal until in recent times, everyday reality has outrun the wildest dreams of past centuries.

There is no reason to suppose that this pattern will not continue into the future, even though we may, indeed, have learned to master local circumstances and evade local disasters only by exposing ourselves to fewer but bigger—even global— disasters. Nonetheless, when, amid the multiplicity of errors, an innovation turns up that satisfies human needs better than before, it is highly contagious and tends to displace less effective sorts of behavior, just as biological mutations, when they prove advantageous to the survival of a particular organism, also tend to spread.

The miracles of interdependence that characterize the earth's ecosphere today arose from processes of selection operating on apparently random genetic mutations. The global interdependence of contemporary humanity results from selections operating upon a diverse array of culturally directed behavior. We have the advantage over other organisms of being capable of a vastly expanded range of mistakes, simply because we interpose words, numbers, and other symbols between ourselves and the outer world. This makes human behavior far more changeable than anything genetic mutation and organic evolution can match. (Mutations in viruses and other micro-organisms are almost as quick, but so far scientists and doctors have kept ahead of nearly all viral mutations so that humanity remains the sovereign disturber of ecological relationships on the face of the earth.)

Another way of describing our role on earth is to say that historical, cultural evolution supplanted biological evolution as the principal engine for changing the face of the earth, from the time our ancestors became fully human and began to combine tools with words to organize the hunt. But historical change, by selecting successful behavior and discarding mistakes, still conforms to the older pattern of evolution in the sense that no one knows the upshot, or foresees the future accurately, even though individual choices and actual experiences of ordinary people, as well as of political leaders and administrators, do add up to making the future into whatever it will be.

In a time when winds of change are blowing very strong, we must rest content with knowing that foresight is always imperfect and that choices must always be made in ignorance of their full consequences. That is the price we pay for being able to make the world over by changing our own behavior, individually and collectively, in response to cherished hopes and shared purposes, framed in words. Our capacity to err is our capacity to learn and thereby achieve partial and imperfect, but real, improvement in the conditions of human life.

The possibility of overcoming the age-old inequity between town and country seems inherent in our contemporary circumstance. To achieve that goal, some way of checking the rural population growth will have to be found, along with who knows what else to bridge the gap that now divides the poor peasantry of the earth from the urban rich. Checking the social decay that exists in contemporary urban society may turn out to be quite as difficult as learning how to accommodate the demands of the peasant majority of humankind. Avoiding ecological catastrophe on a global scale may be hardest of all, since bringing the rural majority up to an urban standard of living would enormously intensify pollution, while the alternative of depressing existing urban standards to peasant levels appeals to no one.

A humane and comfortable outcome cannot be counted on. Moral and practical dilemmas are with us always and will continue indefinitely into the future. All one can say with confidence is that hitherto human history has been a success story, despite powerful back eddies and recurrent disasters. One can believe, but one cannot know, that the trend will continue, even though, or just because, the problems and possibilities of our age are so enormous.

NOTES

1. Slaves were important in these polyethnic societies. Unlike other elements of the population, they were free-floating, isolated individuals, torn away from their native social context and brought into a totally new environment, sometimes, but not always, by force. This characteristic fitted them for positions of trust as servants and bodyguards in private households, and for serving in the highest offices of state. Slave plantations, of the sort we associate with slavery, were exceptional, though such agricultural factories did exist in a few places and for short periods of time. Slave labor was also sometimes used in mines. But throughout Eurasia, slaves normally served in the households of powerful men, up to and including imperial sovereigns. Rulers relied upon enslaved and isolated individuals, wholly dependent upon royal favor for their positions of power, to counterbalance overmighty subjects, whose kinship and other ties to civil society gave them an independent power base of their own.

2. Children commonly suffer less acutely from diseases like smallpox and measles than adults do. This is probably because children become vulnerable to such infections only when the antibodies they inherit from their mothers' bloodstreams begin to fade away. Whenever such infections are

continually present, therefore, the disease is likely to develop while remnants of inherited resistances are still available to diminish the severity of the attack. Hence endemic diseases tend to be less lethal than epidemics; and a population thoroughly and persistently exposed to a given infection, though ill more often than more isolated populations, can nevertheless count on fewer deaths from the disease in question.

3. But the production of food was usually elastic, at least within limits, and it seems unlikely that population growth was a response to an expanded food supply rather than vice versa. Instead, increased availability of labor in the fields could normally be counted on to produce larger harvests, though expansion of agricultural production in this fashion was always subject to the law of diminishing returns.

4. Many customary practices, justified by religious and other ideas, diminished disease risks, and medical doctors sometimes helped, too. Public health measures probably prevented deaths in some cities as early as the fifteenth century, when quarantine for plague became common in Mediterranean ports. Inoculation against smallpox was even more effective. It probably spread among caravan personnel early in this millennium, though it became a recognized technique among European doctors only early in the eighteenth century, and not all accepted it then. But the effect of these measures was far eclipsed by the triumphs of scientific medicine in the nineteenth century, at least in European lands. The impact became worldwide after World War II, when doctors, under the aegis of the World Health Organization, waged extraordinarily effective campaigns against malaria and smallpox, along with an array of other serious infections. The effect of this medical campaign, of course, was to accelerate population growth throughout the Third World, raising rates of growth for some populations above anything ever recorded in earlier times.

1989 AND ALL THAT

Robert W. Tucker

In 1989, the division of Europe came to an end. Within a period of scarcely four months, a structure of power that had largely defined Europe and that had been the principal political conse- quence of World War II collapsed. The end of the Soviet Union's domination over the states of Eastern and Central Europe was as unexpected a development as it was sudden. Despite the Soviet government's earlier insistence that it was now prepared to en- tertain new relationships with these states, at the beginning of 1989 few observers doubted that there were still strict limits to the change Moscow was prepared to admit in a region long identified as a vital interest. At the close of 1989, the bounds of Soviet toleration had apparently grown so broad that it was no longer clear whether there remained any line beyond which change, however displeasing, could be expected to evoke the threat of military response by the government of Mikhail Gor- bachev. Even the prospective withdrawal of a state from the Warsaw Pact no longer appeared to constitute an intolerable provocation to Moscow. Given the changes that occurred in Eastern and Central Europe during the course of the year, the continued effectiveness of the Pact could not, in any event, be counted on. The events of 1989 deprived the Pact, for a number of years an increasingly unreliable military alliance, of any remaining effectiveness.

The prospect of German reunification formed a case apart. Of all the changes to which Moscow reconciled itself, the re- unification of Germany stood out as the great exception. Even this prospect, however, did not once evoke the threat of a military response by the Soviet government. Instead, it was met by the plaintive forecast that reunification would give a new lease on life to the conservative opposition to Gorbachev. A novel tactic for the Soviet Union to take in response to unwanted change, it, too, was abandoned in early 1990, and German reunification was accepted.

What made the events that marked the end of Europe's postwar division so remarkable is that except in one country—Romania—they were unattended by armed violence. Although in each instance a communist government relinquished its claim to a monopoly of power and undertook to inaugurate democratic processes, the change occurred without a shot being fired. Regimes that were initially imposed and subsequently maintained largely by force were ended bloodlessly in an unprecedented display of restraint by rulers and ruled alike. The result defied expectations long accepted by many in the West as articles of faith of how communist states might one day be overturned. Instead of coming as a result of defeat in war, change came in the wake of popular, though peaceful, demonstrations. Nor was this triumph of restraint substantially diminished by virtue of the critical role that Moscow undoubtedly played in facilitating change by pressuring communist governments to accept popular demands that they relinquish power.

The events of 1989 not only brought to an end the division of Europe, they also brought to an end the postwar role of the Soviet Union in Europe, for that role depended above all on the once clearly recognized division of the Continent and, of course, the political-military consequences acknowledged to follow from that division. These consequences no longer obtain, however, and this despite the continued presence of Soviet forces in Europe. The view that they still do obtain, if admittedly in attenuated form, must depend on the possibility that the Soviet government—whether that of Mikhail Gorbachev or of a successor—may yet employ military power to prevent unwanted developments. If that prospect cannot be entirely ruled out, it nevertheless now remains so small that it may be all but discounted, for the military power needed to stay the developments that have now been set firmly in train—including German re-unification—would have to be very considerable. To succeed, the effort required would greatly tax the Soviet Union's resources and, by doing so, place in further jeopardy, if not simply put an end to, efforts of domestic economic reform. The suppression once again of popular aspirations to freedom and self-determination in Eastern Europe would be seen as vindicating those opposed from the outset to liberalization in the Soviet Union. At best, such suppression would set the clock back 30 years in Soviet relations with the West. At worst, it would directly threaten a general war in Europe, if only because those circumstances that formerly assured the Soviet Union that military intervention could be undertaken in reasonable safety no longer exist. The division once clearly recognized, if not legitimized, is no longer so. The once acknowledged power, if not the right, to intervene is no longer acknowledged and would now be very dangerous to exercise.

The end of Europe's division signals as well the end of the great conflict that has dominated world politics since World War II. It does so not because, as the conventional view has it, the Cold War arose out of the division of Europe and will therefore end when this division is ended, but because the abandonment by the Soviet Union of its core external interest marks the onset of the long-term decline of Soviet global power and influence. The principal cause of the Cold War was the essential duopoly of power left by World War II, a duopoly that quite naturally resulted in the filling of a vacuum (Europe) that had once been the center of the international system and the control of which would have conferred great, and perhaps decisive, power advantage to its possessor. What gave the resulting conflict its particular intensity, of course, was the profound ideological gulf that separated the Soviet Union and the United States. But the root cause of the conflict was to be found in the structural circumstances that characterized the international system at the close of World War II.

Although not the principal cause, Europe has unquestionably been the principal symptom and stake of the conflict. For this reason, as long as a divided Europe persisted, the Cold War could have been expected to persist. Even if that division had earlier been brought to an end, although in circumstances other than those that in fact have marked its end, the Cold War could have been expected to persist in some form. For it is very difficult to imagine even a reformed, though still vibrant and powerful, Soviet Union's long resisting the temptation to gain ascendant influence over a Europe that, whatever the extent of its economic integration, continued to lack political unity. Barring a radical change in America's outlook and policy, this nation could be expected to counter such Soviet aspirations.

It is not so much, then, the end of Europe's division that signals an end of the Cold War as it is the circumstance that above all led to this end: the decline of Soviet power. Nor does it matter here that this decline did not occur overnight, that its root causes are profound, and that its consequences might well have been put off for a number of years and remained unacknowledged by a different Soviet leadership. What does matter is that these consequences were acknowledged and acted upon in Europe by the present leadership. Once drawn they have become all but irreversible in the Continent that gave rise to the Cold War.

In relinquishing its core interest in the world and in doing so without apparently obtaining in return anything even approximating a quid pro quo, the Soviet Union has signaled, as clearly as it is possible for a great power to do, that it is no longer prepared to play the role to which it has aspired since the 1950s and in pursuit of which the Soviet people have sacrificed so much. That this abandonment of interest has yet to extend clearly to the periphery of Soviet interests in the developing world cannot detract from the significance of what has occurred at the core. The pretensions to superpower status cannot be realized at the periphery, and this however tightly Moscow might—despite every rational expectation to the contrary—hang on there. For the Soviet Union, the key to superpower status must be found in Europe or not at all.

The conclusion that the Soviet bid for at least a true equality in superpower status has come to an end and that Soviet power and influence have now entered a protracted period of decline may seem at odds with the vast panoply of nuclear and conventional arms that remain at Moscow's disposal. These arms not only continue to represent perhaps the single greatest concentration of military power, they continue to be augmented by an effort the magnitude of which has yet to undergo substantial change despite the straitened condition of the Soviet economy. Even so, these considerations no more than qualify the declining prospects for Soviet power and influence, for unless this or a succeeding Soviet leadership were to somehow use the military power remaining at the disposal of the Soviet state in one last desperate throw of the dice, a gamble Moscow was unwilling to take in far more auspicious circumstances than obtain today, that power would prove a wasting asset. It would prove a wasting asset because the several elements that constitute the basis of military power and that assure its continued effectiveness are almost all in decline. Whereas only yesterday the political-psychological shadows cast by Soviet military power were still seen to be lengthening, today they are instead seen to be shortening, not only because of the striking erosion occurring in the domestic base and the virtual abandonment of an ideology that once provided the justification for an expansionist foreign policy, but because the significance of military power itself is increasingly seen to have changed.

What happened in 1989 could not but strengthen a growing uncertainty over the role of force in world politics, and above all in the relations of the developed powers. The end of Europe's division, the passing of bipolarity and of the conflict that arose from it, and the dramatic decline in the power and influence of the Soviet Union, are events that would normally be associated with the outcome of a great war. That they have instead unfolded peacefully is perhaps the most compelling evidence to date that the international system itself is in the process of profound transformation and that the principal feature of this transformation is the declining role of force.

II

A debate has already begun over the causes of the great events that have brought the postwar order to an end. The debate is significant, for it raises the issue of the lessons to be learned from the victorious outcome of the Cold War. The nature of those lessons will vary greatly, depending on the nature of the causes considered to have brought the Cold War to an end. If the end is seen to be largely the result of the ripening of contradictions that are internal to the Soviet regime, contradictions in which foreign policy played no more than a modest role, there is little to be learned save that in such conflicts as we have just experienced we must have a great deal of patience while entertaining little expectation of what we can do to alter the nature and disposition of the adversary.

On the face of it, this view appears implausible. It does so if only because of the known significance with which Soviet governments have invested their foreign policy aspirations and endeavors. For at least a generation the primacy of foreign policy has been almost axiomatic to Moscow. In the name of this primacy Soviet governments have undertaken and justified a massive and sustained arms buildup, one the momentum of which even today has yet to be decisively broken. They have done so at great cost and with the avowed objective of an expanding world role. Soviet governments not only have attached the highest priority to the pursuit of this role, they also have received a substantial measure of such domestic legitimacy as they have enjoyed.

The moderate success of Soviet foreign policy in the 1970s represented the regime's only visible achievement. Even that success, however, proved of limited duration. Within a very brief period in the early 1980s, the tide began to turn against Moscow. The principal result of the relentless accumulation of arms and the attempt to use these arms to press for advantage wherever the opportunity arose was to provoke a general reaction against the Soviet Union. In the United States a new administration began a massive rearmament effort with the intention of demonstrating to the Soviets that they could not expect to use their arms to gain further advantage. Moreover, the debate that arose in the United States, and particularly the harsh rhetoric adopted by the Reagan administration, conveyed the message that if Moscow persisted in its behavior of the late 1970s, it was in for a difficult time. To add persuasiveness to this message, the Reagan administration engaged in several demonstrative uses of force. A second Cold War was thus joined.

The results of this renewed conflict were almost everywhere apparent by the mid-1980s. In the principal theaters of contention the Soviet Union's expansionist thrust came to a halt. By the time of Mikhail Gorbachev's accession to power in 1985, the Soviet Union had very little to show for a decade and a half of effort to achieve if not a position of primacy, then at least one of true parity with the United States. The paucity of results could not on any reasonable calculus counterbalance or justify the costs. Politically, the principal result of the Soviet push for an improved position of power and influence was to alienate much of the world and to set the stage for the defeats of the early 1980s. Economically, the effort had imposed an enormous drain on what had already become a chronically ailing economy. The prospect had to be faced of falling further behind the economies of the West. That prospect could not be separated from a future in which the maintenance of a competitive, let alone a superior, arms position relative to that of the West would become increasingly difficult. Judged by the Soviet reaction, the Strategic Defense Initiative (SDI) drove this point home with a vengeance. Moscow had long before chosen to maintain a position of isolation and autarky. By the mid-1980s it could see, as never before, the consequences of this self-imposed exclusion from the global economy dominated by ever more prosperous Western societies—societies that could appear only as a standing reproach to a progressively impoverished Soviet society.

It was in these circumstances that the great conversion occurred. Doubtless, these circumstances do not account for the whole of this conversion. To maintain, however, that they had no more than a marginal effect in prompting the changes that have brought the Cold War to an end is implausible. They must instead be seen as having played a critical role in effecting these changes. If this is the case, the Western response to Soviet behavior was also critical in causing the conversion that brought the Cold War to an end.

What, then, are the lessons to be learned from the outcome of the long conflict? Three stand out. One is the vindication of a policy of largely moderate measures. Another is the narrowing uses of military power. Still another suggests that what we *were* was quite as important as what we *did* to bring about the desired outcome. Each of these lessons deserves brief consideration.

The Soviet Union was not brought to "new thinking" by a confrontationist United States. Despite the frequent charge of critics, the Reagan administration did not pursue a confrontationist policy toward the Soviet Union. It did not do so by the rearmament program it initiated on coming to office, a program that was also the most significant foreign policy action of the first Reagan administration. The intent of that program was not to put the adversary on notice that we were now after military superiority, but to demonstrate to Moscow that it could not expect to use its arms to gain further political advantage. As such, the measures taken to build up our arms were both reasonable and moderate. To be sure, the administration's early rhetoric often appeared to intimate a penchant for confrontation. But its rhetoric was seldom an accurate guide to its policy. This was true as well of the largely rhetorical change from the preceding administration's strategy of "countervailing" to the Reagan administration's declared strategy of "prevailing." Whatever the precise significance of the shift, and it was never quite clear, it did not portend the adoption of a confrontationist stance. Nor did the policies pursued in the central theaters of contention, in Europe and in the Persian Gulf, ever verge on the confrontational. Had they done so in Europe in the early 1980s, given the low state of the Alliance, the result might well have been to give the Soviet Union an important and unexpected victory and to breathe new life into an offensive that was already waning.

Rhetoric apart, the case for believing that the Soviet Union was brought to new thinking by a militant, if not a confrontationist, American response rests largely on the Reagan Doctrine and SDI. Whereas the former was presumably offensive in intent and designed to demonstrate the reversibility of communist revolutions in the Third World, the latter was charged with having as its objective to regain strategic superiority and, by so doing, to demonstrate to Moscow that it could not expect to be a serious technological competitor with this country.

That the Reagan Doctrine was significant in pushing the Soviet Union to the edge is very difficult to credit. However unlimited and indiscriminate in commitment the Reagan Doctrine appeared, qua doctrine, and whatever the potential it held out for a policy that might prove immodest in means and imprudent in calculation, this potential was not sought after in practice. The Reagan administration did not employ its doctrine to resurrect a policy of global containment. The policy-implementing doctrine was instead marked by caution and moderation. The means committed to policy scarcely betrayed the ideological determination that the rhetoric of the doctrine's architects suggested. The modest results of the policy reflected the modesty of the means committed. Ironically, in 1989, it was where the Reagan Doctrine was never applied or intended to be given application—Eastern Europe—that its promise was unexpectedly realized, and where it was initially applied—Central America—that its results remained remarkably meager.

SDI provides an apparent exception to this record, in that it was a measure the adversary may well have believed, and indeed gave every appearance of believing, was intended to recapture strategic superiority. Whether it was with this intention that President Reagan undertook his initiative is doubtful. Instead, the president's commitment to SDI was more likely motivated by his deep animus toward nuclear weapons and deterrent arrangements and his desire to restore a lost security. Even so, given the strategic relationship between the Soviet Union and the United States, the commitment to SDI appears an immoderate measure, though one that in all likelihood significantly contributed to Moscow's new thinking. Mr. Reagan's determination not to compromise it despite the change subsequently occurring in Soviet policy contrasts markedly with his willingness—a willingness that startled critics and supporters alike—otherwise to respond to this change.

These considerations on the whole vindicate a policy of moderate measures in bringing the Cold War to an end. At the same time, they point to the narrowing uses of military power, at any rate among the great states, for the concluding phase of the Cold War seemed to demonstrate with almost a startling clarity that if arms continue to serve a vital defense function in the relations of the great powers, this appears to be the only remaining function they serve. In looking back on the 1970s and early 1980s, it is clear that a remarkable event occurred. An "aspiring second" had made its grand bid, had seen that bid eventually being countered by its adversary, and had sensed the prospective decline of its power and influence in the world. It seems only reasonable to assume that by the outset of the 1980s, the Soviet leadership must have concluded that the Soviet state was on a declining, perhaps even a rapidly declining path relative to the United States (and, for that matter, to Western Europe as well). In the past, such perception has represented a moment of great danger to the stability of the international system. It did so in the years prior to World War I when German political opinion became increasingly persuaded that relative to Great Britain and Russia, German power and influence were on a declining path.

On this most recent occasion, however, a similar perception did not result in war. Nor did it result in the serious threat of war. The years of the early 1980s were marked by a Soviet Union that was notably circumspect in its behavior. Although many Western military experts considered the Soviet Union to enjoy at the time both a strategic and a conventional arms advantage over the Western Alliance, the period passed without any serious attempt by Moscow to use its presumed advantage for political gain, let alone for the purpose of provoking a showdown with the United States. The revival of the Cold War did not give rise to the intense crises that marked the classic Cold War of a generation earlier. By comparison, this second Cold War seemed little more than a pallid reflection of the first, as is apparent when one contrasts the earlier crises over Berlin or missiles in Cuba with the later Euromissile crisis.

What may account for the marked restraint shown by Moscow at a time not only when it was presumed to enjoy an advantage in arms, but when in all likelihood it could see that this advantage was almost bound to prove a wasting asset? One explanation, of course, is that Soviet leaders simply did not attach great importance to the pursuit of an expanding world role, that whether they achieved a position of true parity with the United States was not a critical matter to them. This being the case, there would have been no incentive to take the kinds of risks entailed by the attempt to substantially improve upon their position. But this response must then account for those considerations earlier invoked, and particularly for the enormous sacrifices made over a generation on behalf of a relentless arms buildup, sacrifices that made little sense unless intended to support a greater world role.

It seems far more plausible to assume instead that the Soviet leadership was intent on gaining a greater role and that to the pursuit of this objective it attached the highest priority. That it nevertheless acted with such marked caution and restraint even once it began to see its hopes fade may be attributed in part to the endemic leadership crisis experienced during the years in question. A prolonged season of aged and sick Soviet leaders introduced an element of restraint that otherwise might well have been absent. But if this is the principal explanation of our deliverance from peril—if a younger, more energetic, and more determined leadership would have reacted to the vision of imminent decline by pressing for a successful resolution of the contest—then there is indeed little to be learned from the outcome of the Cold War save that chance governs all.

Surely a more useful lesson may be learned from this outcome, one that bears out the view that in great power relations the utility of military power has dramatically narrowed. The offensive and expansionist purposes to which military power could once be put by one great power against another have been progressively deprived of credibility. The lesson may be illustrated by a comparison of two events in the Cold War, the Cuban missile crisis and the Euromissile crisis. Separated by a generation and attended by different circumstances in the military position of the parties relative to one another, both events conveyed the same lesson: the difficulty of using military power other than for defensive purposes. In both instances, the Soviet Union sought to use military power, however passively, in order to alter the political status quo to its advantage. In both instances, the attempt failed. That in the first instance the United States enjoyed a position of strategic superiority (and in the immediate theater, conventional superiority as well), while in the second it was perceived by many, including the administration then in office, to suffer both a strategic and a conventional arms disadvantage, made little apparent difference to the successful outcome of each. On both occasions, the side pressing for political advantage proved unwilling to run the risks that were entailed. In the later occasion, it was unwilling to run these risks despite the military advantage it allegedly—and, on the ground at least, almost assuredly—enjoyed and despite its awareness that this advantage was in all likelihood a wasting asset. This experience of a generation does not and cannot afford the kind of ironclad assurance we should like to have about the utility of military power today in the relations of the great powers. But in the contingent world of politics, it is perhaps the next best thing to such assurance.

If the two lessons drawn here respecting the outcome of the Cold War are apposite, the third and last lesson will scarcely provoke much dispute—namely, that what we were was as important as what we did in gaining the desired outcome. What we did established the conditions necessary for allowing what we were to work its eventual effects. In this, the original prophecy of George Kennan appears to have been largely fulfilled. In his 1947 "X" *Foreign Affairs* article, Kennan had asked what might happen to the Soviet regime if the Western world found the strength and resourcefulness to contain Soviet power for a sustained period of time. Kennan answered by holding out the strong possibility that Soviet power, "like the capitalist world of its conception, bears within it the seeds of its own decay, and that the sprouting of such seeds is well advanced." The United States, he declared, could influence and further this development to the degree it could "create among the peoples of the world generally the impression of a country which knows what it wants, which is coping successfully with the problems of its internal life and with the responsibilities of a World Power, and which has a spiritual vitality capable of holding its own among the major ideological currents of the time." Provided that we could fulfill this promise while at the same time containing Soviet encroachments, Kennan believed that we would "promote tendencies which must eventually find their outlet in either the break-up or the gradual mellowing of Soviet power."

In the more than four decades since the "X" article appeared, the conflict that Kennan addressed has followed a tortuous course. Its duration has been much greater than scarcely anyone, Kennan included, had anticipated. The strategy adopted for coping with Soviet power and ambition proved to be an invitation to controversy and a source of dissatisfaction. Criticized for being either too aggressive or too defensive, containment long ago lost what popularity it initially enjoyed. All but disavowed by administrations since the late 1960s, containment came to have only practitioners, though few defenders. The man who initially articulated the American strategy for the Cold War soon became disillusioned with the manner in which that strategy found expression in policy. In time, Kennan viewed American policy as having no better than a remote relationship, if that, to his original conception. Even more, he came to conclude after the early 1960s that the circumstances attending the Soviet-American competition bore no more than a remote relationship to the circumstances of the immediate postwar years.

Yet the strategy of containment survived the pervasive criticism regularly, and often justifiably, made of it, just as it survived the occasional excess to which it was carried in practice. The postwar order was an order inseparable from containment. With some exaggeration, it may even be seen as the order of containment. For all its defects, that order has been an impressive achievement. Not the least part of this achievement was that of enabling a prosperous Western civilization to work its eventual subversive effects on those who once so confidently proclaimed its imminent demise.

III

It is only in retrospect that we can appreciate the extent to which an entire worldview was conditioned by the great conflict that dominated the postwar period. Such was the pervasive influence of the Cold War on political vision that its effects often extended even to those who decried this influence. Ironically, the criticism regularly made of American foreign policy, that those responsible for its conduct saw virtually every issue through East-West lenses, was not infrequently true as well of those who made the charge. After more than four decades, the truths born of the Cold War have long ceased to have only a relative character.

The sudden end of the conflict has, not surprisingly, given rise to a situation for which it is difficult to find a real precedent. Arguments to the contrary notwithstanding, there does not appear to be an instructive modern historical parallel of a hegemonic conflict simply being terminated by the default in time of peace of one side. Yet this is what has happened in the present instance. By its actions in Central and Eastern Europe, and by the increasing signs that it is prepared as well to abandon positions held elsewhere, the Soviet Union has largely withdrawn from the conflict that had come to be seen as almost interminable. In doing so, it has transformed the landscape of world politics almost beyond recognition. It has turned believers in the political truths of the postwar world into skeptics who sense, even when unwilling to acknowledge as such, that they have lost their once secure moorings. Nor does the sense of being put adrift extend simply to surface political phenomena. It reaches as well to the deeper forces at work in world politics.

Any speculation over the character of world politics in the coming decade (and quite likely in the following decade as well) must begin by addressing the question of how far it is reasonable to expect Soviet power and influence to decline. A brief answer is very far indeed. While the Soviet Union will continue to pose a security threat of sorts, simply by virtue of its continued possession of formidable military power, the usefulness of this power has already markedly declined and may be expected to decline still further in the years ahead. Having abandoned its most important geostrategic asset outside the Soviet Union, Moscow has already weakened its military position relative to that of Western Europe to an extent that finds a meaningful parallel only in military defeat.

Yet it is not the growing debility of its external position that creates the principal doubt over the persistence of the threat that once confronted Western Europe, important as the weakening of its external position undoubtedly is, but the steady erosion of the Soviet domestic base. The many developments—political, economic, environmental, ethnic, ideological, and spiritual— that have marked this erosion need not be entered into here. Almost every conceivable pathology a society—and an empire— can suffer from has now made its appearance in the Soviet Union. That a society suffering from the several crises that now plague, and that will continue for years to plague, the Soviet Union may nevertheless somehow find the moral and material resources to pursue an assertive foreign policy seems altogether implausible. Instead, the expectation must be that the Soviet Union will increasingly follow a passive and contractive foreign policy and that it will do so whether the government of Mikhail Gorbachev remains in power or not. In either event, the retrenchment of Soviet power and influence in the world will in all likelihood continue. Indeed, this retrenchment may be expected to continue even should the Soviet domestic scene not worsen. But since that prospect is itself implausible, we may not unreasonably anticipate the time, which cannot be far removed, when the Soviet Union will for all practical purposes no longer actively function as a great power in the world.

If this estimate of the Soviet future is reasonably well founded, what are the consequences that may be expected to follow from it? The principal consequence will be evisceration of the Atlantic Alliance. When alliances lose their common adversary, their normal fate is to break up. If this is not to be the fate of the Western Alliance, the principal foundation of the postwar order, either the persistence of the old adversary and the threat it held out or a new adversary must be assumed. The former assumption, though, can no longer be realistically made, while the latter assumption presupposes a new world of multipolarity in which the glue holding the Alliance together is the threat of protectionism and the eventual collapse of the international economy.

That a multipolar order will succeed the now passing bipolar order is clear. That the emerging multipolarity will differ markedly from the multipolarity of the 1970s and 1980s is equally clear. Whereas the multipolarity of yesterday took on meaning within the broader context of a persisting bipolarity, the multipolarity of tomorrow will not do so. Yesterday, Germany and Japan were great powers when judged by their economic productivity, their trade balances, and their financial surpluses; they were scarcely such when judged by their continued security dependence on the United States. Tomorrow, these states will be great powers not only in the sense that they already have been such for some time; they will be great powers as well in that the political impact of their economic power will no longer be qualified by a security dependence that imposes substantial constraints on their freedom of action in foreign policy.

In the case of Germany, this change is already apparent. In time, it is bound to appear yet more striking. The sudden recession of Soviet power has effected a revolution in the position of the Federal Republic and of the soon to be unified state of Germany. What formerly constrained West Germany as no other major state in the postwar order was constrained is now gone. For almost half a century, the threat of Soviet military might conditioned, as did no other factor or combination of factors, West Germany's behavior. It is the virtual disappearance of this threat that has suddenly given rise once again to the "German problem." In upsetting, if not simply destroying altogether, the postwar balance of power that had obtained for so long in Europe, the Soviet Union liberated the country that was the principal reason for, and object of, that balance. To be sure, the German problem has arisen as well because a reunited Germany is seen to constitute a striking increase in size and power over the Federal Republic. But of far greater importance is the realization that a unified Germany will be largely free of the constraints that formerly bound a divided Germany. And while a new Germany may have every reason to behave with moderation and circumspection, the means of constraining it to do so are no longer apparent.

The singularity of Germany's transformed position is that it holds out the prospect not only of a greatly enhanced freedom of action but of a freedom to pursue an expansionist foreign policy in the name of the essential principles of legitimacy on which the postwar order has been based. This is clear enough in the case of a policy of reunification, a policy that would merely fulfill the decades-long Western commitment to German self-determination. It is equally true, however, in the case of a policy that is likely to lead to German economic preponderance over the states of Central and Eastern Europe. The instruments for achieving such preponderance would be those that have long been considered entirely legitimate. They would presumably be employed in pursuit of an end—economic growth and development—avidly sought after by these states. To the objection that the successful pursuit of this end by Germany would result in the marked extension of German power and influence, the position may be and is taken that in the present international system, such extension does not carry the implications and entail the consequences it once did. Unless German economic preponderance in Eastern Europe threatens to take a military expression, the prevailing view seems to be, it is to be considered desirable. And since the possibility that it would again take a military expression appears virtually excluded, the conclusion is commonly drawn that there is no problem that needs to be addressed. Indeed, those who insist there is a problem, and that it arises simply from Germany's disproportionate economic power, are themselves often seen to harbor less-than-creditable motives. This is why West German Chancellor Helmut Kohl can declare: "There is a difference between understandable misgivings and fears and what is disguised as fear but is really economic jealousy." But if those holding the latter view must be discredited, those holding the former view must be educated and shown that, the issue of borders apart, there are in fact no "understandable misgivings and fears," and that talk to the contrary comes from those who are, in Kohl's words, "deliberately slandering the Germans."[1]

A rather more detached view nevertheless leads to much the same conclusion that these misgivings and fears over German power and influence are largely groundless. It is roughly this: Those who worry about the danger of a new disequilibrium in Europe do so because they continue to think of Europe in terms of the old politics with its obsession with the balancing of power.

But the old politics presupposed a reliance in the last resort on forcible methods for achieving the ends of statecraft. Once that presupposition is no longer relevant, as it presumably will not be relevant in the emerging international order, the concern about equilibrium and the careful balancing of power also appears irrelevant.

There is no easy response to this view, once the essential premise that underlies it is accepted. And that premise does appear increasingly persuasive. The forcible methods that traditionally defined and dominated European politics do indeed seem relegated to the past, now that the last great representative of these methods has apparently abandoned them. It is, after all, the Soviet government that has repeatedly declared that it is time to begin "the gradual dismantling of the outdated model of the European balance of forces"[2] and that has moved dramatically to make good on its words. This development cannot but have a crucial bearing on the judgment made of Germany's expanding economic, and political, role. For if that role holds out the prospect, as many contend, of altering the balance of power in Europe, the balance it alters is presumably a new one—a balance that is ultimately judged in economic terms rather than, as it once was, in economic and military terms.

Nor is this all. A unified Germany, no longer menaced by Soviet military might and confident in its role as Europe's most powerful economy, would have no reason to jeopardize a position from which growing power and influence over Central and Eastern Europe seem all but inevitable by attempting to give this position a military dimension as well. It may be argued that this power and influence no longer hold out quite the same attractions that great powers and their statesmen once found so difficult to resist, but then neither do they hold out the old risks. A German push for the revision of frontiers or for the acquisition of nuclear weapons would surely revive the specter of these risks and by so doing provoke once again a hostile coalition against it. Why should Germany be tempted to take these paths, given all of the advantages of its present situation?

Thus the new reality in Europe is not the emergence only of a powerful German state, but of one that, so long as it eschews the old and disastrous ways, is likely to have few constraints placed on its freedom of action. Moreover, the commitment to the values of liberal democracy apart, a united Germany has every reason to eschew the old ways, for the new ways hold out the promise of achieving in substantial measure the perennial ends of statecraft. From this perspective, Germany has nothing to gain, though much to lose, by balking at the acceptance either of restrictions on arms, both conventional and nuclear, or of guarantees of now firmly sanctioned postwar borders.

Although Germany is free of the constraints of a bipolar world, the consequences of this freedom continue to be obscured. The principal consequence is that a unified Germany may now choose whether to pursue its destiny within or outside the framework of the Atlantic Alliance. Neither the Soviet Union nor, for that matter, the major Western states are in a position to determine the nature of that choice. Does the nature of that choice matter a great deal? The prevailing view is that it does. A new German state, the now familiar argument runs, must be firmly anchored to the West through membership in the Alliance; any other arrangement incurs the risk of a resurgence of aggressive German behavior. Above all, it is considered desirable that Germany retain its close ties to the United States, something that is best ensured by the retention of some American forces in the territory of what was once West Germany.

The difficulty with this view is that it not only addresses a past that is very unlikely to recur, it also addresses a future with the means of the past. The prospect is not a Germany bent on military aggression but a Germany bent on economic expansion. This prospect cannot be avoided, or contained, by Germany's continued membership in the Atlantic Alliance. Nor can it be contained by a continued American military presence in Germany. These arrangements may provide a measure of psychological reassurance to Germany's neighbors; even so, such reassurance must be a classic instance of faute de mieux and in time will surely be so seen. The simple though apparently unpalatable truth is that the Alliance ties, with or without American forces, can no longer be expected to serve the functions they once did. Nor can they be expected to elicit the support from German governments they once did. Instead, the prospect must be faced that in time, what plainly resembles a special dispensation for Germany will generate an increasing measure of resentment on the part of those who have long ceased to accept the burdens inherited from a receding past.

IV

In comparison with the change effected in Germany by the end of the Cold War, that in the position of Japan appears much less dramatic. In Europe, the balance of power that dominated the Continent since the late 1940s has been destroyed; in Asia, the balance that has existed since the 1960s—a balance that has comprised the United States, the Soviet Union, Japan, and China—has only been altered, and with effects that are not yet apparent. In Asia, there has not been to date an abandonment of interest and a recession of military power by the Soviet Union that finds a real parallel with the process now occurring in Europe. It may nevertheless be argued that sooner or later, Moscow will initiate a comparable process in Asia and that it will do so with much the same motivation that has moved it in Europe—the need to obtain access to capital and technology. The role that Germany may play for the Soviet Union in the West, Japan may play for it in the East. This being the case, Moscow has every reason to reassure Japan about its basic security and to be forthcoming about particular issues in dispute, above all, the issue of the Northern Territories. This it seems reasonable to expect the Soviet government to do.

The point remains that the end of bipolarity cannot have an effect on Japan that is comparable to its effect on Germany. Just as the threat of Soviet military power never weighed as heavily on Japan as it did on West Germany, the operation of the balance in Asia never constrained Japan's freedom of action as the balance in Europe constrained the Federal Republic. For the same reason, the end of the Cold War does not appear to present the opportunities for the expansion of influence and power in Asia to Japan that it does in Europe to Germany. The decline of Soviet power cannot be expected to alter dramatically Japan's prospects for achieving greater power and influence in Asia. While that power and influence have grown markedly in the past decade and will doubtless continue to grow, they do not hold out the same opportunity that Central and Eastern Europe hold out for Germany. The Japanese remain suspect in Asia to a degree the Germans do not in Europe. In contrast with the Germans, the Japanese have made little effort to come to terms with their past. A persisting cultural isolation from the rest of Asia also provides a striking contrast with the cultural affinity of Germany and Eastern Europe. Were it not for Japan's close postwar relationship with the United States, which has often shielded it from criticism in Asia, the consequences of these factors would be yet more apparent. Even so, their net effect is to limit the opportunities for Japan to use its economic power in Asia to establish a leadership and to exercise an influence that now appears open to Germany in Europe.

Whereas the German problem has arisen because of the persuasion that a unified Germany will be not only a more powerful state than the Federal Republic but one that is free of the constraints that formerly bound a divided Germany, the "Japanese problem" has arisen in the first place because of the conviction that Japan's international economic power has already become disproportionately great and promises—or threatens—to become still greater. This is why discussions of the Japanese problem are almost always prefaced by a now familiar recitation of statistics on trade and financial surpluses, on the growth of Japanese foreign investment, on the prospects of continued growth of the Japanese economy and, in turn, of what that projected growth portends for yet greater economic power in the world. To be sure, critics of Japan's ever increasing power in the international economy do not center their criticism on the fact of growth per se. It is the methods by which Japan has presumably achieved its present position, above all its trade practices, that form the core of their criticism. Yet it is by no means apparent that if Japan were to abandon many of these practices, the Japanese problem would disappear. Provided that Japan nevertheless retained a substantial measure of its competitive edge and therefore its favorable trading position, the likelihood is that the Japanese problem would persist and that critics would give even greater attention than they do today to the need for pervasive change in Japan's domestic economy and polity—change that would have as its general objective the conversion of a nation of producers (and savers) into a nation of consumers. For the real issue that forms the root of the matter, the disproportionate growth in Japan's economic power, would remain.

It has become a commonplace to observe that the transfer of wealth and economic power attendant on Japan's growth is one of the greatest, if not the greatest, that has occurred in time of peace. In marked contrast with earlier and less spectacular transfers, the political consequences of the present shift remain in large measure conjectural. That Japan will enjoy a greater measure of influence in international economic and financial institutions is apparent. What is not apparent are the more profound dimensions of Tokyo's economic and financial ascendancy. To date, Japan has yet to make a serious and determined effort to convert its economic and financial power into substantial political influence. Its reticence in this, however, cannot be expected to go on indefinitely.

The end of the Cold War and of a bipolar world will almost surely prompt Japan to take a more active political role in the international system. Japan will do so if only for the reason that the risks and liabilities attending a greater assertiveness will have diminished and will be seen to have diminished. The constraints on policy that, in the final reckoning, once had to be accepted because of a security dependence will now be increasingly called into question. With the expected change in the Soviet-Japanese relationship, the threat to Japan's physical security must decline almost to a vanishing point. Even if the recession of Soviet power in Asia were to occasion a greater Chinese assertiveness along its borders, which seems unlikely, this would not heighten Japan's physical insecurity. What might appear to do so would be the prospect of an alliance in all but name between the United States and China that had the containment of Japan as its principal objective. But such an alliance, even if it surmounted the obvious ideological barriers in its way, would still not respond to the interests of either party. While it could scarcely serve to contain

Japan's economic power, its predictably traumatic effect on Tokyo could possibly move Japan to seriously consider the need for large-scale rearmament, even perhaps including the acquisition of nuclear arms.

Short of the limiting situation that a Washington-Beijing alliance might well be seen to represent, Japan has no vital interest that would be served by a large-scale rearmament. Its principal foreign policy interests are, and seem likely to remain, those of retaining access to the raw materials it needs and access to foreign markets. Even for the former interest, let alone for the latter, a large military force appears increasingly irrelevant. Although Japan may indeed face a threat of access to raw materials, particularly oil, it is difficult to see how any expansion of Japanese military power might respond to this. The expansion of Japanese power and influence in Asia and in the world does not depend upon Japan's becoming a great military power. If anything, the acquisition of such power would almost certainly prove to be far more a liability than an asset, for it would at once raise fears that have never been stilled. These fears would arise in Asia even if Japan were to have a plausible reason for again becoming an independent military power by virtue of the (altogether unlikely) withdrawal of the American security guarantee.

The same question raised with respect to Germany, then, seems equally appropriate to raise with respect to Japan. Why should Japan be tempted to follow the old ways, or even to appear to do so, given the advantages of its present situation? If those advantages do not appear quite as striking in Japan's case as they do in Germany's, they are still considerable. To lead in the growing economic integration of East Asia is no small matter, and this even if Japanese leadership is looked upon by those led with marked reserve. The criticism persists that Japan has yet to play the political role in the world that is both its right and its duty, and that this continued unwillingness or inability betrays a narrow self-centeredness. In an age when the critical political issues are increasingly economic in nature, this criticism is easily overdone. Japan already plays a political role, even if that role is not the conventional one. And with the end of the Cold War, a more conventional role as well is bound to emerge.

In the new order of multipolarity, neither Japan nor Germany can be expected to have the same relationship with the United States that it had during the Cold War. What will prevent the present relationships from falling apart? Certainly they will not lack reason for doing so. In the emerging order, threats to security will be increasingly defined in economic terms. This being so, threats to security will be implicit simply in the disparate and conflicting economic interests and policies of the major powers. If the persistence of the old adversary and the threat it once held out can no longer be counted on to provide the glue holding the Western Alliance together, may a new threat be substituted? Can the threat of protectionism and the eventual collapse of the present international economy do for the multipolar world that is emerging what the threat of Soviet arms once did for the bipolar world that is vanishing?

There is no disagreement over the nature of the consequences likely to follow from a breakdown of the global economy. Were the growth that this economy fueled suddenly to cease, let alone to contract, the very foundations of the present international order would be endangered. For that order has increasingly come to rest, as never before, on the functioning of a global market that provides the indispensable means for the growth of national economies. The breakdown of that order would at once jeopardize in a fundamental way the political relationships of the major developed powers while opening as well the prospect of a degree of domestic instability these states have not experienced in the postwar era. Can the threat thus held out substitute for the old threat in ensuring the cooperative policies and measures needed to sustain the future international order?

A confident response requires a faith in the beneficent working of interdependence in a world that will continue to be dominated by the right of self-help that states have always laid claim to by virtue of their sovereignty and independence. That the right of self-help may be effectively asserted in the future by ever greater entities—that is, by the three great blocs many expect to form in the years ahead—does not hold out the promise that its effects will somehow prove benign. The possible hazards attending interdependence in a system of sovereign political entities were momentarily raised during the oil crisis of the 1970s and the far-reaching debate it provoked over the necessity and desirability of effecting a more equitable distribution of the world's wealth. In the context of what was then widely seen as a dangerous conflict emerging between the developed and rich states of the North and the developing and poor states of the South, it became clearer than ever that interdependence itself is not constitutive of order and, although creating the need for greater order, provides no assurance this need will be met. Interdependence creates the need for greater order because it is as much a source of conflict as of consensus. While promoting insecurity and competition, it does not itself provide the means for assuaging insecurity and setting bounds to competition. Even if interdependence is beneficial to all parties, its benefits may vary considerably. The perception of marked disparities in benefits may well provide a potent source of conflict.

There are, of course, large differences between the interdependence of North-South relationships and the interdependence of the developed great powers. In the economic realm, the inequality that still marks North-South relationships, and that still can give rise to deep resentment, finds no real counterpart in the relations between this country and Japan and Germany. In the case of Washington, Tokyo, and Bonn, a tradition of working together, as well as a common outlook on many issues of trade and finance, also must enhance the prospects for dealing with the dilemmas of interdependence in the post–Cold War world. Even so, the interdependence of the future is bound to prove quite different from the interdependence of the past, which, after all, gave rise to its share of conflicts and, in the case of trade relationships between Japan and the United States, to a serious and persisting conflict. Given the recession of the Soviet threat, it is not unlikely that the interdependence of the future will be marked less by consensus and more by conflict, for the essential compact that held for roughly four decades between the protector and the protected will no longer hold. Whereas in the past, significant economic differences arising between the United States and its major allies were unavoidably conditioned in the last resort by the security protection this country extended, this will no longer be true.

The interdependence of the emerging order is likely to be characterized not only by more economic conflict among its major actors but by conflict that will not be readily resolved. Conflict will not be readily resolved if only for the reason that the system will no longer have an apparent hegemon. It may be argued that in the economic sphere it has not had a dominant power for some time. Yet the continued security dependence of Germany and Japan undoubtedly served to compensate for the more modest economic position of the United States in recent years. In a radically altered security environment, this will no longer be the case and the consequences of the change in the nature of the American position may soon be laid bare. From an order that, despite all qualifications, had an acknowledged leader, the outlook is for an order that has no real leader but only partners. Experience indicates that this shift is nearly always critical. While a hegemonic power, if determined to do so, can impose a solution on the conflicts arising from interdependence, partners can only disagree.

The fate of interdependence in a world that is no longer dominated by the Cold War and that no longer has a hegemonic power necessarily remains speculative. What appears less uncertain is the nature of power in this world. The decline of military power, by now reasonably apparent, need not be compensated by the corresponding rise in the utility of economic power. Power is not a constant in human history. It may well be that in the international system of tomorrow, power itself will be progressively at a discount and that what military power can no longer do, economic power also will be unable to accomplish. Even so, the power that will remain is likely to be increasingly economic in character and take the form largely of financial and trade surpluses. In measuring power, the wealth of nations will no longer have the significance it once had, in that a nation's power will no longer be roughly proportionate to its collective wealth. Instead, it is the capital and goods at a nation's disposal to employ abroad that must increasingly form the yardstick of power. By this measurement, the power of Japan and Germany will be considerable. By the same measurement, the power of the United States will be relatively modest.

Thus, the ironic outcome of the past half-century is that at the moment of victory, our power and influence are diminished. If the end of the Cold War marked the virtual disappearance of the Soviet Union as a great power, certainly as a great power in Europe, it also marked a visible decline in America's role. That decline, the consequence of the adversary's sudden disappearance and America's peculiar economic position, was only too apparent during 1989 in the unfolding European drama.

V

It is all but inevitable that the end of the Cold War will give rise to yet another debate over American foreign policy. The signs of such debate are already apparent in the emergent dialogue between those who believe that we should once again play a much more modest role in the world and those who believe that America's post–World War II role must be held up as the model for the future. To date, it is the supporters of continuity who clearly appear to enjoy a position of advantage. But this is to be accounted for in part by the persisting view that their position responds, after all, to the natural order of things. Once it becomes clear that this order, the postwar dispensation, is no more and that we now live in a very different world, the advantage that is conferred by the force of the habitual will erode. The advocates of change will then have their day.

The case for having the United States play a far more modest role in the post–Cold War world is rooted in the history of the past 50 years and the vast changes that have occurred during this period. America abandoned a policy of isolation and intervened in World War II because a fascist victory would have threatened the nation's physical security and material well-being. This threat apart, a fascist victory also held out the prospect of a world in which America's political and economic frontiers would have to become coterminous with its territorial frontiers, a world in which societies that shared our institutions and values might very possibly disappear—in sum, a world in which the

American example and American influence would become irrelevant. In such a world, it was believed, America would find it difficult, and perhaps impossible, to realize its promise, since a hostile world from which America was shut out would inevitably affect the integrity of the nation's institutions and the quality of its domestic life. The issues of physical security and economic well-being apart, it was to prevent this prospect from materializing that the United States abandoned its interwar isolationism and intervened in World War II.

It was for roughly the same reasons that, in the years following the war, this country adopted a policy of containing Soviet power. The initial measures of containment, the Marshall Plan and the Atlantic Alliance, formally expressed and thereby made unmistakable the vital American interest in preserving the security and independence of the nations of Western Europe. In the context of Soviet-American rivalry, they formed a clear acknowledgment that the domination of Western Europe by the Soviet Union might well shift the balance of power decisively against the United States and that, at the very least, such domination would result in a security problem that would severely strain the nation's resources and jeopardize its institutions.

Although the circumstances of the late 1940s made the application of containment roughly identical with a conventional balance of power policy, from the outset containment also expressed an interest that went beyond security, narrowly conceived. From the outset, a conventional security interest was joined with a broader interest in preserving and extending the institutions of freedom. The Truman Doctrine expressed these two aspects of containment, that of organizing power and that of vindicating purpose. In its refusal to distinguish clearly between the two aspects, the Truman Doctrine foreshadowed the subsequent history of containment and the refusal to distinguish clearly between the interest in securing a balance of power and the interest in extending freedom. That refusal, in turn, has reflected the conviction, deeply rooted in the American consciousness, that the successful pursuit of the American purpose is, in the long term, the only truly reliable method of achieving both peace and security.

The outcome of the Cold War has at last put an end to the circumstances that required America's intervention, first in a global conflict and then in a protracted contest that came to encompass most of the world. In the 50 years that has elapsed since the abandonment of isolation, the structure of American security, both in its narrower and in its broader dimensions, has changed radically. It has changed radically by virtue of the military defeat (or, in the case of the Soviet Union, the functional equivalent of military defeat) of those powers that threatened the nation's physical security. And it has changed radically by virtue of the progressive triumph of those institutions and values the extension of which has long formed the American purpose—a purpose that has in turn been equated with the nation's greater-than-physical security. The prospect of a world in which the American example and the influence of American institutions and values might decline, let alone become irrelevant, has never seemed more remote.

It is quite true that as a result of nuclear-missile weapons, the United States is physically vulnerable today in a way it was not vulnerable in the interwar period. But this ultimate vulnerability cannot be significantly reduced—let alone removed—by the attempt to retain our postwar role. Against the possibility of attack by nuclear-missile weapons, a possibility that will exist as long as nuclear weapons exist, our present alliances afford little, if any, protection. In any event, that possibility must be considered virtually negligible today not only because our once great adversary no longer lays claim to interests and harbors ambitions that could lead to situations in which nuclear weapons might be threatened, but also because experience has shown how limited the utility of these weapons is save for defensive purposes.

These are the general considerations in support of having the United States play a far more modest world role in the post–Cold War period. The conclusions they suggest are apparent. The reasons that prompted this country to play the great role it did for half a century are no longer valid. A new world has come into being, one in which America's security in both its narrower and its broader dimensions is no longer at serious risk. This being the case, it must be asked, why should this country persist in efforts that respond to circumstances now past? Why should it continue to maintain substantial forces in Europe and in the western Pacific? Whose interests are served by its doing so?

There are, of course, the constraints imposed by a period of transition. But these constraints apart, the case for maintaining a continuity of role rests essentially on the propositions that the world will have a continuing need for a power able to maintain peace and stability and that only this country can fill that need. The United States must preserve a peace that remains fragile. It must do so because it is not only the world's greatest power but the most trusted one. The argument for preserving a continuity of role thus increasingly resembles today the rationale for collective security rather than for alliances. The peacekeeping role we are now urged to pursue is one that is directed no longer against a particular state or states, but against disturbers of the peace regardless of their identity. Accordingly, the interests that are served by accepting this peacekeeping role are those of the international community as a whole.

Although the principal sources of instability are usually described in general terms, it is apparent that they are now considered to be our major postwar allies, Germany and Japan. The need of retaining a substantial American military presence in Europe and in Asia is primarily to reassure the neighbors of these states. To reassure them against what, however? If the answer is to reassure them against the threat of military expansion, the political reality will be that of tacit alliances between the United States and the neighbors of Germany and Japan that have as their object the containment of these two states. In time, such arrangements are bound to generate resentment on the part of those who have been made the objects of these alliances—and this despite their initial approval and even support of them—for the continued presence of American forces will be a constant reminder to both states that they remain less than trusted by others.

On the other hand, if the purpose of maintaining a substantial American presence in Europe and Asia is to safeguard against an economic preponderance that in time may be transformed into political influence as well, the means for doing so seem quite inadequate to the end. There is no apparent way by which an American military presence, whatever its size, can contain the expansion of German and Japanese economic power. In time, this is bound to become clear to those who may have initially experienced a measure of reassurance from the continuation of this presence. When it does, the American presence may retrospectively be viewed not as having impeded but as having facilitated an expansion the consequences of which are viewed with increasing apprehension and even resentment by those who have come to believe they were lulled into a false sense of security.

At the heart of the position favoring a continuity of role is, more often than not, the unspoken assumption that even though the Cold War may have come to an end, all else will go on largely as before. We will remain the leader even though we can no longer lead quite in the manner of yesterday. Our major allies will continue to need us even though we are no longer needed quite as much as before. The satisfactions of our position will persist even though they may no longer be quite as apparent as they once were. Unfortunately, we are due for a rude awakening. The leadership role that persisted as long as the Cold War persisted is very unlikely to survive the end of that conflict. It is unlikely to do so simply because we will not be needed as before. And although the change in role will almost at once be apparent in the case of Germany, it will in a less dramatic manner eventually become apparent in the case of Japan as well.

In principle, it is, of course, possible that this country might retain a leadership role though the functions and frustrations of that role change. This is evidently what many supporters of continuity have in mind. With the ending of the Cold War, the United States will presumably change from leader of an alliance formed to counter the threat of Soviet power to leader of a community of nations that needs the American presence in order to maintain a still fragile peace and stability. In practice, this change in function from that of defending freedom to that of ensuring order is apt to prove critical. Not only is the latter function a considerably more complicated one, it is also a much less appealing one. Certainly it must prove far less appealing to this nation. The American purpose was never seen to imply that we should play the role of policeman to the world. It did imply that we might one day have to free the world, though not to police it. One polices the world because men and nations are recalcitrant, because they often have deeply conflicting aspirations, and because they are usually influenced more by precept than by example—even the best of examples. These are the convictions of a traditional outlook on statecraft; they are not the convictions that have moved this nation.

Even if the neutral role of policeman were more congenial to this nation, the question that it holds out for us would insistently arise. It must not be assumed that the rewards for being policeman to the world will be the same as were the rewards for being defender of the free world. They will not be the same. The deference, such as it was, shown in the past to American interests and wishes is unlikely to be shown in the future, since the principal incentive for according such deference will no longer be apparent. In the past, the security America provided its allies was security against a quite specific threat—a threat, moreover, that the protected could not begin to counter effectively with their own unaided resources. In the future, this will no longer be the case. The function of preserving order may, of course, be considered a security-conferring function as well, but it is not one that is directed against a particular party. Instead, it is directed against a general threat, a threat to peace and stability, regardless of the identity of the party responsible for the threat. This being so, the utility of America to its major Cold War allies will of necessity become ambiguous in the new dispensation. Circumstances may even arise in which the policeman's role will require that we place ourselves in opposition to our former allies.

At best, then, the expectation must be that the American role will be viewed in the future with more diffidence by others than it was in the past. It will be exercised on behalf of those who will find much less need for it than they once did. Even when its exercise appears clearly to respond to need—for example, in the event of a renewed threat of access to the oil of the Persian Gulf— it may elicit little cooperation from those we regard as among the principal beneficiaries. These states will constitute our principal trading partners, states with which we may then, as now, run a deficit. With the Cold War a receding memory, but with financial stringency a persisting reality, how long can we be expected to maintain a role that, while no longer required for our security, is viewed by others with the mixture of ingratitude and resentment that has always been the lot of the policeman?

This, in brief, is the case for why the United States should play a much more modest role in the post–Cold War world. Persuasive though this case is in many respects, doubt must nevertheless persist that it foreshadows the future. Great powers are not in the habit of voluntarily relinquishing the role to which they have become accustomed, and this despite the fact that the circumstances initially prompting the assumption of the role have changed. It may be argued that when the attainment of great power was relatively easy, as it was for this country, the relinquishing of power should prove correspondingly easy, and particularly so given America's historic traditions. But against this view of easy come, easy go, must be set the consideration that the American experience in world leadership has been, on the whole, a remarkably successful one. In statecraft, as elsewhere, success normally leads not to withdrawal but to reengagement.

Still more important than these considerations, it would seem, is the process whereby over time, a role becomes invested with a force and sentiment that render it increasingly invulnerable to criticism and change. Then, too, there is seldom a lack of plausible justification for maintaining a role that has come to be seen as part of the accepted order of things and that has been attended by success. America's postwar role has been so important and pervasive, it is difficult to imagine a world in which that role is substantially diminished. At the same time, it is not difficult for many to imagine the dangers a marked diminution of the American presence would bring in its wake. Although the threat of Soviet arms has receded, the threat of global instability has taken its place. In Europe and, even more, in Asia, this threat of renewed competitions in arms and of heightened tensions can supposedly be kept down only by maintaining the American commitment and presence.

This justification for preserving a continuity of role cannot be effectively turned aside by pointing out that it is quite likely mistaken in its assumptions about the role of force in the international system now emerging, just as it is quite likely mistaken in its assumptions about the principal threat to global stability in the period ahead. Even if it can be shown that these assumptions are probably misplaced, and that the emerging system will be both peaceful and stable, and almost surely in the mutual relations of the great powers, events might always turn out otherwise. There is no way of *knowing*, for example, what the effect would be of withdrawing American forces from Japan. That such withdrawal would lead Japan's neighbors to arm themselves as they have not done in the postwar period and that this response would in turn prompt Japan to new arms efforts seems unlikely. Yet this result cannot simply be precluded. It is even possible that a withdrawal of American forces might in time cause Japan to seriously consider acquiring nuclear arms, and this despite America's continued willingness to guarantee Japan's security.

These considerations reflect the innate caution and conservatism that normally mark the conduct of foreign policy. What may well give them a special persuasiveness is the prospect that the substance of role may be maintained, though at markedly diminished costs. Whether calculated in blood or in treasure, this prospect does appear increasingly likely. To the extent that force is actively employed as a means of policy, the expectation must be that it will be limited to demonstrative uses (Grenada, Libya, Panama, etc.). In time, limitations on the use of military power will be reflected in the size of the nation's military forces. Even if the ancient game itself has not at last changed, it holds out the promise today of having moderated to a degree altogether unexpected only yesterday. This moderation may prove to be the essential condition for maintaining a role that was taken on for reasons and in circumstances that are now a matter of the past.

NOTES

1. As quoted in Alan Riding, "Bonn Balks at Soviet Plea for Vote on German Unity," *The New York Times,* February 4, 1990, p. 22.
2. John Iams, "Kremlin Ready to Cut Troops Without East-West Arms Pact," *The Washington Post,* February 12, 1990, p. A13, 17.

Reconsiderations

THE NAME OF THE GAME

Susan Strange

Imagine a game of poker. It is being played for money. Next night, it is strip poker, played for quite different stakes. The card game apparently has not changed, but the name of the game has.

Something like that happened to international relations in the course of the 1980s. The name of the competitive game between states used to be control of territory. Other states had to be "contained." Buffer zones were needed for protection. Dividing "curtains" hung over big rivers like the Oder and Neisse, or the Yalu in Korea, separating territory on the right bank from territory on the left. Behind each curtain, there were missile bases, guns, and airfields to deter incursions into the territory.

Now the name of the game is world market shares. Export competitiveness is what states need to keep national income rising. And rising national income is what governments need to keep from being thrown out. In order to stay in power, and maintain their authority, governments have to concede to popular demand for participation, or at least for peoples' interests to be taken into account. Social justice involves welfare spending by the state, and that costs money. Rising gross national product, which automatically increases the tax harvest, is the one way government can pay for welfare without raising the level of taxation. Everywhere, from Mexico to the Transkei, from Kiev to Calcutta, people expect governments to see that they get a better standard of living next year than they got last year, and that their voice is more loudly heard in the corridors of power.

In short, more people are demanding more as the price of their acquiescence to hierarchies of power. They want more say and more goods in return for acknowledging the legitimacy of their masters. When rulers first emerged in ancient times, people asked only some security from random violence. To pay the costs of protection, rulers needed land to tax and authority over the farmers creating wealth from the land. So chiefs, lords, kings, and emperors—even popes—coveted land and sought to enlarge their territory. With first the English revolution under Cromwell and then the French Revolution, people began to demand a say in government and the abolition or restriction of absolute rule. Enter the nation-state, self-determination, and the democratic franchise. Territory then became primarily where "our" people lived, not something valuable in itself as a source of either wealth or military manpower. Fighting over it could be justified only in terms of the balance of costs and risks to the people. Thus, by the 1980s, the whole world outside the Middle East saw the futile Iraq-Iran war as a tragic anachronism. Hardly less anachronistic in terms of the mismatch of means and ends, as perceived by the bystanders, was the Falklands war or the U.S. invasion of Panama. Only where the retreat of an empire has left behind a mismatch between people who live on territory and a community that feels emotionally responsible for them—as Turks feel responsible for Turkish Cypriots—are there still places where it looks as though the old game of competition for territory is still played. But it is not really the same game. The reason for the obsolescence of major war, as historian John Mueller has argued, is not just that people fear the catastrophe of nuclear war. It is that the *idea* is dead, or dying.[1]

Elsewhere, the loss of appetite for the control of territory has been a striking feature of recent years. Why did the Soviet Union give up Afghanistan? Why did South Africa give up its claim to Namibia? Why does communal trouble in Kashmir cause so much less apprehension about an Indo-Pakistan war than it would have in the 1940s? Why did the Czechs feel so confident that the Soviet tanks would not be used as they were in 1968? Not so long ago, the postwar retreat from empire by the British, the Dutch, the French, the Belgians, seemed to some Americans the proof of Europe's decadence, or else, perhaps, an enforced concession to pressures from the United States. Now, in hindsight, perhaps the Europeans were just showing a prescient recognition of the changing name of the game, forced on them by a quite exceptional disparity between the benefits of territory and the economic and political costs of holding on to it.

Not since the fifteenth century—or if you count Amsterdam as well as Florence and Venice, not since the seventeenth—has preeminence in the production of wealth been claimed by cities as well as territorial states. Yet the inclusion of Singapore and Hong Kong among the "Asian tigers" underlines the growing irrelevance of territory as the basis of wealth and power. Forced by their very lack of territory to go full-tilt for export competitiveness, Singapore and Hong Kong have recognized the new name of the game more quickly than have the United States, the Soviet Union, China, and India, whose big domestic markets lulled them into a false sense of security and economic success.

Conversely, we find players in the new game throwing away cards that they once valued in order to stay at the table. Three examples come to mind. South Africa—persuaded, no doubt, by its powerful banks and transnational conglomerates—has apparently come to the conclusion that apartheid is a costly handicap in the game, one that it can no longer afford, even if there are all sorts of difficulties in the shedding of it. Canada, fearful of its vulnerability to U.S. protectionism, has put its national pride and separate identity at severe risk by accepting the U.S.–Canada Free Trade Agreement. The Eastern Europeans have come to the conclusion—as even one day, perhaps, the Soviet Union may—that the economic cost of maintaining the leading role of the party is too great and imposes too big a handicap in the struggle for economic growth, export earnings, and political legitimacy.

The big debates these days in most countries are not about foreign policy. They are about industrial policy.[2] The fact that in the United States no one cares to admit that such a thing as industrial policy exists does not make patriotic Americans' differences about its content any less profound; whether there should be state support for manufacturing industry, what is the proper relation between industry and services, and what rules should apply to foreign investment by the United States and in the

United States are hot issues. The old debates between strategists over weapon systems and the disposition of nuclear capability are fading off the front page—because of détente and arms control agreements, it may be said. But why the optimism about this phase of arms control? Surely, because both superpowers came almost simultaneously to the same conclusion: military spending was putting such a deadweight on their economic performance in the competition for market shares that it was preempting those very resources without which social needs and demands could never be met. Both governments instinctively knew and recognized the new game that had to be played.

The game of baseball is essentially the same when it is played professionally as when it is played on a neighborhood lot. Yet while the players in both games behave similarly in some respects, they behave and perform differently in others. So it is with the market-shares game when the players are firms, not states. But the stakes and the goals are the same. As a general rule, although there are exceptions, the winners in both games are those who gain, and hold, the largest shares of the market. Moreover, both firms and states have the problem of reconciling this central aim with a multiple agenda of other objectives. In the case of firms, total market share may be in sales of one product, in a variety of products, or in a combination of a few major products with success in niche markets. A firm has also to decide whether to supply the market from its home base, from a series of local bases, or from a combination of dispersed production bases. These are all strategic decisions—not too different from the choices states make in economic and industrial policy. The aim in each case is to do better than the rivals. And just as some states have shed territory, we can see major companies shedding unprofitable product lines, affiliates, or product divisions, the better to concentrate on the core business.

As more and more enterprises have been drawn into the competitive game of world markets, because they could no longer survive by supplying just the local market, the so-called multinationals have come to occupy a larger and larger part of the current picture of international relations. They are no longer playing walk-on parts, auxiliaries to the real actors. They are at center stage, right up there with the governments.

Indeed, growing numbers of enterprises have begun to resemble states, and sometimes to behave like them, sending diplomatic missions to other firms or to governments; making alliances with other firms or with states; even setting up intelligence departments, which may be described as "research" but may also engage in what governments would recognize as spying. And just as the state was never concerned simply with the pursuit of security, so the transnational corporation is seldom concerned simply with the pursuit of immediate profit. Its products, whether goods or services, are its weapons. Its employees are its armed forces. Its concern is with survival, security against takeover, or dwindling market share. Both firms and states now have the problem of managing multiple agendas; of trading off the pursuit of immediate wealth against the demands of long-term security; and of allocating the proceeds between the bosses, the stockholders, and the workers.

Because this evolution of international business has been going on for so long, it sometimes seems as though nothing new has happened. But the mid-1980s were a milestone as the volume of international production for the first time exceeded the volume of international trade. International trade is when goods or services are bought and sold across frontiers. International production is when goods or services are produced within a country under the global strategy of a foreign-owned and foreign-directed enterprise. When the latter became more important, it marked a significant change in the relation of states to markets and the graduation of transnational enterprises to a significant political role in international affairs—or, as the Council on Foreign Relations prefers to say, foreign relations.

The change is significant because while there is a lot states can do to disrupt, manage, or distort trade, there is much less they can do to disrupt, manage, or distort international production. To put it in a nutshell, states can to some extent control trade because they can bar entry to the territory in which the *national* market functions. They cannot so easily control production that is aimed at a *world* market and that does not necessarily take place within their frontiers. And even when a lot of production for the market is under control—as it was in oil in the 1970s—the market may not be—as the Organization of Petroleum Exporting Countries (OPEC) discovered, to its cost, in the 1980s. When states do try to use their power to influence where and how international production takes place, they find they cannot direct, as with trade. They can only bargain. And the costs to themselves can be very much higher than the rather small costs of indulging in trade protection. For example, when the Brazilian government excluded all the big international computer enterprises from producing in Brazil, it imposed a very high cost on all the local enterprises needing to use the latest and best computers in order to keep up with *their* competitors. When governments have wanted to develop offshore oil fields, they have had to bargain with enterprises possessing the know-how and the risk capital necessary for the operation, and have been obliged to moderate their tax demands and other conditions accordingly. The outcome of bargaining may be to the state's advantage, or to the multinationals'. It is still a bargain. It was much easier—and less costly to the national economy—in war or Cold War to ban some kinds of trade altogether, or in peace arbitrarily to saddle traders with tariffs or quotas.

Henceforward, therefore, diplomacy has to be conceived as an activity with not one, but three dimensions. The first, familiar dimension is the bargaining and exchange of views and information between representatives of governments, the conventional diplomats. The second, newer dimension is the bargaining and exchange of views and information between representatives of enterprises. And the third is the bargaining and exchange of views and information between a government representative on one side of the table and a representative of an enterprise, whether based in the same or in another state, on the other.

A good illustration of three-dimensional diplomacy can be seen in the responses in 1989 by both states and firms to political change in Eastern Europe. Besides the comings and goings of heads of state across the divide, there was much parallel activity—no less important to the reforming national economies—by American, European, and Japanese firms. While Fiat was proposing a new plant in the Soviet Union, Isuzu was busy negotiating in Poland. Daimler-Benz/Messerschmitt/Bolkow/Blohm was looking for Eastern partners in engineering; IBM was doing a deal with Robotron in East Germany, just as the West German fashion house Escada was doing in clothing.

Meanwhile, around the world, firms are every day reported negotiating with other firms, making alliances (just as states do) to beat the opposition. Some, of course, fail—like the AT&T-Olivetti alliance. Others are more successful. For example, a Finnish cable maker combines with a Dutch competitor to create an enterprise that will be big enough to sell on world markets. A Mexican glassmaker, Vitro, buys into a U.S. one, Anchor, to challenge Corning. AT&T and Sun Microsystems make a strategic alliance to win the race to establish new software standards. Mitsubishi tries once again to forge a powerful alliance with Daimler-Benz. In every case, the negotiations—about what resources each partner will allocate to the alliance, and about how each will share in the risks—are not fundamentally different from the sort of interallied negotiations so well documented in international relations during, for example, World Wars I and II. These interfirm alliance negotiations, moreover, not only are similar to the old-style international bargaining between allies; they also have important consequences for states and their international relations. The U.S. Defense Department finds it needs the collaboration—to the point of possible dependence—of foreign-owned firms for the development of new weapon systems. The French government's indirect control over French industry is much weaker now that French companies have negotiated all sorts of deals with foreign enterprises.

Ingredients of Change

So much for the essence of the major change in recent years. It was the product of a combination of changes, each one a necessary ingredient of the result. But because of the extreme specialization practiced by the social sciences, and because of the deafness of each group of specialists to the others, the connection between these diverse ingredients has not always been clearly perceived.

For firms to play their part in change—and such a large part—it was necessary that many more of them become mobile, no longer so firmly rooted in just one national economy, serving just a local market. They were pushed into mobility by the accelerating rate of technological change, and pulled into it by the accelerating mobility of finance. Their transition to transnational status was coincidentally eased by the falling real costs of intercontinental communication and transport. Therefore, a word of explanation is in order about each of these ingredients.

The push factor—the acceleration of technological change— meant two things. First, it meant that a firm had to face the approaching obsolescence of its existing plant or production processes much sooner than it originally expected. Unless it was to lose market share or profitability, it was obliged to recoup the costs of past investment more quickly than it could possibly do by producing only in and for the local market. The only feasible approach was to adopt a global strategy of production, whether by setting up a relay affiliate to reproduce in other markets what it had learned to do at home, or by farming out part of that process to a workshop affiliate in some other country where taxes or labor costs were lower, or where the firm had reason to believe that, if it were an insider rather than an outsider, its market share would be less vulnerable to government interference.[3]

Second, it meant that firms had to be prepared to compete in the production of new products. The fax machine is a good example. It was unknown ten years ago. Ten years before that, the big innovation in business communication was the telex. Now telex has been made all but obsolete by fax. In the market for office machinery and equipment, none of the major competing firms could afford not to produce fax machines. Thus, whether the firm needed to produce new products or to produce in a new location, it needed to raise new capital.

A necessary condition for either strategy was that the firm be able to make use of its reputation for creditworthiness, its ready access to OPM (other people's money) in the other countries in which it wanted to expand production: in other words, that national financial systems for providing enterprise with capital gave way to an integrated international financial system. That was the key change in the international political economy, the change that over the past two decades has proceeded faster than any other process of change. Instead of a series of national credit-creating structures linked together by ancillary markets for foreign investment—whether by bonds, shares, or trade credit—there was created a single integrated global market for capital. In this market, although the buyers and sellers and their intermediaries may be physically separated, they are connected by computerized communications systems that make information on any local change in market responses instantly known in every other part of the global financial system. The result is that the local financial markets are now ancillary to the global one, not the other way around. Peter Drucker put his finger on it when he said that "capital movements rather than trade . . . have become the driving force of the world economy," and that the world economy was in control, rather than the macroeconomies of the nation-state.[4]

The growth in this system of interbank transactions across the exchanges means that for a firm to make the transition from a national to a transnational producer of goods or services, it does not have to undertake to move capital from one place to another. Through its bank, it can arrange to raise capital on the spot at short notice. The interbank system takes care of the modalities.

One political consequence of the new opportunities for firms to exploit their creditworthiness on a global scale—and of the new imperatives pushing them to do so—is that it has greatly reduced the erstwhile differences between the state and the enterprise as borrowers. We have come to accept as normal the raising of $30 billion for the Nabisco takeover—a sum hitherto associated only with bond issues by governments. Although there is nothing new in multinational corporations raising capital for their global operations, there are other things that are new: the scale on which they do so, the number of them doing it, and the frequency with which they raise funds offshore. This means that firms and governments are increasingly competing much more directly with each other for a share of the same global pool of credit. When most governments need to borrow to supplement taxes and solve their fiscal problems, and when more and more corporations need to raise more capital to stay in the poker game of market share, both are vulnerable to secular increases in the cost of doing so—that is, the price of borrowing OPM, otherwise known as the long-term rate of interest.

And where, once upon a time, governments could, if they wished, manipulate their national capital markets—in the interest of their foreign allies, for example—now, the markets are master over at least the weaker and smaller governments. For example, where the French government in the nineteenth century could effectively ensure that the czarist Russian bonds were issued in Paris and bought by French banks (which then passed them on to a gullible French public),[5] now, even the U.S. government cannot insist that U.S. banks back the Baker Plan with their clients' money. In 1982, to save Mexico from involuntary default, the U.S. government had to find the bulk of the rescue money from its own resources—and even then the bankers had to have their arms twisted hard to join in.

There is another way in which one of the ingredients of change has all but eliminated a major difference between the world of states and the world of business. The "diplomatic bag" or privileged messages to and from headquarters was symbolic of the special hold that governments liked to claim over international channels of communication. The claim was often disputed. Rothschild's in London used pigeons to get news of the victory at Waterloo to London bankers quicker than Wellington could get the news to the British government. Now, the technical revolutions in communications and information systems mean that governments are no better off and no more speedily informed of important news, political or economic, than are the news media or the managers of international business.

These managers needed to have a global communications system in order to manage international production and to implement the global strategy that is their distinguishing characteristic. They also needed reliable, swift, and unrestricted means of transport for executives and for specialized technicians. It would be hard to imagine international production having grown so large and so fast without the international airlines. It would also be hard to imagine this change if fashion—and, more than fashion, the general pattern of consumer tastes and preferences—had not become as standardized as it is today. Rock music recordings; blue jeans; compact cars; lightweight, multigeared bicycles; lager beer and hamburgers; paper tissues and diapers; and the TV sets that advertise them—the taste for all of these products is worldwide.

Given this global standardization of demand for a common range of new products, the firms concerned will protest, local preferences still differ and have to be catered to if a firm is to hold its local market share. This is where the improved technology of manufacturing has stepped in to reconcile a grand strategy with specialized production to suit local market tastes. The computer has made unnecessary the annual process of shutting down the factory and laying off workers while the assembly line was reprogrammed to introduce rather minor design changes for next year's model. With the aid of computers, the same machines and the same workers can now be switched quickly and easily to produce shorter runs of different models or of marginally different products. Had this not been so, the standardization that has helped firms survive through international production would have been much more difficult.

Political Consequences

Three important political consequences have stemmed from the change in the name of the game. Each has been noted and written about in recent years, but the common connection with the central and fundamental change in the nature of competition between states has not always been sufficiently recognized.

The first is the improvement since 1945 in the life expectancy of states, mainly as a result of the predators' loss of appetite for territory. Many new states have appeared; few old ones have departed. Whatever may happen to the government in power, the political system, the ruling party, or the economy, a state in existence today does not expect to disappear from the political map. Only with divided nations, as in Korea or Germany, may a merger replace two states with one. But this is different from

being forcibly eliminated or partitioned, having whole provinces
amputated, or being taken over by another state, as often happened in the past. In the 1920s, for instance, the great powers
thought it necessary to guarantee the territorial integrity of
China. Half a century later, the gesture seems not so much futile
as unnecessary. Already in the 1930s, Hitler's demand for
lebensraum sounded faintly theatrical. It was not really the loss
of territory imposed by the Treaty of Versailles that was so
bitterly resented not only by Hitler but by many Germans; it was
the sense of injustice in being treated differently from other
states, in having their just claims to self-determination taken so
much less seriously. And by the end of World War II, it was
already clear that, except, perhaps, for the Soviet Union, the
allies had lost the sharp appetite for territory that the victors of
1918 had shown. By 1990, the USSR had also changed, and even
West German Chancellor Helmut Kohl had come to accept the
frontiers of 1945—including those of Poland—as permanent.

The other side of the coin has been a much more rapid
change in the cast list of major enterprises. New ones have
appeared and have grown more quickly than they did 50 years
ago. Long-established ones have disappeared more suddenly. If
the world of states has become less predatory, the world of
business has become more so. Think of Chrysler and the American Motors Corporation (AMC), of the German AEG; of the
Bond empire; of Slater, Walker, or Continental Illinois, shrunk
to a shadow of its former self. One reason is that the competition
has become more international. A comfortable position of dominance in the national economy can be more easily challenged by a
foreign firm. And what were national firms have blossomed as
multinationals—in brewing, for example, where Heineken and
Fosters (unlike the American brewers) have become global producers. Another sector where this has happened is in accounting
and consultancy, where Peat Marwick and Price Waterhouse
were able rapidly to become global and not just national market
leaders. In many cases, the secret of success or failure lay in
finance, and in the ability or inability to take advantage of financial opportunities. Those that failed were often unsuspectingly
vulnerable to merger or takeover—often by a foreign firm.

Those that escaped death often did so because they were able to use finance to switch to another occupation. Cunard became a hotel group; P&O a construction and ferry operator.

The asymmetry in life chances for states and firms produces new kinds of risks in trilateral diplomacy. Choice of a sickly corporate partner may be just as damaging for a state as making an alliance with a weak or vacillating state once was. Wherever possible, having a variety of competing corporate partners ensures against such risks. The dilemma comes when one corporation has such technical preeminence that there are other costs to partnership with its inferior rivals.

The other side of the coin relates to the corporation's choice of partner from among rival states. At the beginning of the 1980s, it seemed as though transnational corporations looking for compatible host states in which to locate their operations went shopping for tax breaks and docile, ill-paid labor. By the end of the decade, experience had demonstrated that neither could compensate for administrative incompetence or for complex official meddling with prices, either by internal price control or by tariffs and other barriers to imports. "The state's most crucial task by far is to provide the rule of law," concluded a 1989 survey of Third World development by *The Economist*.[6] And the worse its performance in this respect, the more likely it was to be playing the role of supplicant to foreign firms; the less it was in a position to bargain, still less to dictate. The rule of law the state enforced, moreover, had to be one that appeared reasonably stable, one that was not subject to frequent arbitrary alteration. It was not so much that transnational corporations necessarily preferred to deal with authoritarian regimes as that authoritarian regimes, like Lee Kuan Yew's in Singapore, understood the value to the firm of reducing political uncertainty—and the importance of leaving price mechanisms alone. Even efficient, purposeful state intervention, not with prices but with credit allocation, as practiced by South Korea, though it worked rather well in the short term, also stored up trouble for the future. It produced too few, too oligopolistic enterprises and a repressed but rebellious work force and student body. A question mark hangs over its rule of law in the longer term.

In a word, what the corporate partners were looking for was the combination of political stability and economic nonintervention. Tunisia and Thailand were two countries that filled their bill, and benefited in consequence. Neither was large, and whereas, as the decade began, some corporations were dazzled by size—and the prospect, however distant, of a large, local market for their goods—by the end, many were sadly disillusioned by experience with the big-nation partners, such as Brazil, the Soviet Union, or China.[7]

Some firms were more fortunate. When, as sometimes happened, they could carve out a comfortable monopoly role—in socialist state-planned economies, for example—they could extract the appropriate rents and use their privileged position in the protected market to increase their total global output and sales, thus reducing the unit costs of incorporated research and development. The danger, as with Fiat in the Soviet Union, or 3M in China, was that the monopoly might not last forever and newcomers might be let in to challenge the efficiency of the monopolist.

The clear political implication for the state was that population—like territory—was no longer a dependable source of strength or a particularly desirable asset in the global game of competition with other states. There was a time, in living memory, when governments still thought that more births, to produce future cohorts of conscript soldiers, was a rational choice for the state in its pursuit of military power. Corporations will look back to the time when they assessed markets by counting heads, not evaluating household disposable incomes, as an age of comparable folly.

The third political implication of the changing game is bad news for the international organizations on which such fond neofunctionalist hopes reposed. The development literature already reflects a widespread acceptance that the developing countries' call for a new international economic order (NIEO) is a dead duck, as is their hope of a debtors' strike. At least in Latin America, the latter held an appeal for a little longer into the 1980s than the NIEO. The reason for disillusionment is the same in both cases: competition between states for market share conflicts head-on with demands for solidarity, whether between debtors or between exporters. It is not hard to hear the hollow ring in the UNCTAD publicity material of the late 1980s that proclaimed a new role for UNCTAD in the 1990s. The Group of 77 may have 134 members, but it is no longer a group.[8] Neither, for the same reason, is the Group of 24. Each state is playing a lone hand in the game. That is why a decade that began with the sustained acclaim for multilateralism ended with an undignified scramble to conclude bilateral deals—a scramble, it is only fair to point out, that was conspicuously led by a U.S. government fearful of *le défi japonais*. The failure of Western developed countries to respond in effective concert to Eastern European revolts against the dominance of communist parties is one among many indications of the prospective decline—or at least arrested growth—of international economic cooperation.[9] Of course, *some* cooperation is not totally incompatible with competition or even conflict. But the salience for the state of success in the competition for market share suggests that much recent discussion of economic policy coordination has been historically illiterate and, in consequence, grossly overoptimistic.

This is partly a result of the short horizons of policymakers in liberal democratic states. When the head of state cannot reasonably expect to outlast a decade in office—Mrs. Thatcher has been the exception to this (among other) rule—the long-term gains of accommodating national interest to wider considerations of the world economy in the name of international economic coordination seem hardly worth the short-term political cost. Robert Pringle, who used to run the Group of Thirty office in New York and therefore has had close experience with attempts at coordination, has observed that the democratic processes of policymaking in modern industrialized states actually make policy coordination more difficult than it was 100 years ago, when the sterling-gold standard was managed by autocrats insulated from populist pressures.[10]

Moreover, the very constitutions and political systems of states are designed to achieve national consensus or acquiescence, not international consensus. The perceptive Japanese journalist Yoichi Funbashi found the same principal—and essentially political—impediment in both the United States and Japan. In the United States, he said:

> Congress should reorganize its present hydra-type jurisdiction over trade issues—for example, the Senate Finance Committee and the House Ways and Means Committee should be assigned a greater role in international economic policymaking. Only a full partnership between the executive and legislative branches will provide the means for constructive policymaking. . . . Public testimony by the Managing Director of the IMF [International Monetary Fund] should also be encouraged.

Funbashi also advocated parallel changes in the policymaking processes in Japan and Germany, whereby all political parties would be enrolled in the discussion of key issues.[11]

The problem of monetary coordination has also been directly and specifically addressed by Mac Destler and Randall Henning.[12] They propose reforms aimed at increasing the leverage over fiscal policies of those responsible for the exchange rate. For though taxation may seem to be a domestic matter, it nevertheless often substantially affects the capacity of governments to comply with G5 or G7 agreements.[13]

Misperceiving Change

There is a curious paradox about American perceptions of recent change in international affairs as compared with British perceptions of change between the 1920s and the 1960s. While the British, to their cost, failed dismally to comprehend their own decline, and thus to adjust to it, the Americans have perceived decline where there was little or none—at least in the near future. To be more precise, what the United States has been experiencing is not so much a loss of power as a shift in the basis of power. For far too long, the Americans have encouraged a succession of British governments, from Churchill's to Thatcher's, to think that they still represent a great power. This perception added to British leaders' own self-deceiving arrogance, hid from them their identity of interest with other Europeans until it was almost too late. It allowed them to cling to the two absurd ideas that the commonwealth was some sort of substitute and that they had some sort of substantial special relationship with the United States. If British misperceptions of change

have had such lamentable results for the British, American misperceptions may be no less unfortunate—and not only for the
Americans.

That statement calls for clarification, but I can be brief. Paul
Kennedy in *The Rise and Fall of the Great Powers,* somewhat more
explicitly and persuasively than Mancur Olson in *The Rise and
Decline of Nations,* gave expression to rather inchoate American
emotions of which a sense of unmerited humiliation was perhaps
the dominant one.[14] Everyone knows the sources: Watergate,
Vietnam, OPEC, the Iran hostages, the meteoric success of
Japanese exports. The argument appealed directly to those
emotions. It was simple and therefore gained widespread acceptance. The United States had been humiliated and put down in
its own estimation because it had suffered the inevitable decline
in power that awaited any state that overstretched itself militarily
and allowed its free-riding allies to gain an economic lead over it.
The proof was there for all to see: a rather dramatic fall since the
1950s in the U.S. share of world exports and in the U.S. share of
world production of manufactures. There was also the corresponding rise in Japanese exports, in industrial production, and
in the presence of Japanese corporate names among the top ten
international banks and automobile producers.

Among American writers on international affairs, especially
economic affairs, an immediate connection was made in which
the deteriorating state of international economic relations was
directly ascribed to this supposed American decline. They recalled Charles Kindleberger's rather cautious hypothesis in *The
World in Depression* that the failure to prevent or recover quickly
from the financial crash of 1929 was due to the combination of
Britain's inability, through weakness, and America's unwillingness to act as leader in restoring stability to the world economy.[15]
In other words, it was the lack of a stabilizing hegemon.

An associated proposition, popular with liberal economists,
was that postwar prosperity and the unprecedented growth in
world trade in the 1950s and 1960s was the direct result of
American hegemony. At this point, some made a logical jump in
attributing the prosperity to the process of trade liberalization
led by the United States in the General Agreement on Tariffs

and Trade. A much stronger case, however, can be made that prosperity was due to the liberal access to credit for international trade and investment, also led by the United States, starting with the British Loan of 1945 and the Marshall Plan, and continuing into the 1960s with the birth of the Eurodollar market.

Right through the 1980s, the bracketing of American hegemonic decline and the erosion of international economic order and stability prevailed. I have been convinced, however, that this interpretation of change was not only wrong but just as maleficent as German beliefs in the 1930s that their economic difficulties could be blamed on the Jews and the Versailles diktat.[16] In short, it was a plausible but ill-founded myth. It was ill founded because the indicators quoted ignored the continuation of American industrial growth on other shores—in Europe, in East Asia, and in Latin America. The sum of output under American management and direction produced within the territorial United States did *not* necessarily mean a loss of power, but meant a shift in location. It may have hurt American workers or modified the capacity of the U.S. government to tax or control it. The shift in power, however, in favor of American enterprise and at the expense of the American government, which found it difficult to cope with the effects on the U.S. balance of payments of American industry's moving offshore. The result showed in a loss of market share for those American enterprises that still produced at home. There were also, it was true, some new industrial sectors, like semiconductors and VCRs, where the Japanese or the newly industrializing countries beat the Americans, whether producing at home or abroad, in capturing market share. But there were still many important sectors—aircraft and aerospace, optic fibers, pharmaceuticals, entertainment, data banks—where American technology and market share were unchallenged. Leadership did not require dominance in every sector of the world market; nor did it require the dominance only of the stay-at-home firms. Leaders were often U.S. firms that had been quickest to produce transnationally as well as in the territorial United States—like IBM—or that had not hesitated to make strategic alliances with foreign manufacturers of components—as Boeing did with Rolls-Royce, for instance.

And when it came to the erosion or deterioration of the international economic order loosely known as the Bretton Woods system, almost every writer who studied international organization came to the same conclusion. It was not weakness of the United States that accounted for the breakdown of the gold-dollar exchange (i.e., fixed exchange rates) regime in 1971–1973. It was the decision of President Nixon to correct the U.S. trade deficit by forcibly devaluing the dollar. The OPEC oil price rise, inflicting a shock to the system and to American *amour propre,* was the response to the U.S.-led spurt of inflation, originating in Vietnam and exacerbated by commodity speculation after the dollar devaluation. The disorder of the 1970s and 1980s, the persistent asymmetry between Japanese and other surpluses and the U.S. deficit, was the consequence in large part of the failure of successive U.S. administrations to take hard choices in monetary management.[17] For example, the budget deficit could have been cut—but policymakers did not want to stint on defense.[18] Or it could have been financed by U.S. savings, not by Japanese—but policymakers did not want to risk a recession in consumer spending.

As to the decline in standards of behavior in matters of international trade—the resort to VERs ("voluntary" export restrictions), to bilateral deals, to retaliatory threats and unilateral judgments on dumping by trade partners—this, too, could not be blamed on the insubordination of other states to a weakened American hegemon. Rather, it was the hegemon itself that had changed its mind about the national interest—instead of keeping to liberal, nondiscriminatory rules, it negotiated trade-managing deals, first for steel in the 1960s, then for textiles in the 1970s, and for semiconductors in the 1980s. Leading U.S. scholars who studied these events were agreed on this.[19] And it was the United States under Ronald Reagan that scuppered the United Nations Conference to Reform the Law of the Sea, and that stonewalled any extension of international commodity agreements.

If the decline of international economic order could be ascribed to anything, therefore, it was to the impunity with which the United States could break the agreed rules, not to U.S. weakness in enforcing them. The instinctive grasp that the Roosevelt, Truman, and Eisenhower administrations had shown of the Gramscian principles of hegemony—that to increase your own power in society, you recruited class allies by giving them insignificant rewards and concessions: what the British call "putty medals"—seemed to have progressively eluded subsequent presidents. It had cost the United States nothing to agree in the 1940s that the head of the IMF should always be a non-American, even though the United States had all the decision-making power. By the 1980s, the United States was refusing to make room at the top for the Japanese in the Asian Development Bank, even though it would have made little difference to policy decisions. It seemed as though the Americans had quite liked leadership when they could patronize their associates in Europe and Japan. But, like some mothers who dote on babies but can't get on with teenagers, they unaccountably lost the appetite for leadership as stroppy adolescents—first the French under de Gaulle, then the Germans and Japanese—dared to question the wisdom of Uncle Sam's policies.

Closely associated with the misperceptions of American decline has been the idea that by the end of the 1980s, a multipolar world was replacing the bipolar world that had dominated international relations since Yalta. Because, clearly, obtaining agreement among five or seven heads of state or finance ministers was apt to be more difficult than making a horse trade between two, this notion also had an exculpatory appeal. It did not, however, stand up against the record of recent history. The 1986 Reykjavík summit, at which Reagan nearly agreed with Gorbachev to move toward the total abolition of nuclear weapons without even pretending to consult the North Atlantic Treaty Organization (NATO) allies, was one clear indication that in matters of security, the world was still bipolar. Another came with the 1989 arms control agreements, where, again, the allies on each side were informed only after the deal had been done. Moreover, the idea that 1990 is in any way comparable to the multipolar world of 1910 does not bear close scrutiny. Then, there were indeed five great powers—France, Germany, Russia, Britain, and the United States—with Italy, Austria, Turkey, China, and Japan playing relatively minor, dependent roles. All the great powers—and some of the minor ones, like Japan—had powerful navies. They all had armed forces that could be mobilized for war. None had any one weapon that the others could not possibly hope to resist. The nuclear superpowers equipped to send large numbers of intercontinental ballistic missiles against any assailant are so obviously in a class of their own that the point hardly needs making.

Multipolarity, however, has another significance when it comes to misperceptions. It contributes to the persistent idea that an increase in protectionism in the United States and the European Community in the 1970s and 1980s presages the buildup of economic blocs similar to those of the 1930s—the Nazi German trade bloc in southeastern and central Europe, the dollar bloc in the Western Hemisphere, the British Commonwealth sterling bloc, and the Japanese Co-Prosperity Sphere in East Asia. First, there is a historical misrepresentation here. Only when combined with military domination were these blocs really exclusive in the sense of totally keeping out other trading partners. The fear of trade wars escalating into military conflicts, therefore, is unfounded. Second, the internationalization of production described earlier makes the idea of trade blocs totally obsolete in an era when IBM, Nissan, McDonald's, and Hilton are established global enterprises. Their operations can be hampered by protectionist trade policies. They will not be brought to an end.

The last major misperception contributing its share to a paralyzing mental isolationism of much American intellectual discourse today is the perception—encouraged, alas, by the Paul Kennedy book—that once begun, decline—or, indeed, any trend in international affairs—has a momentum that makes it hard to reverse. To any historian, this is an unsustainable proposition. Since I do not accept the notion of either absolute or relative American decline—certainly not in the present and near future—I need deal only with the associated notion of irreversible trends in the relation of authorities, especially states, to markets.

It is true that there has been a trend, since the early 1960s or even late 1950s, in which governments have retreated, leaving the allocation of costs and benefits, of risks and opportunities, to markets. The trend culminated in the adoption of flexible exchange rates in the 1970s and in the move to deliberate deregulation, initiated by the United States in the same period. There was a similar trend in the 1920s, but it was reversed in the 1930s and, in rather dramatic fashion, in New Deal America. I believe that the October 1987 crash of the world's stock markets, though it proved less catastrophic than some feared at the time, nevertheless marked some sort of turning point, back to regulation. Certainly this was the case in financial markets, though it was not necessarily so in sectors like air travel where unfriendly oligopolists, sustained by governments, still exploit consumers. Agreement among central banks through the Bank for International Settlements in Basel is one indication. Another is the lead given, significantly, by the U.S. Securities and Exchange Commission, to its counterparts in other countries to tighten rules on transfers of illegally acquired funds and on falsification of information by financial institutions.

The danger in this determinist notion is that it reinforces a harmful mood of defeatism in the face of social and political problems—like the U.S. budget deficit, for instance. During the German invasion of France in 1940, the French called it "Je m'en foutisme"; it was expressed by a dismissive shrug of the shoulders, abdication of personal responsibility for what was going on. Paul Kennedy recently compared the present hard choices facing America with those facing late Victorian and Edwardian Britain. The British, he said, had had a fatal tendency to lapse into a sluggish complacency whenever they were given breathing space in periods of relative tranquility. They drifted along, hoping for the best, but doing nothing to solve underlying problems. Does he mean, then, that we can expect a change in American policies only *after* some catastrophe? Will it really take financial chaos, widespread bankruptcies, and mass unemployment to create a will for constructive political change?

Perhaps the liberation of Eastern Europe, and the sudden obsolescence of NATO and Warsaw Pact arsenals, at least in large part, now creates a window of opportunity for a reversal of American political defeatism. There is the chance both that progress can be made with the deficit and that more Japanese funds still can be liberated for investment in developing countries and Eastern Europe, thus reinvigorating economic growth and presenting the United States with a chance to regain its old élan without suffering catastrophe first. It would be worth spending billions, not millions, of dollars in Central and South America to check the drug menace at its source—the poverty of Latin American farmers. The long-term danger of American decline through neglect of basic education, the starving of academic research, and the neglect of urban poverty—all these are also Kennedy's prime concerns—could conceivably be banished in the 1990s. What is needed, of course, is a revolution in American minds. If only the hindering blinders of misperception could be cast aside, Americans might again perceive the enormous power they still have to lead and to revolutionize the government of the world market economy.

To sum up, perhaps the greatest misperception is that the international system of states has not changed—even that it never will. By the end of the 1980s, a metamorphosis of the international political economy had begun: the old, close relationship between state, civil society, and economy is in the process of being replaced by a new relationship between authority and economy, and between authority and society. A global business civilization had emerged, a new international economic order, in which authority is far more dispersed, less precisely defined, but not totally absent. What, more precisely, does it mean?

The International Business Civilization

In the first place, it is now worldwide, in that the closed societies of China and the Soviet Union began opening up to it in the 1980s. By the end of the decade, the alternative path of central planning of the economy was everywhere being abandoned—not only in the Soviet bloc, but in Burma and in several African states. In Europe and Latin America, big state enterprises were being broken up or privatized. Foreign investors were newly welcome. In the summer of 1989, before the autumn revolutions, Soviet managers were sent to the London Business School. All this did not mean, as some wishfully thought, that socialism as an idea was on the rubbish heap. Freedom for the socialist countries was a victory not for undiluted American capitalism, but for the forces of the market, which promised to put more goods in the shops, and popular demands for participation in government—in short, for some form of democratic socialism within the world market economy. It *was* a victory in the sense that the whole idea of creating a separate, centrally planned economic bloc insulated from world markets was abandoned and implicit assent given to joining up with the business civilization.

However, to say that the business civilization became world-wide is not to say that it is universal, that everyone belongs to it, as people in a territorial empire are its subjects. Civilizations are not like that. Indeed, at this point it may help to distinguish rather more clearly between the concept of civilization and that of empire. They are not the same, though historically they have usually—but not always—closely coincided. A civilization may have a territorial base—China in Confucian civilization, for example. Or it may have just an ideological base in a belief system, presided over by a central authority, in which case it could be called a nonterritorial empire—the Mormon and Catholic churches and the religion of the Aga Khan are examples. The nearest example of the combination of a civilization with a formal, territorial empire of subjects and an informal, nonterritorial empire of *cives* (citizens with civic rights and duties) was Rome. It had a core, south of the Alps, which extended west to Spain and east across the Adriatic, and where the *cives* predominated. In its northern periphery, in Wales or Brittany, or across the sea in North Africa, or among nomads like the Romany (i.e., Gypsy) people, most people were subjects. Among them, old ways, old religions and customs, old social hierarchies, persisted side by side with the new. Willy-nilly, however dissident, it is clear that these peoples were also part of Rome's informal empire, its civilization, for besides the relics of Roman power in the shape of military camps to keep order in the marches of empire, archeologists are still finding the relics of Roman civilization: villas that were outlying farmsteads, with baths and heating systems, coins, and ornaments—all witnesses to common civilized tastes and economic behavior. One could make the same point about ancient Chinese or Islamic civilizations; though sustained by military and political power, they were not coterminous with it in either time or space. And when Britain, with its sterling standard, was the geographic core of the business civilization in the nineteenth century, its tentacles reached out beyond the political empire—for example, into Argentina and the Middle East. And in outlying parts of that civilization, its level of concentration was often low, diluted by dissidents. The robber and folk hero Ned Kelly was not the only "new" Australian in the nineteenth century who rejected the values of British business civilization along with the authority of the government of New South Wales. "Waltzing Matilda" tells of the swagman caught stealing sheep who drowns in the creek, shouting defiance. "You'll never take me alive!" said he.

The international business civilization of today is the same. Its core is in New York—not Washington—and in Chicago and Los Angeles. There are Ned Kellys in each of these places, but these are also the cities where the social and political elites most wholeheartedly accept the values, the mores, the customs, and the taboos of the civilization—as, of course, do their counterparts in London, Tokyo, São Paulo, Sydney, and Taipei. The values are both economic—efficiency, speed, and responsiveness to demand in the production of goods and services—and social—openness to competition and opportunity for social advancement regardless of race, parentage, and soon, perhaps, sex. Particularly on the last issue, practice, as always, falls short of ideology. Women are not yet given equal opportunity; nor are blacks, as a head count of business-class passengers on any airline will show. But the significant point here, as with the other values of the civilization, is that the core is in the lead in bringing about social and economic change. American women have more opportunities than Japanese women; American blacks have more opportunity than Japanese of Korean or Ainu origin. And there is little doubt that where the core has led, the civilization will follow. A harbinger of future sea-change in the late 1980s was the first appearance of a Japanese woman, the Socialist Party's Takako Doi, on the political scene.

A central concern of the civilization is with the securing of property rights, for individuals and for firms. In the realm of ideas, the business civilization has given and, on the whole, despite environmental protests, still gives the benefit of any doubt to science. The scientists exercise authority in a way that in other civilizations the priests have done. The fact that—like priests—they do not always agree does not apparently lessen the legitimacy of their claim to pass judgment.

There is an important point here. The scientists with authority do not have to be American. But in most every field of advanced scientific research, the largest concentrations of authoritative scholars is in the United States—at the Massachusetts Institute of Technology, the Mayo Clinic, Woods Hole; in Silicon Valley and the San Francisco area for advanced electronics; at the Livermore laboratories. Between them, their influence over the preferred directions for scientific inquiry is felt worldwide. Their presence explains why, however poor the showing of American education at the lowest, primary levels, its standards in higher education, especially in the great graduate schools, are superlative. And the research communities based in the territorial United States are often attached to universities, dependent on the U.S. government, on U.S.-based foundations, and on state legislatures and fee income of predominantly American students. This means that the indirect authority exercised in the United States by the government, federal and state, in scientific matters is certainly greater than the governmental authority in any other country.

If the scientists wield one kind of authority in the civilization, the banks and the financial markets wield quite another. In earlier business civilizations, and when they were more fragmented into a series of predominantly national systems, governments reserved to themselves the authority to decide how much credit should be created. Banks were allowed some power to decide on the allocation of the credit they created, but generally not on its amount. Now, with the growth of global capital markets, of Eurobonds and Eurocurrency loans, all governments have given up a large part of their control over the rate at which credit is created. The fact that the U.S. government really has little choice but to bail out the savings and loan institutions for fear of the social consequences of not doing so is just one indication of a significant shift in authority over the world market economy from state to market.

Within the civilization, social groups are increasingly built up within firms, not around places. They are not nearly so closely linked to local communities as they were even 50 years ago. The friendships made by corporate executives and technologists are more and more within the enterprise or, beyond the enterprise, within a particular sector of economic or professional activity. These social networks are increasingly transnational, creating new conflicts of loyalty.[20] The situation for many individuals is becoming much more akin to the civilization of Christendom in the Middle Ages. Then, people had multiple loyalties—to family, to church, to prince, to politico-economic groups like Guelphs and Ghibellines, to guilds, and so forth. Now, once again, individual choices have constantly to be made between conflicting claims. The apparent resurgence of nationalisms long suppressed in some parts of Eastern Europe—Transylvania, for instance—does not change the secular trend in most societies today toward a more fragmented social map.

The notion of citizenship is also undergoing subtle change. At the core of the business civilization in America, there are grades of entitlement to the status of citizen. At the bottom are illegal immigrants who live and work in the country under various degrees of threat to their way of life. At the top are the passport-carrying, job-holding, bona fide U.S. nationals. In between, there are participants in the business civilization who, as residents, enjoy, de facto, many of the rights of nationals. They can come and go freely. They have access to the courts, to schools and universities, and, through health insurance, to doctors and hospitals. Some gain entitlement through wealth, as businessmen; others through knowledge and education, as experts in the arts or entertainment, as well as in science and technology. And outside the United States, there are citizens of the business civilization who may be Swedish, Japanese, Israeli, Brazilian, or of many other nationalities, but who, culturally speaking, are almost identical with the American model. If their command of the grammar of the language is wobbly, or if they speak with a foreign accent, these are weaknesses that have been shared by some top officials and leaders of the U.S. government. As in Rome, in fact, there are grades of citizenship, degrees of entitlement, uniting, not separating, participants in one global civilization. Japanese businessmen dress like Americans. Their wives dress like American wives. Their children jump to the same music, follow the same fads and fashions, eat the same junk food, are even beginning to experiment with the same dangerous drugs. In every country, people are introducing more and more American words into their local languages. They are copying Americans in the taste for travel, for foreign cuisine, for jogging, for a freer and easier style of life.

Who Governs?

The big question for political economists is, Where, in this civilization, does authority lie? As I have said, it has already been diffused among nonstate authorities—the markets; the bankers; the scientists; the corporate executives in manufacturing, transport, insurance, the media, and entertainment. But among the governments of states, who has most authority? According to the defeatist school of decline, the United States has lost power to other states, to Japan or to the G7. The truth is that its main loss of power has been to the market, the balance of power tipping from state to market. Diffusion of the international business civilization from its core in America to the rest of the world has brought dilution of government. Like an oil slick, Washington's authority has gotten thinner at the center as it has spread to the periphery. But this has meant a growing asymmetry in managing and shaping the basic structures of the civilization between the United States and other governments. As other economies and societies have become integrated in the business civilization, their range of choice in policymaking has been constrained much more than that of the United States. Thus, when it comes to product liability, trading with socialist countries, access to U.S. government contracts and subsidies, or, most important, the upward or downward trend in interest rates, the U.S. government is still in a position to exercise substantially more authority than the government of any other state. When the United States raises interest rates, others follow. When Japan does the same, or when the Tokyo stock market plummets, the global reverberations are minimal.

The trouble is, of course, that on the important issues for the preservation of the economic order—for the business civilization—the United States has failed to use its authority, or else has used it for narrow, short-term national interests, losing sight of its long-term national interest as the core and leader of what could also be called a nonterritorial empire. These failures were actually greater in the 1980s, in the gung ho Reagan years, than during the seemingly more dangerous Nixon and Carter administrations.

In the postwar years, and especially in the 1980s, there have been three really important failures and two rather important secondary ones. The three important ones were the failure to secure for the economic order a rule of law based on elementary justice; the failure to maintain a soundly based stable currency; and the failure to create an administration that was both efficient and wise enough to maintain some balance between the interests of the United States as the inner core and those of its fellow *cives* in the peripheries. The two secondary ones are those that concern Paul Kennedy and his followers, and they relate particularly to the economic and social health and prosperity of the core, as distinct from the civilization—in other words, the United States.

The civilization's rule of law has been visibly unjust in the Rawlsian sense, in that it has condoned a lot of financial crime. It has let a lot of rascals get away with too much loot. Some of the rascals have been heads of states—the shah and his family, the Marcos couple, and quite a few leaders of African states. Some of them have been drug barons. Some have been bankers and financial wheeler-dealers. Now, it may be said that fraud and embezzlement have not been a monopoly of the West; the peoples of communist states were also robbed by their rulers. But *tu quoque* is no excuse. Those regimes fell. The lesson is that this sort of visible injustice undermines authority. And it is a pity, because in some ways the United States has tried to extend and sometimes has succeeded in extending to other parts of the civilization its own administration of justice—in compensating victims of air disasters or (after Bhopal) in extending industrial and product safety rules to the affiliates of U.S. companies. Some of the worst financial criminals have also been punished—eventually: Michele Sindona, for instance, and Ivan Boesky. And Britain owes it to the United States that some London-based rascals were caught and punished. A major task for the next decade, therefore, is to devise and see enforced new rules not only against the laundering of illegal drug money but against capital flight of embezzled public funds.

The affront of financial injustice has been exacerbated by deeper and more widespread injustices—those of income redistribution resulting from seven lean years of unresolved foreign debt problems (1983–1990). The reputation of the civilization for openness and equal opportunity within the power of government to secure it has suffered severe, long-term damage as workers have had their real wages and food subsidies cut while the rich and powerful, aided by foreign banks, have evaded taxes and exchange controls and stashed their fortunes abroad.

This is the direct result of the second failure, which is monetary and financial. No civilization lasts long that depends on money for production and exchange and fails to nurture confidence in the stability of that money. No capitalist civilization lasts long that depends on the creation of credit for economic growth, but does not make sure that there are not sudden interruptions in the flow of that credit and that access to it is not distorted by discriminatory structures. The business civilization of the 1980s continued to use U.S. dollars as a medium of exchange, while sustaining the value of dollars by preempting (with relatively high real interest rates) Japanese savings to finance a payments deficit—and to some extent a budget deficit. The problem is familiar and needs little explanation. The obdurate budget deficit came of trying to get a quart of defense spending plus welfare spending out of a pint pot, while fearing to bring about an economic slump if consumption were too severely discouraged by trying to increase U.S. savings to take the place of Japanese savings. The high interest rates came of failing either to restrain government or firms from expanding their borrowing or to restrain banks from lending to them. Credit creation has been insufficiently disciplined, but the consequences have been concealed from Americans by policies that practiced Keynesian pump priming at home—notably by Reagan in 1983–1984—and monetarism abroad. Americans were saved the necessity of adjusting to the built-in volatility of the financial structure by inflicting it on other citizens of the business civilization.

A new decade holds out a wonderful and unexpected opportunity for the United States to escape this catch-22 situation. It offers a chance to begin to restore financial order and confidence in the power of authority over unruly markets. The opportunity is the disintegration of the Warsaw Treaty Organization and the chance made possible by the Soviet Union to make big cuts in spending on aggressive weapons, especially in Europe.[21] Progress with the budget deficit would calm Japan's doubts about the long-term sustainability of its capital exports. Consultation between the Securities and Exchange Commission and other regulatory authorities that look to the United States for a lead could be speeded up. And the authority, already growing, of the G7 central bankers in calming nervous markets and checking volatile exchange rates could be reinforced. There now is a way out of this particularly dangerous wood.

The third requirement for a durable civilization, or for a loosely linked nonterritorial empire, is a competent bureaucracy. By that I mean an administrative and policymaking system that manages judiciously to balance the short-term demands of the core against the longer-term interests and needs of the whole civilization. Necessarily, such an administrative machine has to be insulated to a certain extent from day-to-day pressures. It has to be able to take a long view. It has to be dedicated and incorruptible—but subtle. It has to have a sense of mission, and a pride in its own achievements.[22] The British, for the one part of empire they really valued, India, created a special branch of government. One part, the India Office, was in London. Its independence from daily politics attracted to it some of the best civil servants, John Stuart Mill included. The other part served under the viceroy in the Indian Civil Service, recruiting long-service English officials, often straight from school, and an increasing number of educated Indians. In some degree, the system succeeded in creating a dual, but not a divided, bureaucracy. The government of Britain was separated from that of India. In the latter, crucial matters, like security, money, and law, were decided on broader grounds than the interests of the core—although it is only fair to add that not much account was taken of the interests of the Indians.

The nearest the business civilization has come to an India Office solution is the side-by-side existence in Washington of the U.S. State, Treasury, and Defense departments and the Federal Reserve Board with the secretariats of the IMF and the World Bank. The dominant influence of the United States in these two organizations is clear for all to see. The technical competence of their multinational staff is high. But both—the IMF especially—have been handicapped by having to pretend that their "recommendations" are technical rather than political, and by always having to play second fiddle to the agencies of the U.S. national administration (the Treasury and State departments and the White House). Whenever U.S. national policymakers took an initiative—to Mexico, to Brazil, to India, for example—international organizations were immediately overshadowed and financially outgunned. Yet unlike the international bodies Walter Bagehot might have called ornamental or symbolic, such as the United Nations General Assembly, these organizations are highly political—more so than other functionally effective ones, like the International Telecommunications Union or the International Maritime Organization. They therefore need to be able to carry through policies once agreed on and, at an earlier stage of interagency, interfactional bargaining, to associate closely with the necessary parts of the U.S. national policymaking machine.

Nor has this discordance between the international and the national bureaucracies been helped by the deterioration in recent years in the caliber of the latter. American officials of the federal government are too often political appointees rather than career people. Moreover, they are paid too little, stay in office for too short a time, and, outside the regular foreign service, are too often not well informed on international issues.[23] All these defects could be remedied. Non-American liaison people could be attached to any office dealing with transnational policymaking.

The other discordance in current policymaking that affects foreign and defense policy, and trade and financial questions, concerns domestic U.S. politics—but it has global consequences. It is the gap between Congress and the executive. This is a big subject and cannot be adequately dealt with in this essay. But the essence of the problem is that present arrangements do not involve senators and representatives at an early enough stage in the formulation of policy, with regard to either trade, monetary strategy, the reform of financial regulation and surveillance, or the tactics of negotiation in arms control. These are only some of the main issues where U.S. leadership is essential for the good government of the civilization. David Abshire, who has thought hard about these matters, also suggests separating, within the Washington bureaucracy and especially the National Security Council staff, the functions of strategic planning from the day-to-day conduct of business.[24] (This, incidentally, is something many well-run firms have learned to do.)

In the longer term, the logic of the global business civilization suggests that the business interests that have most to gain from its prosperity, and most to lose if it fails, should also be involved in the policymaking process. This is not a new idea; at the national level, syndicalism and corporatism were both much debated in the 1930s. In several European countries today, neo-corporatist practices that grew out of those debates have been institutionalized. And behind the scenes, in recent years, there has been growing evidence of the power of business interests in pushing policy changes on sluggish politicians. The fears of European multinationals that if progress in the European Community continued to be as slow as it was in the 1970s and early 1980s, they would be fatally handicapped by their narrow bases in national markets is widely credited with giving Lord Cockfield the necessary backing for the Single European Act. The fears of South African multinationals that their chances of surviving on the world stage were being seriously undermined by the practice of apartheid have undoubtedly played a part in giving South African President F.W. de Klerk the necessary backing to start negotiating with the African National Congress. So far these are still only isolated instances. There is a long way to go before effective institutional expression could be given to transnational syndicalism or corporatism. The problem emerging from the 1980s, therefore, is how to translate the reality of corporate power in the world market economy into a share of political responsibility for its better government. There is no question that some reform is urgent. That much is clear from the defects revealed by the experience of the 1980s in international policy coordination. As Kindleberger has observed, these arrangements have proved good in crisis but poor on trend. When the boat is in danger of sinking, all those in it lend a hand with bailing out the water. But when it comes to deciding which way to sail and how to get going, disagreements are rife, and unresolved. And the reasons for that are obvious to any politician or student of politics. Under the present policymaking system, leaders win elections and governments survive by listening to national concerns, not by worrying about the general good of the business civilization.

In the meanwhile, what we have to think about is how to devise a wholly new system of government for the business civilization of the next century, for the informal empire whose core is still in the United States, however much it may need the consent and cooperation of its junior partner Japan, just as it once needed the consent and cooperation of Britain. That is the task for the 1990s.

NOTES

This essay is in part the product of intellectual osmosis; I have benefited subconsciously from the ideas and insights of my colleague Professor John Stopford of the London Business School.

1. See John Mueller, *Retreat from Doomsday: The Obsolescence of Major War* (New York: Basic Books, 1989).
2. See Richard Rosecrance, *The Rise of the Trading State: Commerce and Conquest in the Modern World* (New York: Basic Books, 1986).
3. See C.-A. Michalet, *Le Capitalisme Mondial* (Paris: Presses Universitaires, 1976).

4. Peter Drucker, "The Changed World Economy," *Foreign Affairs*, vol. 64, no. 4 (Summer 1986), pp. 768–791.

5. See Herbert Feis, *Europe, the World's Banker, 1870–1914* (New Haven, Ct.: Yale University Press for the Council on Foreign Relations, 1964).

6. "Poor man's burden: A survey of the Third World," *The Economist*, September 23, 1989.

7. There are many examples of such disappointed hopes. One, told blow by blow in James Mann, *Beijing Jeep: The Short, Unhappy Romance of American Business in China* (New York: Simon & Schuster, 1989), began with AMC's attempts to build jeeps in China. Once the plant had been built in 1984, the government tried to grab most of the profits by raising AMC's tax bill, inflating the firm's phone bill, and throwing sand in the works by refusing it foreign exchange for spare parts. In 1986, a new local manager staved off disaster by using political leverage. But by 1990, the venture was again in trouble as a new national austerity program cut back both demand and imports.

8. See Miles Kahler's "International Political Economy" in this volume.

9. Behind a façade of "coordination" by the European Commission and the other international institutions, the plain truth was that aid for Eastern Europe was predominantly bilateral and uncoordinated. Neither in the United States, Britain, or France, nor yet in West Germany, was there found the leadership or vision of how the transition, economic and political, could be managed as a multilateral exercise.

10. Robert Pringle, "Financial Markets and Governments," WIDER Working Paper, no. 57 (June 1989).

11. Yoichi Funbashi, *Managing the Dollar: From the Plaza to the Louvre* (Washington, D.C.: Institute for International Economics, 1988), pp. 247–248.

12. I.M. Destler and R. Henning, *Dollar Politics: Exchange Rate Policymaking in the United States* (Washington, D.C.: Institute for International Economics, 1989), p. 162.

13. The thoughtful studies by Funbashi and by Destler and Henning both recognize the decisive role of political institutions and policymaking processes within states when it comes to international policy coordination. They contrast sharply with the stupefying platitudes produced by some economists who try to use "pure" economic analysis to illuminate these matters. See, for example, David Currie, Gerald Holtham, and Andrew Hughes Hallett, *The Theory and Practice of International Policy Coordination: Does Coordination Pay?* (London: London Centre for Economic Policy Research, 1989).

14. Paul Kennedy, *The Rise and Fall of the Great Powers* (New York: Random House, 1987); Mancur Olson, *The Rise and Decline of Nations* (New Haven, Ct.: Yale University Press, 1982).

15. Charles Kindleberger, *The World in Depression, 1929–1939* (Berkeley, Ca.: University of California Press, 1973).

16. See Susan Strange, "Still an Extraordinary Power," in R. Lombra and W. Witte, eds., *Political Economy of International and Domestic Monetary Relations* (Ames, Iowa: Iowa State University Press, 1982); and "The Persistent Myth of Lost Hegemony," *International Organization*, vol. 41, no. 4 (Autumn 1987), pp. 551–574.

17. See, for example, R. Gilpin, *The Political Economy of International Relations* (Princeton, NJ: Princeton University Press, 1987); J. Odell, *U.S. International Monetary Policy* (Princeton, NJ: Princeton University Press, 1982); and J. Gowa, *Closing the Gold Window* (Ithaca, NY: Cornell University Press, 1983).

18. See D.P. Calleo, *The Imperious Economy* (Cambridge, Ma.: Harvard University Press, 1982).

19. See Gilbert Winham, *International Trade and the Tokyo Round Negotiation* (Princeton, NJ: Princeton University Press, 1986); M. Hudson, *Global Fracture* (New York: Harper & Row, 1977); and B. Nowzad, *The Rise in Protectionism*, IMF Pamphlet No. 24 (Washington, D.C.: International Monetary Fund, 1978).

20. I recall an early personal instance from 1947. The British embassy in Washington called a press conference of British correspondents and refused to invite my colleague, an American by nationality who was employed by a British Sunday paper. I had to threaten to boycott the meeting in order to make the embassy change its mind.

21. David Hendrickson's call for a revision of U.S. defense priorities, shifting the emphasis from "attacking" weapons like Midgetman missiles to "retaliating" ones like submarines, aircraft, and cruise missiles, suggests one principle on which this might be done. In the past arms reduction has been stymied by insistence on reciprocity and equal cuts, with inevitable disagreement about what, between conventional nuclear weapons, was "equal." See David I. Hendrickson, *The Future of American Strategy* (New York: Homes and Meier, 1987).

22. The Ottoman Empire solved the problem in part by creating an artificial class of janissaries, specially chosen and trained from childhood but drawn from all over so that they could not be identified with a master race. The system made it hard for them to indulge in nepotism and dynasty building.

23. *Leadership for America: Rebuilding the Public Service,* Report of the National Commission on the Public Service, Washington, D.C., 1989; also a speech by Paul Volcker, chairman of the commission, "Public Service: The Quiet Crisis," Francis Boyer Lecture, American Enterprise Institute, Washington, D.C., December 7, 1988.

24. David Abshire, *Preventing World War III: A Realistic Grand Strategy* (New York: Harper & Row, 1988).

Reconsiderations

A NEW WORLD AND ITS TROUBLES

Stanley Hoffmann

Someone—an American—has been lying for almost 50 years on a procrustean bed, with a big gun under his pillow and eyes trained on the window, through which a Soviet intruder might burst in. Today, as he is getting up from that bed, he discovers a Soviet in the room, but with an olive branch; he also notices that there are many other people all around him, that his gun is of little use in the crowd, and that the furniture has been rearranged. A bit dizzy, he congratulates himself on having apparently deterred any break-in, but he finds it difficult to make sense of the changes and the bustle, and he experiences some painful bedsores.

Many of the trends discussed in this volume are anything but new. Scholars, scientists, and policymakers (especially when on their annual visit to the United Nations General Assembly) have often referred to them. But their minds, at least in this country, were really elsewhere: on the Cold War, on the ups and downs of containment, on the fortunes of the enemy. In a sense, the "long peace" that John L. Gaddis has written about was a substitute for a war.[1] National security concerns dominated the foreign policy of the two antagonists. In the USSR, the contest combined with the dispositions of a centralized command economy in building up an efficient war machine that absorbed a huge share of the country's resources and left the civilian economy both below, in priority, and behind, in quality. In the United States, as William H. McNeill observes, "the arms race . . . provided the principal stimulus for . . . remarkably effective political management of the economy." Certainly, the events of recent years amount to the recognition, by the leaders of the Soviet Union, of the USSR's defeat in that long confrontation—both on the ground, where, in Robert W. Tucker's words, "the Soviet Union has signalled, as clearly as it is possible for a great power to do, that it is no longer prepared to play the role to which it has aspired since the 1950s and in pursuit of which the Soviet people have sacrificed so much," and in the mind, insofar as the new thinking entails a repudiation of almost all the assumptions that had fed a diplomacy and a strategy of bipolar rivalry aimed at hastening the victory of one "social system" over the other that Marxist-Leninist ideology, now in full retreat, had predicted. As in a hot war, the leaders of the two rivals either concentrated on their conflict or treated the trends and troubles elsewhere in the world as opportunities or perils in that conflict.

However, in other respects, the contest was not a war. Indeed, the common triumph of the superpowers was their ability to avoid one. This feat had little to do with the "structural" properties of bipolar systems (Athens and Sparta were the two "poles" of a Greek city-state system that destroyed itself in the Peloponnesian war); rather, it resulted from nuclear weapons and from the plans, ideologies, and expectations of these particular rivals. The fact that the conflict was not a war, and therefore did not end with the losing side's formally begging for peace, is both an advantage and a drawback. It is an advantage insofar as it ought to facilitate that "integration of the Soviet Union into the world community" that both Soviet and American leaders have said to be one of their new objectives. But it is a drawback for the following reason: states fighting a war always aim at returning to peace—through victory or compromise—and therefore usually make plans both for the reconversion of their economies and for the shaping of the postwar order. The "long peace," precisely because of its length, distracted statesmen—and, often enough, scholars as well—from thinking enough about either. Our "victory" has left us dazed.

As a result, there exists today a certain nostalgia for the Cold War, not unlike the romantic nostalgia for the days of sacrifice, discipline, and community so often displayed by veterans, or by the British after the Blitz: things were simpler when. . . . The need for each "camp" or "bloc" to preserve its coherence compressed, suppressed, or repressed differences of interests and aspirations within each. But at the same time, because the Cold War was not a violent interruption and disruption of ordinary life, but a regular form of politics for almost half a century, it warped our definitions of security and stability in ways that wars do not. To be sure, we have gradually understood that military security is not a zero-sum game; theorists of arms control taught both us and the Soviets that nuclear weapons create mutual interests even among rivals. Nevertheless, our approach to security remains predominantly military—in matters of economic security, have we ever succeeded in getting much beyond the need to protect ourselves against a sudden disruption of the flow of oil?—and predominantly "bipolar"—preparing, as McNeill puts it, for high-tech war rather than low-grade local violence. And we have tended to equate stability—the goal of nonrevolutionary statecraft in peacetime—with the structures put in place in order to fight the Cold War, the institutions of containment. Even though their main purposes have now disappeared, we find it difficult to imagine new and different structures aimed at achieving if not stability (a somewhat absurd objective in a fluid world), at least moderation.

When we try to establish a balance sheet of the Cold War, it is its duality that stands out. As a quasi-war, it did great damage to both superpowers, although not to the same degree. In the Soviet case, the fit between the regime and the contest delayed modernization and wasted resources to a catastrophic degree. In the United States, much of the relative decline of American power can be attributed to the diversion of resources toward the military, and away from increasingly serious domestic problems. As a result, neither power is in mint shape as it faces the international problems of the future. Insofar as the Cold War was not a war but a way of life, of organizing a dangerous but not warlike international system, its end leaves us without a clear sense of priorities or criteria for allocating resources, and without a clear picture of all the things that happened while we were manning increasingly irrelevant barricades.

And so we find ourselves today confronting simultaneously two agendas for which we are unprepared. The first is one we always knew, vaguely, that we might have to face someday—it is, after all, what the architects of containment had been aiming at: the liquidation of the Cold War, beyond the (difficult enough) routine of arms limitations agreements. Here, the old superpowers remain the central players—although even here they must make room for the main beneficiary of their armistice: a reunited Germany. The German problem and European security are the key issues; what makes these so tricky is that the main stake is the relative influence of the two rivals in the heartland of their former contest, as well as their future weight in the new European order. It is an extremely important agenda, but essentially transitional: the answers to both these questions are already emerging, through the retreat of the Soviets and the rise of Europe. The second agenda is one for which we are not prepared at all; it is the "postwar" and global agenda, to which I shall turn now.

II

I will begin by describing, insofar as it is possible, the main trends that are at work. A convenient starting place is the phenomenon often referred to as the diffusion of power, and the perspective provided by the long-dominant theory of international affairs, Realism. That theory looks at the international system as a milieu in which states compete, seek to increase their power, try to prevent the rise of rivals or hegemons through unilateral moves as well as through balances of power, and depend for their survival and success above all on military might and the economic underpinning of it.

From that perspective, power has been largely concentrated, since 1945, in two "poles," the United States and the Soviet Union. The "diffusion of power" means that this will no longer be the case. But where has power gone? Here, we must make an important distinction: between two arenas that exist, or "games" that go on, simultaneously.[2] One is the traditional strategic-diplomatic arena, which corresponds to the Realists' analysis, with its emphasis on the actors' quest for relative gains, or (in the case of great powers thirsting for total security) absolute gains in a zero-sum contest. The other is the modern arena of economic interdependence, in which state actors are interested in relative gains, to be sure, but within a world economy, whose continuing growth is in their common interest, and in which my gains may well require that you make some yourself. The stakes are clearly not the same: physical security, the control of territory in one case; market shares, the creation and expansion of wealth in the other. Nor are the necessary ingredients and possible uses of power the same.

In the strategic-diplomatic arena, we have moved from bipolarity to a much more complex and unprecedented situation. Here, the main actors are still the states; it is in this realm that the United Nations and the various regional organizations have been least effective. The most impressive groupings have been the rival alliances (one of which is now almost defunct, and the other, as Tucker and Ronald Steel point out, is likely to lose most of its purposes)—but neither the Warsaw Pact nor the North Atlantic Treaty Organization (NATO) could ever have been regarded as an independent actor anyhow. The United States will remain the most important player in terms of global military power, and the United States and the Soviet Union will keep the capacity to destroy the planet several times over. But the Soviet Union's economic weakness and political turbulence have reduced its ability and will to be a worldwide challenger; and the number of active players has increased and will increase some more, because of the proliferation of military technologies—nuclear and conventional. A return to bipolarity would require a new Soviet-American confrontation; but the condition of the Soviet Union makes this highly unlikely in the foreseeable future. Neither a success of perestroika, a period of revolutionary turbulence and disintegration, nor a repressive regime attempting to reimpose order and control is a good candidate for a return to global ambitions. Security concerns and balances are most likely to be regional than global; and while the United States, because of its military preeminence and its capacity to project might abroad, might see itself as the "sun" at the center of the solar system, there is no obvious need for the "planets" to turn around it in such a fragmented system—now that the somewhat artificial and never totally effective unity imposed by the Cold War is waning. In this system, nuclear states and states with an abundance of conventional forces will be the powers of importance in each region. Besides states, the only significant actors in this realm will be private individuals in the business of arms sales.

The picture is quite different in the arena of economic interdependence. Here, the term "diffusion" is both misleading and imprecise. It is misleading insofar as it conceals the emergence of the new "international business civilization," analyzed in this volume by Susan Strange, Robert Heilbroner, and Miles Kahler—a worldwide phenomenon spreading out from the industrialized nations of North America, Western Europe, and East Asia. Diffusion of power suggests dispersion, whereas this "supranational capitalism" of banks and enterprises is to a large extent both concentrated in its origin (a limited, although slowly growing, number of countries) and a unifying force, at least because it does not respect borders, particularities, and traditions. Indeed, as Heilbroner points out, it is this force that periodically rearranges the distribution of economic and political power.

The term "diffusion" is imprecise because it lumps together a variety of phenomena. One is the fact that many key decisions about the world economy are made not in the political realm of states, but by private agents—investors, corporations, firms, banks, speculators, merchants, mafias—either without much control by state authorities or with enough influence to manipulate them. Another fact, which results in part from the previous one—but to which state, trade, business, and fiscal policies contribute as well—is the internationalization or multinationalization of production, finance, and communications. A third one is the mutual entanglement of state economic capabilities, either in the form of "pooled sovereignties" (as in the European Economic Community or EEC) or in the form of states whose power is each other's hostage (as in the U.S.–Japan relationship). A fourth is the inability of many states to reach their national economic objectives by national means alone (a fact that may well, as

Strange argues, be less true for the United States than for most other states). Present-day Western Europe shows all four phenomena at work. They amount to a decomposition of sovereignty, the ability of the state to command and control that may still exist in the traditional arena. Thus, diffusion here means not only, as in that arena, that the field of major state actors is becoming more crowded, but two other things as well. First, in contrast to the situation in the strategic-diplomatic domain, there are serious rivals for the United States: the losers of World War II, who became the main beneficiaries of American protection during the Cold War, Japan and Germany (or an EEC in which Germany will be the principal actor). Second, all the state actors, in different degrees, are exposed to the vicissitudes of a global market they do not control.

International politics today is not the preserve of states and businesses: we have to move beyond, or rather under, the two arenas or stages where actors play. The diffusion of power has a third and quite different dimension, which, like the emergence and eminence of the sphere of economic interdependence, moves us far away from the Realist analysis of international politics. Realism reduces world affairs to a game played, in Raymond Aron's words, by diplomats and soldiers on behalf of statesmen. Today, we note a worldwide trend (uneven, to be sure, like the "international business civilization")—a trend so messy that there is no adequate term for it. "Democratization" is not quite right, because it brings to mind the spread of representative systems based on consent; in fact, despite recent surges, their triumph is far from universal. "Populism" would be better, were it not for the word's baggage of connotations derived from peasant and farmers' movements in nineteenth century Europe and America. Maybe demands for "people power," or for "citizens' say," is the best approximation: the information revolution so many of the authors of this volume mention does, on balance, make the control of people's minds and moves by governments more difficult, and it is popular demands and pressures that set much of the agenda of the governments' foreign policies. The notion, inseparable from Realism, that this agenda is "objectively" set by the map of geography and by the map of alignments dictated by the "security dilemma" is obsolete. The agendas are either dictated by domestic imperatives or delicate attempts at reconciling these with external constraints.

This third form of diffusion of power is important above all for explaining a shift in stakes, or state preferences and goals, that many of the contributors mention. It is a shift away from traditional goals of conquest, control, and coercion. The decline in the utility of force, stressed here by a . . . realist Realist, Robert Tucker (who for so long had firmly remained in the camp of traditional power analysis), would not have occurred if it had not been for the three factors that were central to Kant's philosophy of history and ethics of foreign policy: the increasing destructiveness of war; the attractions of "greed," or commerce, that is, economic issues to which force is not relevant; and the rise of popular participation. The last raises domestic obstacles to the pursuit of imperial policies, and it also fosters mass resistance among the victims of such policies, which force is often unable to crush. It is a shift toward those economic stakes that are likely to bring to the nation or to its citizens the wealth and welfare people aspire to—which means that the control of market shares is more important, in a world where firms are endlessly mobile, than that of territory, and that access to resources and markets through trade and investment is seen as far more effective and sensible than access through force.[3]

If the diffusion of power is a first way of apprehending the sea-change, a second and perhaps more fruitful one is to look at the world in terms of a contest not between two domineering states, but between three levels. There is the global level, where the "world business civilization" operates, with its own logic and instruments, outlined here by Strange and Heilbroner. There are the states, which try to exploit this logic and its carriers in order to increase their countries' wealth, or to increase their power and influence over others (since wealth is more than ever a source of power); but the states are, with respect to the world capitalist system, in a doubly uncomfortable position. On the one hand, they are still engaged in another "game": the traditional one, of security fears, calculations, and contests, whose logic is that of Thucydides, not Adam Smith. On the other, they are trying to prevent the logic of world capitalism from depriving them of financial, monetary, and fiscal autonomy and from magnifying the differences between rich and poor states, as well as between modern sectors, fully integrated in the global economy, and backward ones. Thus, the world economy is not their single obsession, and they are ambivalent about it.

Moreover, they are besieged by more than the uncontrollable forces—private, at home and abroad, as well as public, in the form of foreign trading and investing states, abroad—of a world economy that is only partly denationalized. They are also under pressure from the third level, that of the people.

The people, to be sure, count on their state to play the game of wealth effectively, and want the benefits of growth that the economy dangles before their eyes. But the global requirements of efficiency are not those of equity, and wealth for the nation and for some of its members may be very different from welfare for most. Participation, equity, and wealth: people want all three, but often they can have only two of these, and sometimes none at all. To keep the engines of growth working, there is often a need, in the advanced countries, to attract immigrants as manpower. All of this exposes the state to a double danger. When its political and economic system leads to poverty and stagnation, there is a risk of rebellion, or of such pressure from below that the system collapses (consider the end of the Stalinist system in the 1980s); but when the state's participation in the global economy leads to inflation, unemployment, growing inequalities, or an "invasion" of inassimilable aliens, a populist backlash is always to be feared.

The world economy is thus one of the factors that may disrupt the connection between national unity and territorial boundaries that McNeill discusses: either when national unity and identity are challenged by mass immigration, or when—as may be the case in the destitute but populous countries of North Africa or black Africa, or Mexico—masses of the poor leave for richer places. To use Albert Hirschman's classical categories, voice (of the "natives," against the intruders) and exit (of the poor) may undermine loyalty to a state deemed incapable of protecting its own people. But there is also a second factor that can break the connection. The "fit" between people and state is often missing—for example, in the case of an obsolescent empire, like the Soviet Union, in which many national minorities want to have states of their own, or in the case of weak or artificial postcolonial states, as in Africa and Asia, where different ethnic groups ask for independence. Both insofar as the loyalty of citizens is based on the state's economic performance and insofar as it is based on cultural and emotional ties, the rise of people power can be not only a threat to the state, but also a cause of international conflict: either when other states are made responsible for economic injustice, when secessions and local nationalisms provoke external interventions, or when a state succeeds in diverting its people from domestic grievances by indoctrinating them against an external devil.

These are, of course, broad trends described with broad brush strokes. In today's Japan, national homogeneity has been carefully preserved, and the people appear still satisfied with the strategy, aimed at national wealth rather than individual welfare, that has been selected, in the world economy, by the governments they have confirmed in power for so many years. In China, the regime still—but for how long—seems to have the power to keep demands for economic change compatible with the preservation of a bureaucratic and authoritarian system of command. But there is yet a third way of looking at the global dynamics at work: a simultaneous movement of unification and fragmentation. The capitalist economic system tends to unify the world by internationalizing and integrating the markets of goods and capital, and by creating a sort of world elite of managers, private and public. Still there is a fragmentation of the world into states, with the trappings of sovereignty, including currencies, armies, and national rules and welfare systems for labor: formal fragmentation, if you like—the kind for which Marx, who saw states as mere façades concealing class relations, had little understanding. And there is another kind of fragmentation that he grasped extremely well in his analysis of world capitalism: the substantive one. It results both from the dynamics of the global market, which tends often to exacerbate inequality both among and within states (Susan Strange writes about different "grades of entitlement to the status of citizen"), and from the dissatisfaction of many people with "their" state, precisely because, for ethnic, religious, or ideological reasons, they do not recognize it as theirs, or else because the government has failed to feed, employ, enrich, or protect them, and thus has broken the bonds of consent.

III

One reason for offering this rather abstract picture is to point out that a post–Cold War world will be anything but harmonious. We are entering a new phase of history. It is assuredly not the "end of history,"[4] a silly notion based on a series of mistaken assumptions (that the death of communism means the definitive triumph of Western liberalism, the end of ideology, and the coming of a "boring" era of material concerns and unheroic squabbles); it is a period in which the discrepancy between the formal organization of the world into states and the realities of power, which do not resemble those of any past international system, will create formidable contradictions and difficulties.

Miles Kahler has indicated why even the shift from traditional goals and tools to economic ones is not likely to lead to peace and quiet. First, there is a huge array of possible "traditional" quarrels, in a world where there is at least still one ideology of violent conflict—Islamic fundamentalism—and where the disappearance or decay of secular ideologies leaves nationalism, over much of the planet, as the only glue of loyalty. The Arab-Israeli conflict, Kashmir, and Cyprus are daily reminders of gloomy forms of permanence. Evidence of the declining utility of force for the superpowers and for other major actors, such as the nations of Western Europe and Japan, may not deter those for whom passion overruns cost-benefit analysis, and those for whom force seems the only alternative to despair, humiliation, or destruction. If one remembers that the increased economic capabilities of smaller states, alluded to by Joseph Nye in his latest book,[5] allow them to buy or build formidable modern arsenals and to make themselves largely independent of arms shipments by fickle superpowers—and if one believes, as Tucker and I do, that the latter, no longer chasing each other all over the world, may play less of a moderating role in such regional conflicts now that their potential as triggers of a superpower collision has vanished—there is then no reason to expect that the traditional arena of world politics will be empty or boring—except, perhaps, strangely and happily enough, in Europe, prophets of recurrent doom notwithstanding.[6]

Second, the realm of interdependence will also breed conflicts that could be serious. As Kahler says, elites depend on popular satisfaction for their survival in power, and the disruptions and distributional conflicts the "world business civilization" may bring with it could "cause some states to define their security requirements more broadly rather than less," or to divert domestic turbulence toward conflict abroad. Among the advanced countries, the different strategies chosen by the main players in the quest for market shares and wealth may become incompatible if they lead to permanent imbalances. This is already the message of the so-called revisionists who point out that the Japanese brand of neomercantilism—which subordinates the interests of consumers to those of producers, entails a deliberate and long-term strategy aimed at gaining the lead in advanced technologies, and results in a "continued displacement of industrial sectors and the shift of technological capability toward Japan"[7]—may not be reconcilable with America's consumer orientation, lack of industrial policy, and lesser "ability to adapt quickly to changing circumstances."[8] Conflicts over trade and industrial policy ultimately involve as stakes both the power of states, since wealth is a component of power (even though the uses of economic power are often constrained or capable of boomeranging), and the fate of labor at home. Without the restraining force exerted by the Cold War, and by the need of Western Europeans and Japanese for American protection, such conflicts could become acute.

The potential for trouble, not between the "North" and "South," but between the advanced countries and certain groups of less-developed ones, is equally serious. It is often said that the poorer among the latter cannot cause much harm, whatever they do. This maybe true, in cases other than oil, if harm is defined in purely economic terms. But radical anti-Western ideologies could turn fiercely against the institutions and agents of Western capitalism; also, the weakness and heterogeneity of some of these states, and the pressure of increasing populations, may well lead to violent regional conflicts, as well as to formidable quarrels over immigration and refuge to and expulsions from the richer countries. Two of the problems that have become urgent, drugs and the environment, could all too easily lead to confrontations between advanced states eager to protect their health and their future, and states such as those of South America that need to cultivate drugs, or to forgo strict protection of the environment, in order to develop.

Third, the conflicts between state and people must be taken seriously, too—not only because popular or populist attacks on ill-constituted states and unacceptable governments, or governmental attempts to divert such attacks, could lead to interstate troubles, but also because the victory of "people power" is neither a guarantee of moderate behavior abroad nor at all guaranteed. Popular victories can trample over minority rights and create nationalist explosions. Conversely, democratic revolutions may wilt if the winners get bogged down in party squabbles and parochial issues, or else caught between the "demands" of the world business civilization and domestic discontent, and replaced by authoritarian or military rulers. This, in turn, may be bad, both for regional peace and for the cause of human rights.

IV

It is not possible for Americans to walk away from these problems simply because none of them concentrates the mind and creates a danger for our physical security comparable to the Soviet threat. The role of the United States will have to be quite different from that of the past 40 years, and the reasons Tucker give for rejecting both a policy defined in traditional balance of power terms and a mission of world policeman are compelling. However, an American total retreat toward domestic reform would be a serious moral and political mistake, comparable to the return to isolationism in 1919–1920. Indeed, the scope of American involvements abroad (however much the end of the

Cold War may allow us to reduce them)—"ethnic empathy toward various parts of the world, popular sympathies for the underdog,"[9] and the pressure of interests affected by the global economy—make such a full retrenchment unlikely.

On the other hand, the changes in power that have been stressed in this volume limit the ability of the United States to set the rules and to provide the solutions. As John Zysman noted in a recent article,[10] the shift from military to economic influence hurts the United States, insofar as others depend less on American military technology, and in the economic realm a United States deep in debt is far from the free giant it was after the war; our ability to extract foreign policy gains from economic power has dropped, and we depend increasingly on foreign sources for important products and technologies. While Strange is right to point out the assets the United States still enjoys, the various failures of American policy that she criticizes and blames for the fate of international economic organizations have their roots in the place that is the real locus of America's decline: not imperial overstretch, nor any catastrophic fall in aggregate figures of material resources, but the domestic components of power—low savings; insufficient productive investments, especially in leading sectors; the obsession of business with short-term profits; a poor system of technical education; and, above all, a failing capacity to mobilize tangible and intangible resources, which results from the bad state of American infrastructure (especially urban), popular resistance to taxation, and a lack of leadership.

The United States, after a decade of celebration of its ability to deal with the world's problems by its own means, finds itself in a bind. The three principles that have guided its foreign policy—American exceptionalism, anticommunism, and world economic liberalism—are of little help, because others are less receptive, or because "victory" has made anticommunism irrelevant, or because the market itself is the problem (as in U.S.–Japanese relations) or provides no answers (as in ecological matters). Persisting with the trade and budget deficits increases American dependence on creditors; eliminating those deficits would require either measures that would disrupt the world economy (protectionism) or decisions that would bring about a complete and painful reorientation of American fiscal and industrial policy. If U.S. statesmen do not address the domestic issues that deeply worry the people but that, in the absence of leadership, leave it adrift, America's ability to affect world affairs positively will decline further, and we will find ourselves on a road comparable to that on which the Soviet Union is now skidding. However, if the United States addresses its internal problems, the resources it will need to raise will not be available for external purposes. America faces a heavy bill, the product of the weaknesses of its own unregulated and often uncalculating economic systems, of those of its decentralized and byzantine political system, and of the Cold War.

The tensions, contradictions, and conflicts described here will therefore not be manageable unless we find the methods and found the institutions of planetary governance that are now indispensable. Laissez-faire and the invisible hand are not capable of resolving such issues as population growth and movements, the environment's destruction, famines and epidemics, and the distributional effects (among and within states) of the "business civilization." It is of course true, as Susan Strange argues, that the demands of the people and the short lives of democratic governments make multilateral cooperation difficult, but they also make it necessary. At this stage, the states remain the only legitimate public authorities and mobilizers of public resources, but the problems they face—those I have just mentioned, but also those of "megascience" and large-scale technology, discussed by Kenneth H. Keller—demand cooperative solutions. Moreover, the very dynamism of the world economy and its restless reallocation of wealth and power require the same kind of political control at the global level that the "political realm" of authority, the state, provides at the country level; and that control, too, can come, so far, only from a pooling of state efforts.

It is therefore, to use Richard N. Gardner's terms, for a "comeback of liberal internationalism" that one must plead.[11] Each person may have his or her own favorite blueprint, but the main directions are clear. Among the advanced countries (including—or rather and also—the Soviet Union), the main tasks will be, first, the establishment of a new security system in Europe, which will probably be a mix of a much-reformed NATO no longer dominated by the United States, a Western European defense organization, and an organization set by the Conference on Security and Cooperation in Europe (CSCE); second, an agreement among the main suppliers of arms and advanced technologies to restrict such sales drastically, to strengthen the nuclear nonproliferation regime, and to establish regional arms limitation and conflict resolution regimes; third, a deal to redistribute power—now still largely in the hands of the United States—among the main actors in the international financial and economic organizations, the United States, Japan, and the EEC.

The end of the Cold War and of the straitjacket of worldwide East-West security concerns should allow the advanced countries to concentrate their efforts on social, economic, and political conditions in an increasingly diversified "South." Both ecological imperatives and the issue of the population pressure of the poor and the refugees require a set of bargains, thanks to which ample resources will, through multilateral assistance and with the participation of the leading private firms, be made available to the developing countries, in exchange for commitments on environmental protection, health care, energy efficiency, agricultural productivity, and human rights. The demands on the resources of the richer states—caught between the needs and expectations of their own people and the fear of external chaos—will be both so large and so conflicting that organizations for regional and global cooperation will have to be strengthened, through guaranteed revenues, the creation of independent secretariats, and frequent high-level meetings.

Robert Tucker asks whether a world without a central threat and a hegemon will be able to create order. It is not certain. What is proposed here is very much a halfway house: not a world government for which states and peoples are unprepared (and that the managers of the world business civilization would not like), but a new experiment in polycentric steering, in which the three major economic powers—plus the Soviet Union if it overcomes its problems, and perhaps China once it begins to turn its potential into effective power (something that would require drastic political changes)—would form a central steering group, and in which regional powers would play comparable roles in their areas. Nothing like this has ever been tried—but then, the hidden theme of this essay has been the advent of discontinuity in international affairs.

Two big question marks remain. First, will a development of multilateral diplomacy and institutions not merely add a layer to the three—the global market, the states, the people—that exist already, and simply add cooperative inefficiency to market inequities, state erosion, and popular discontent? Will it help global unification or make for more fragmentation (including, now, among international and regional agencies)? The risk exists; the example of the EEC shows that where the will can be found, the danger can be overcome. Second, will the United States be willing to commit itself, and sufficient resources, to such a path? The answer could be yes, on two conditions: if adequate leadership can at last be provided—leadership that would understand and explain that, as Kahler puts it, "unilateral American action is likely to be less effective, and the workings of an untrammeled market . . . less desirable than . . . international collaboration"; and if domestic reform to provide for the underpinnings of power is undertaken. Without such reform, popular turbulence and resentments against competitors will mount. To be sure, such reform will require fiscal sacrifices, and while it absorbs attention and funds, America's own contributions to the needs of others might remain limited. But none of America's problems at home or abroad can be solved if "people power" is equated with no new taxes; and in the immediate future, one of the welcome effects of the diffusion of power is the ability of Western Europe and Japan (already the largest donor of foreign aid) to play a larger role.

V

The world after the Cold War will not resemble any world of the past. From a "structural" point of view—the distribution of capabilities—it will be multipolar. But the poles will have different currencies of power—military (the Soviets), economic and financial (Japan and Germany), demographic (China and India), military and economic (the United States)—and different pro- ductivities of power—demographic power is more a liability than an asset, the utility of military might is reduced, only economic power is fully useful because it is the capacity to influence others by bringing them the very goods they crave. Moreover, each of these poles will be, at least to some extent, mired in a world economy that limits its freedom of action. What we do not know is what relations are going to develop among these actors, what institutional links they will set up to manage their relations with one another, and their relations with the rest of the world, in a context of vigilant, demanding, and often turbulently mobilized masses. The fate of this new world will depend on the ability of the "poles" to cooperate enough in order to prevent or moderate conflicts—including regional ones, and to correct those imbal- ances of the world economy that would otherwise induce some states, or their publics, to pull away from or to disrupt the momentum of interdependence. Above all, it will depend on domestic currents that remain highly difficult to predict. Since foreign policy today is so largely shaped by domestic demands and expectations, the most dangerous remaining tension, and the most difficult to overcome, is that between the global dimen- sion of the issues that foreign policy will have to deal with and the fact that political life remains, at best, limited to the horizons of the state and is, often, even challenging the unity, the borders, and the effectiveness of the state.

The world is like a bus whose driver—the global economy— is not in full control of the engine and is himself out of control, in which children—the people—are tempted to step on either the brake or the gas pedal, and adults—the states—are worried passengers. A league of passengers may not be enough to keep the bus on the road, but there is no better solution yet.

NOTES

1. See John L. Gaddis, *The Long Peace* (New York: Oxford University Press, 1987).
2. On this distinction, see my *Primacy or World Order* (New York: McGraw-Hill, 1978). I realize that the distinction is, in reality, far from perfect. In the

realm of economic interdependence, states try to combine the logic of competition (the quest for relative gains) with that of a world economy that, as Robert Heilbroner points out, has rules and a dynamism of its own. Chaos or crises caused, in that realm, either by aggressive state competitiveness or by economic recessions and dislocations can spill over into the traditional arena.

3. On this shift, see Carl Kaysen, "Is War Obsolete? A Review Essay," *International Security*, vol. 14, no. 4 (1990), pp. 42–64.
4. I am referring to Francis Fukuyama's notorious essay, "The End of History?" *The National Interest*, no. 16 (Summer 1989), pp. 3–18.
5. See Joseph Nye, *Bound to Lead* (New York: Basic Books 1990), ch. 6.
6. For such a prophecy, see John J. Mearsheimer, "Back to the Future: Instability in Europe after the Cold War," *International Security*, vol. 15, no. 1 (Summer 1990), pp. 5–56.
7. James Fallows, Chalmers Johnson, Clyde Prestowitz, and Karel van Wolferen, "Beyond Japan Bashing," *U.S. News & World Report*, May 7, 1990, p. 54–55.
8. Edson W. Spencer, "Japan as Competitor," *Foreign Policy*, no. 28 (Spring 1990), p. 165.
9. Charles W. Maynes, "America without the Cold War," *Foreign Policy*, no. 78 (Spring 1990), p. 13.
10. "Redoubling the Bet," BRIE Working Paper, no. 38 (Berkeley: University of California, January 1990), p. 20.
11. "The Comeback of Liberal Internationalism," *The Washington Quarterly*, vol. 13, no. 3 (Summer 1990), pp. 23–39.

ABOUT THE AUTHORS

Mark Falcoff—Resident Scholar in Foreign Policy, American Enterprise Institute

William H. Gleysteen, Jr.—President, The Japan Society

Robert L. Heilbroner—Emeritus Professor of Economics, The New School for Social Research

Stanley Hoffmann—Professor of Government, Harvard University

Miles Kahler—Professor, Graduate School of International Relations and Pacific Studies, University of California, San Diego

Robert G. Kaiser—Assistant Managing Editor for National News, *The Washington Post*

Kenneth H. Keller—Volvo Distinguished Visiting Fellow, Council on Foreign Relations

William H. McNeill—Emeritus Professor of History, University of Chicago

Itamar Rabinovich—Senior Research Fellow, Dayan Center for Middle Eastern Studies, Tel Aviv University

Nicholas X. Rizopoulos (editor)—Vice President, Studies, Council on Foreign Relations

Tony Smith—Professor of Political Science, Tufts University

Ronald Steel—Professor of International Relations, University of Southern California

Roger D. Stone—Whitney H. Shepardson Fellow, Council on Foreign Relations

Susan Strange—Professor of International Relations, European University Institute, Florence

Thomas P. Thornton—Adjunct Professor of Asian Studies, The Paul H. Nitze School of Advanced International Studies, Johns Hopkins University

Robert W. Tucker—Emeritus Professor of American Foreign Policy, The Paul H. Nitze School of Advanced International Studies, Johns Hopkins University

Crawford Young—Professor of Political Science, University of Wisconsin-Madison